# MEDIA, CRISIS AND DEMOCRACY

# MEDIA, CRISIS AND DEMOCRACY

## Mass Communication and the Disruption of Social Order

*edited by*

# Marc Raboy and Bernard Dagenais

SAGE Publications
London · Newbury Park · New Delhi

First published 1992

SAGE Publications Ltd
6 Bonhill Street
London EC2A 4PU

SAGE Publications Inc
2455 Teller Road
Newbury Park, California 91320

SAGE Publications India Pvt Ltd
32, M-Block Market
Greater Kailash – I
New Delhi 110 048

**British Library Cataloguing in Publication data**

Media, Crisis and Democracy: Mass
Communication and the Disruption of
Social Order. – (Media, Culture & Society
Series)
  I. Raboy, Marc   II. Dagenais, Bernard
  III. Series
  302.23

  ISBN 0–8039–8639–4
  ISBN 0–8039–8640–8 (pbk)

**Library of Congress catalog card number 91–051187**

Typeset by The Word Shop, Bury, Lancs.
Printed in Great Britain by The Cromwell Press Ltd,
Broughton Gifford, Melksham, Wiltshire.

# Contents

# Notes on Contributors

**Marc Raboy** is associate professor in the Département d'information et de communication, Laval University, Québec, Canada. A former journalist and community organizer, his books include *Missed Opportunities: The Story of Canada's Broadcasting Policy*, *Movements and Messages: Media and Radical Politics in Quebec*, and *Communication for and against Democracy* (edited with Peter A. Bruck, 1989).

**Bernard Dagenais** is associate professor in the Département d'information et de communication, Laval University, Québec, Canada. A former senior communications officer in the Quebec civil service, his books include *La crise d'octobre 1970 et les médias: un miroir à dix faces*, and *Le communiqué, ou l'art de faire parler de soi*.

**Peter A. Bruck** teaches communication and cultural studies at Carleton University in Ottawa, Canada, and at the University of Salzburg, Austria. He is currently heading the internationally comparative research program 'Economy and Future of the Print Media' established by the Republic of Austria, and does research on news formats and socio-cultural formations in Europe and North America.

**George Gerbner** is professor of communication and dean emeritus of the Annenberg School for Communication, University of Pennsylvania, USA. He chaired the editorial board of the *International Encyclopedia of Communications* and is the author of numerous books, articles and reports on violence in the mass media.

**Julian Halliday** is instructor in communication studies at Muhlenberg College, with a cooperative appointment at Cedar Crest College, both in Allentown, Pennsylvania, USA. He writes and teaches on cultural studies, media criticism, and critical and interpretive theory.

**Karol Jakubowicz** is director of programmes for Polish Television, after serving as chair of the Broadcasting Reform Commission appointed by Poland's 'Solidarity'-led government. His career has alternated between work as a media practitioner and scholarly research, and he has published widely in Poland and abroad.

**Sue Curry Jansen** is associate professor and head of communication studies at Muhlenberg College, and co-operative professor of communications at Cedar Crest College in Allentown, Pennsylvania, USA. She is the author of *Censorship: The Knot that Binds Power and Knowledge*.

**John Keane** is director of the Centre for the Study of Democracy and professor of political science at the Polytechnic of Central London, UK. He is the author of several books, including *The Media and Democracy, Democracy and Civil Society* and *Public Life and Late Capitalism*.

**Douglas Kellner** is professor of philosophy at the University of Texas at Austin, USA, and the author of books on social theory, politics, history, and culture, including *Critical Theory, Marxism and Modernity* and *Television and the Crisis of Democracy*.

**Mustapha Masmoudi** is a journalist, media consultant and member of parliament in Tunisia. A former ambassador to UNESCO and member of the International Commission for the Study of Communication Problems (MacBride Commission), he is recognized as one of the architects of the 'New World Information and Communication Order'.

**Armand Mattelart** is professor of information and communication sciences at the Université de Haute Bretagne, Rennes II, France. His books include *Multinationales et systèmes de communication, Mass Media, Ideologies and the Revolutionary Movement, L'internationale publicitaire* and *La publicité*.

**Michèle Mattelart** is a lecturer at the Université de Paris III, France and an independent researcher. She is the author of *Women, Media, Crisis: Femininity and Disorder*, and co-author (with Armand Mattelart) of *Le carnaval des images,* and *De l'usage des médias en temps de crise* and *Re-Thinking the Media*.

**Lorna Roth** is a cross-cultural communications and education consultant based in Montréal, Canada. She lectures in northern communications and Canadian broadcasting policy at Concordia University, and supervises Mohawk teachers in Kahnawake and Kanehsatake for the Native Teacher Training Program of McGill University.

**James Schneider** is assistant professor in communication studies at Muhlenberg College, with a cooperative appointment at Cedar Crest College, both in Allentown, Pennsylvania, USA. He teaches courses in film theory and criticism, communications studies, and media production, and directs an alternative film program.

# Acknowledgements

This book grew out of the international conference on 'Media and Crisis' held at Laval University, Québec, in October, 1990. We wish to thank all the participants in that conference for providing a stimulating and collegial environment in which many of the ideas now presented here could be aired and tested.

The project's development was greatly facilitated by the constructive comments and logistical advice of Paddy Scannell, on whose initiative it was originally proposed for publication in the *Media, Culture and Society* series.

The Social Sciences and Humanities Research Council of Canada provided support for the participation of Armand and Michèle Mattelart, enabling them to produce the inaugural lecture presented here as the concluding chapter to the book. Material support was also provided by the Faculty of Arts of Laval University, the Ministère des communications du Québec, and the Solicitor General of Canada.

Chapters 2, 8, and 11 were translated from their original French versions, with the very generous assistance of the office of the vice-rector for research and the Faculty of Arts of Laval University.

MR
BD

# Introduction: Media and the Politics of Crisis

*Marc Raboy and Bernard Dagenais*

## On Crisis

The centrality of the media of mass communication to social life is something that we take for granted in the late twentieth century. The actual function one can attribute to media – their role in society – is highly contested, however.

Debates over the relationship of media to society have to do in good measure with diverging views of the nature of society itself. In the 1990s, one of the flashpoints of this debate concerns the juncture of 'modernism' and 'postmodernism' (cf. *Media, Culture and Society*, 1991) – that is to say, have we indeed crossed the threshold into an entirely new era, or are we rather in a later stage of the one that began politically with the great revolutions of the late eighteenth century, economically with the industrial transformations of the mid-nineteenth century, and culturally with the new artistic movements of the early twentieth century?

In short, is the present moment one of continuity or rupture with the past? Despite the intellectual attractiveness of the prospect of debating this question, we would propose that society evolves in a process of continuity *and* change, and that this process does not lend itself to such neat characterizations.

It is clear that such a process is not smooth. But we can nonetheless seek to understand it. We would propose the notion of *crisis* as a paradigm for understanding the dialectics of continuity and radical change (rupture), the thread (both real and imaginary) connecting social order and disorder in our times. This idea is suggested in M. Mattelart (1986).

The notion of crisis *as an analytical category*, Edgar Morin wrote in 1976, has spread to every horizon in the twentieth century: society, the family, value systems, the economy, the environment, the struggle with nature . . . all have been scrutinized from the perspective of crisis. A moment of crisis – by definition, a decisive moment – provides a unique opportunity for making a diagnosis, according to Morin (1976).

While we essentially agree with this view, the focus of this book will necessarily be more narrow than the panorama proposed by Morin. Our concern is with *the politics of crisis*, in which, we shall argue, communications media play a central role. The notion of crisis is encountered in the literature in various guises pertinent to our consideration.

The question was addressed, for example, by the great Italian political philosopher Antonio Gramsci (1930), for whom situations of conflict between the 'representatives' and the 'represented' in society engendered a crisis of ruling class hegemony, a crisis of authority, or a general crisis of the state:

> In every country the process is different, although the content is the same. And the content is the crisis of the ruling class's hegemony, which occurs either because the ruling class has failed in some major political undertaking for which it has requested, or forcibly extracted, the consent of the broad masses . . ., or because huge masses . . . have passed suddenly from a state of political passivity to a certain activity, and put forward demands which taken together, albeit not organically formulated, add up to a revolution. (Gramsci, 1930: 210)

For Gramsci, a 'crisis of authority' arises when the ruling class no longer commands a social consensus, and must resort increasingly to coercive force to maintain its dominance. 'This means precisely that the great masses have become detached from their traditional ideologies, and no longer believe what they used to believe previously' (Gramsci, 1930: 276). This analysis begs the question: how does this come about? and indicates the importance of the means of exercising ideological hegemony.

Closer to our own day, Offe (1984) asks why the policy-making capacity of the state (ie its 'welfare state regulatory strategies') is so limited in effectiveness in late capitalist societies? For Offe, like Gramsci, the notion of crisis is central to the maintenance of hegemony:

> the tantalizing and baffling riddle . . . is why capitalist systems have so far been able to survive – in spite of all existing contradictions and conflicts [crises] – even though an intact bourgeois ideology that could deny these contradictions and construct the image of a harmonious order [bourgeois hegemony] no longer exists. (Offe, 1984: 36)

His answer lies in the view of policy making as a form of crisis management. Crises, for Offe (1984: 36), are 'processes in which the structure of a system is called into question'. One view of crisis, which Offe calls the 'sporadic' view, holds that 'crises endanger the identity of a system', especially when events occur that lie outside the boundaries developed by the system. This view sees crises as 'particularly acute, catastrophic, surprising and unforeseeable events' requiring intervention. 'The crisis is thus seen as an event or a chain of events confined to one point in time or a short period of time. This makes it difficult to describe the *tendency towards crisis* or *crisis-proneness* of a social system' (Offe, 1984: 37). By failing to link events with social structures, it fails to see the crisis as *characteristic* of the general state of affairs.

An alternative, or 'processual', approach conceives crisis at the level of 'mechanisms that generate "events"': according to this approach, crises are seen as 'developmental tendencies' that can be confronted and counteracted (for example, by policy measures). Here, the crisis-prone tendencies of the system are related to its overall characteristics. Crisis and administrative (state) intervention are traditionally pitted as opposites, but they are linked by what Offe (1984) calls the continuing 'crisis of crisis management'.

In an important essay first published in 1981, Jürgen Habermas described social modernization as a process of economic growth and organizational accomplishment that 'penetrates deeper and deeper into previous forms of human existence . . . disturbing the communicative infrastructure of everyday life' (Habermas, 1985: 8). To the extent that modern society is also marked by a seemingly endless series of crises – real and perceived, general and specific – this is a good way of characterizing the media–crisis relationship.

**On Media and Crisis**

Crisis can be defined as a disruption, real or perceived, of social order. In the dictionary sense, the term is also used to refer to a decisive or critical turning point in the course of events, as well as 'a state of affairs in which a decisive change for better or worse is imminent' (*Oxford English Dictionary*, 1971: 1178). It is especially applied 'to times of difficulty, insecurity and suspense in politics or commerce'.

A state of crisis is distinguished from its opposite, normalcy, by the threat (or promise) of change that the crisis implies. Whether change is deemed to be desirable or not is evidently a question of ideological orientation and political interest, but the very labelling of some situation as a 'crisis' is itself an ideological and political act. So is the failure to attribute crisis status to a particular situation. Making these choices and structuring the way they are presented in the public sphere has become one of the essential functions of mass media.

If a situation of crisis is, axiomatically, a moment of importance for the society concerned, it is, by corollary, necessarily worthy of media attention. The nature of that attention then becomes, itself, an element of the crisis, insofar as 'the status and significance of a historical event . . . is inseparable from the equivocal discourses that traverse it' (Pêcheux, 1988: 633).

The role of media will vary greatly depending on the nature of the particular crisis and the nature of the particular society concerned. As all social institutions, media thrive on stability and are threatened by change. But the contradictions inherent to the relationship between their specifically ascribed function as agents of social discourse and their economic status as purveyors of commodified knowledge/information distinguish media from other social institutions: in a certain sense, media thrive on 'crisis' and are threatened by 'normalcy'.

The tendency is, therefore, for media to seek out crisis where it does not exist, and to obscure the actual forces of change that threaten media privilege along with entrenched social privilege in general. Paradoxically, this means that media will tend to pay even more attention to a fabricated crisis than to one that can stake a material claim to reality. For social actors, provoking a crisis thus becomes a form of empowerment or social control. But the ensuing access to media attention is unequally skewed, to the extent that the media themselves are socially positioned.

In a powerful and provocative essay first published in France in the wake of the events of May 1968, Guy Debord (1983) described modern society as one in which public life was reduced to a spectacle. Reviewing his earlier observations recently, Debord (1990) argued that the most significant social fact of the intervening 20 years was the *unbroken continuity* of the spectacle.

Debord characterizes the spectacle as 'the autocratic reign of the market economy which had acceded to an irresponsible sovereignty, and the totality of new techniques of government which accompanied this reign . . . The establishment of spectacular domination is such a profound social transformation that it has radically altered the art of government' (Debord, 1990: 2, 87).

Henceforth, all discussion of what the world's rulers do is organized through the spectacle, through the unilateral and uni-directional communication via the mass media of the results of decisions that have already been made. Only that which is recognized by the spectacle has historical validity; only those consecrated by the spectacle are entitled to speak with authority.

According to this view, those who consume the spectacle cannot act. The only reliable knowledge is that which one gains by direct experience. But, given the pervasiveness of media, to what extent can one participate in modern society on the basis of direct experience alone?

**On Media, Crisis and Democracy**

If ever a political designation has been ideologically charged, it is the term 'democracy' (cf. Raboy and Bruck, 1989). Even a cursory review of the vast array of existing and hypothetical models of democracy would be far beyond the scope of this chapter (cf. Held, 1987). But our examination of the relationship between media and crisis becomes particularly meaningful when considered in light of the evolving debate on the nature of democracy. Let us then state very briefly what democracy means to us.

In the most simple and conventional sense, a democracy is deemed to be a political system in which the majority of a given population exercises power. The obstacles encountered by systems organized along these lines have led to various critiques that highlight shortcomings such as the tendency of the majority to dominate minorities, of elites to control power

\

institutions in the name of the people, of the state to negotiate social peace in the interests of the elites.

We would take a different approach. We consider democracy to be a value rather than a system. As a normative concept, democracy implies equality, social justice and political mechanisms for people to participate meaningfully in making the decisions that affect their lives.

Democracy implies an ongoing struggle, in the political, economic, social and cultural spheres. If, as we have argued above, crisis is a structural feature of modern society, and media are the agents of social communication by which a crisis is made public, then the media–crisis relationship becomes a key factor in the struggle for democracy.

Challenges to the status quo in all types of society tend to be framed in terms of crisis. Crisis is a structuring concept: by labelling a situation as one of crisis, one declares the presence of a threat to the prevailing order. This declaration is usually accompanied by a political positioning with respect to the projected change.

Invoking a state of crisis has, at least in the past half-century, been the classical strategy for legitimating the silencing of media criticism, and the tendency is for media to go along. On the other hand, a serious limitation of contemporary mainstream media is their reluctance to recognize and legitimate an actually existing crisis whose logical outcome would empower those who do not currently form part of the dominant social elites.

Not all crisis is mediated, let alone media-created. Society has not yet reached a condition of stasis, and the forces of social change really do exist. The media themselves, however, constitute a contested terrain in the struggles surrounding the conceptualization, definitions, and transformation of society and democracy in different parts of the world.

As we shall see, the actual role of media with respect to the quality of democratic public life is increasingly problematic. On the one hand, it can be argued that media are most important when and insofar as the issue of democracy is at stake (cf. Keane, in this volume). On the other, one can wonder, along with Debord for example, whether media have not in fact negated the possibility of democracy.

The complicated texture of this problem was made dramatically apparent (if not quite transparent) during the major international crisis that marked the period during which this was being written: the Persian Gulf war of 1991 (see also chapters by Kellner and Masmoudi in this volume).

## A Case in Point: Media and the Gulf War

Media coverage of the Gulf War must be placed in its historic context. During the single year 1989, the global mediatization of political crises reached saturation point. Live television coverage of the different manifestations of the pending collapse of the iron curtain suggested to the viewers of the world that 'the civic function of televised information (is) precisely to go beyond appearances and reveal the real nature of a society' (Ramonet, 1991).

With the outbreak of the Persian Gulf crisis in August 1990, people expected the kind of coverage they had become accustomed to in Berlin, Beijing and Bucharest. The audience was primed. The technology was in place. But there was a major difference: information here was subject to pre-media control.

In the crises of 1989, the global media were tacitly supportive of the forces provoking the crisis. The contrary was the case in the Gulf War. Proliferation of images in one case, silence and blackout in the other. But, as Ramonet reminds us, news blackouts are not new. From the beginning of the 1980s alone, no western power allowed the media to be present during military foreign operations (Israel/Lebanon 1982; UK/Falklands 1982, US/Grenada 1983, France/Chad 1988, US/Panama 1989).[1]

Even so, can we really claim that 'being there' through the eye of the camera (as in Beijing, etc) provides meaningful information, usable in the exercise of democratic citizenship? For local populations perhaps. If publics were to be informed of pending political choices, rather than after the fact, their intervention could perhaps influence those choices. As it is, we are allowed to see only that which we can no longer do more than absorb. This is consumerism in its purest form.

In the case of the Gulf War, television audiences were reduced to unabashed voyeurism. Journalists were, in the best of cases, witnesses. CNN's famous announcement of the start of the bombing of Baghdad was a virtual exercise in *non*-communication (to parody Lasswell): it could not communicate with any degree of accuracy who was bombing what, with what means and to what effect (Ramonet, 1991). Yet CNN set the standard.[2] Never before had an international event generated so much media coverage – and so little information, so much media criticism – and so little understanding (cf. *Le Monde Diplomatique*, 1991).

Almost immediately, the role of the media became the story – in some respects even 'bigger', more controversial, than the story of the war itself, as if to say: 'We know we have little input to policy processes; but we *feel* like participants because of our consumption of media. Perhaps if we take a critical approach to media, we can feel we are helping to make policy as well.'

The speed with which media coverage of the crisis shifted from the story itself to the 'media-in-the-story' was truly stunning. The war period of 16 January to 5 March, 1991 especially, produced an outpouring of hundreds of press articles and countless audiovisual reports about the media. If the media were unable to cover the war, they made up for it by covering themselves.[3]

The media discourse on itself was remarkably homogeneous, in its emphasis and stressing of the following points: the denunciation of censorship, the criticism of the limitations of television as an explanatory medium, the anxiety over the effects of spectacularization and the tendency to approach war as a kind of sporting match, and the recognition of the limitations and constraints of technologically determined journalism.

If nothing else, the Gulf War demonstrated once and for all the communicative incapacity of television and the continued importance of print media as means of reflective information. Television 'informed', in a crude sense, but gave viewers nothing to hang on to: 'Overinformation led to disinformation. The avalanche of news – often uncooked – broadcast "live and in real time" made viewers hysterical with the illusion that they were being informed . . . Being there was not enough to know what was going on' (Ramonet, 1991).

Critics concurred that the missing ingredient of the war coverage was the war itself. Coverage was of the *crisis*, in the abstract.

Management of information in wartime is 150 years old. But never before have we been able to give ourselves such an *illusion* of being informed. In this respect, television coverage of the Persian Gulf War was purely ideological in the Althusserian sense of ideology as 'a representation of the imaginary relationship of individuals to their real conditions of existence' (Althusser, 1971: 162).

A certain managerial tendency has considered serious policy questions – especially regarding war and diplomacy – to be beyond the purview of ordinary citizens, ever since Walter Lippmann published *Public Opinion* on his return from the Versailles conference of 1919 (Lippmann, 1922; see also Burnham, 1941).

A state of crisis encourages this tendency. Then, in addition to the public's declared incapacity to decide due to its lack of technical expertise, one must factor in the need for secrecy, censorship, or suppression of information in the name of national security (cf. Masmoudi in this volume). The media become not a forum for public discussion of policy issues, but a means of massaging the public with reassurances that the authorities have the crisis well in hand. Surfing on the waves of public opinion, the authorities are then able to execute all manner of political agendas, under the cover of crisis communication. But we would do well to recall that such exceptional measures are one of the basic features of totalitarianism (cf. Mattelart and Mattelart, 1979: 55).

This is precisely what happened during the Gulf War, with the preponderance of retired military analysts and other experts seconded to supplement the official information streaming from the Pentagon, the White House, and (for local purposes) other 'allied' capitals. In the face of the general ignorance and professional helplessness of the journalistic milieu, these experts became the oracles of the information we needed to know.

Former White House communication chief (under Ronald Reagan) Michael Deaver candidly explained the strategy to a reporter from *Le Nouvel Observateur* in June 1991:

The military successfully integrated a communication strategy (to its activities) . . . They understood that it was just as important, if not more, to look after the journalists as to deal with logistics or pure military strategy . . . Millions of people saw the representatives of the government speak with assurance while reducing the press to a bunch of assholes asking stupid questions. (de Rudder, 1991: 6–7)

The Gulf War not only rewrote von Clausewitz, it also gave new life to the Hollywood good-guy/bad-guy model of conflict representation (which had, as it turns out, suffered an only temporary blow with the end of the Cold War; cf. Halliday et al. in this volume). The tendency to flatten a complex and multi-textured phenomenon into simple formulations, for example by blackening Saddam Hussein and his regime, obscured all possible consideration of the real meaning of the war, of US designs and motives, of the manipulation of public opinion and disinformation (see Warren, 1991; Kellner in this volume).[4]

The tendency was thus for most people to think as they were told, prompting one critic to remark: 'This represents a historic triumph for propaganda; it no longer needs to bother suppressing or distorting inconvenient facts' (Salutin, 1991: 36).

The facts, meanwhile, were available for those who wanted them in an array of small, independent print media (including some prominent ones such as *The Village Voice* and *Le Monde Diplomatique*) and, in disjointed and decontextualized fashion, in much of the mainstream press as well.

But, significantly, the strongest criticism *in* the media was levelled *at* the media. Characterizing the press as 'a claque applauding the American generals and politicians in charge', and television as 'the most egregious official lap dog during the war', Anthony Lewis of *The New York Times* wrote that government control and censorship alone could not explain the media's performance: 'We glorified war and accepted its political premise, forsaking the independence and scepticism that justify freedom of the press' (Lewis, 1991).

Lewis Lapham, meanwhile, wrote in *Harper's Magazine* that the bulk of the war coverage 'was distinguished by its historical carelessness and its grotesque hyperbole' (1991: 12), concluding that 'a servile press is a circus act, as loudly and laughingly cheered by a military dictatorship as by a democratic republic' (Lapham, 1991: 15).

Trite as it may seem to say, the Gulf crisis drove home not the horror and insanity of war but the emptiness of mainstream media news coverage, especially television. Possibly for the first time, the extent to which media spectacle has substituted for public participation in politics received some essential comment (if not quite an extensive airing) in the media themselves.

In sharp contrast, western media coverage of the unfolding of the failed coup in the Soviet Union in August 1991 was rich and expansive. By comparison to the Gulf War, there were three important differences in the circumstances surrounding the Soviet event: first of all, Soviet authorities were unable to control the flow of information and the media enjoyed easy direct access to oppositional forces and important arenas of action (such as the streets of Moscow). Second, western media audiences in this case did not need to be called upon to support policy decisions of their own leadership and could be unproblematically addressed strictly as spectators. Finally – and no small point as far as the media institutions were concerned – no one was going to argue with their trumpeting that the Russian Revolution was good news this time around.

## Media, Crisis and Democracy: Mass Communication and the Disruption of Social Order

The Gulf War illustrated dramatically some of the ethical and political questions raised by media intervention in a context of crisis. The chapters of this book suggest that these questions are not specific to a particular situation, but are rather endemic to our era, and that they are furthermore fundamental to the continued quality of democratic public life.

Seen another way, the contributions to this international collection suggest that the relationship between media and democracy can best be understood by referring to the notion of crisis. As one of the key structuring elements of social and political life in the late twentieth century, crisis can be seen as synonymous with both modernity and progress. But situations of crisis are more revealing about society and its structures than situations of normalcy. This, the book shows, is particularly true insofar as the role of media in society is concerned.

Returning to the classical origins of liberalism that lie at the root of modern media theory, John Keane argues that the threat to the sovereignty of the nation-state that is deemed to accompany a state of crisis actually subverts the democratic foundations of the media. He proposes instead a new understanding of the relationship between democracy and information. Keane's chapter turns around the relationship between communication and civil society – a theme that characterizes much of his work (see eg Keane, 1988) – and ends with some reflection on the possibility of a truly international civil society (cf. also Bruck and Raboy, 1989).

Keane's is the first of several contributions in the book that emphasize the relationship between crisis situations and state security measures from the perspective of the relative freedom of media activity (see also Masmoudi in this volume). As crisis situations tend to mobilize for security measures, a classical strategy for legitimating clampdowns has been to invoke a state of crisis (cf. Gerbner in this volume). In this context, media become an extension of the state, ensuring 'that a latent crisis becomes manifest' (cf. Keane in this volume).

The most sophisticated argument of this type in recent decades was the mid-1970s formulation of a 'crisis of democracy', put forward by the

high-powered 'Trilateral Commission' of business and political leaders of
Europe, Japan and North America (Crozier et al., 1975). Its specific
emphasis on the role of the media is central to the arguments in this book
by Kellner and the Mattelarts.

But Keane emphasizes that there is no longer a single 'centre' of state
power in modern society; that power is diffuse, and diffused throughout
civil society. This corresponds to the notion of hegemony discussed in the
opening section of this introduction – and indicates an even more critical
role for media in maintaining traditional power relations.

The notion of 'sovereignty' is central to Keane's argument: for Keane, it
is clearly the people (through the institutions of civil society) who must be
sovereign if democracy is to be meaningful – regardless of the implications
of that reality for the state. In this sense, he would appear, on superficial
reading, to be at odds with our next contributor, Mustapha Masmoudi, for
whom the state appears to be the legitimate incarnation of the popular will
– and thus, a legitimate exerciser of communicational authority.

The distinction between these two essays centres around the authors'
respective geopolitical contexts. As one of the architects of the UNESCO-
led project for a New World Information and Communication Order,
Masmoudi writes from a Third World perspective in which the state is the
instrument of progress, modernization and a collective project. Nonetheless wary of any suggestion of state interference in the free circulation of
information, Masmoudi (a professional journalist as well as the former
Tunisian ambassador to UNESCO) struggles with the inevitability of
conflict between the untrammeled exercise of media activity and the higher
reason of state. His call for a codified ethic governing media behaviour in
time of crisis has a welcome pragmatic tone, especially in light of the Gulf
War, which also directly informs his chapter.

Interestingly, both Keane and Masmoudi mention media *accountability*
as a crucial condition of their playing a democratic role, and as assurance of
media responsibility, especially in time of crisis.

Masmoudi's essay also dovetails with that of Douglas Kellner, whose
focus is on the hegemonic role of mainstream media in the United States.
Elsewhere, US television is seen by critics as a beacon of US imperialism;
within the US itself, according to Kellner, it acts as a restraining
mechanism on the exercise of political democracy.

Like Masmoudi, Kellner uses embryonic case material from the Gulf
crisis to illustrate his thesis (well developed in earlier works, cf. Kellner,
1990). Kellner relates the performance of US media vis-a-vis the Gulf to a
political economy analysis of the role of media under capitalism. This role,
according to Kellner, constitutes a crisis of democracy which only a radical
alternative to dominant mainstream media can overcome.

Here the perspective is firmly rooted in a context critical of the way in
which the free flow of information has been integrated into a media system
based on commodification and control. Kellner makes his argument
strongly, and pits it against that of the Trilateral Commission, for whom

too much media independence constituted a threat to the liberal democratic model of societal management. In Kellner's argument, the crisis is that there is not enough democracy – in spite of a proliferation of what passes for information.

As did Keane, Kellner evokes the need to create alternatives if media are to fulfil their democratic function. And here too – with the aid of the counter-examples provided by the Gulf War experience – the notion of crisis allows us to see the emergence of possible spaces of *resistance* within the media/spectacle society.

As Kellner shows, the demonization of Iraq/Saddam/Islam/ the Arab world in general was an essential part of the mediatization of the Gulf crisis. In their discussion of media representation of the end of the Cold War – written before the outbreak of the crisis in the Gulf – Julian Halliday, Sue Curry Jansen and James Schneider demonstrate the importance of representation of the other in media/crisis politics. The end of the Cold War had a perverse effect on western (US) media by removing the state of permanent crisis under which they had flourished since 1945. This itself brought about a new 'crisis of representation' – which culminated in the construction of a new all-encompassing enemy in Hussein.

Halliday, Jansen and Schneider look at the framing of the changes in eastern Europe from the perspective of different types of media discourse: academic, news and advertising. Their argument focuses on the importance of mythology in situating the individual social subject in history. Between the discourses of explanation (which one finds in certain mainstream academic literature) and those of assimilation (as in certain forms of popular culture – where they situate advertising), we find the framing of crisis events which denote 'a dramatic disturbance of order'. The frightening implication of their thesis is that western media have come to rely on crisis denotation as a way of identifying and, especially, targeting the foreign 'other' necessary for maintaining the structures of power. This analysis helps account for the replacement of the 'threat of peace' in eastern Europe with the bogeyman of Saddam in the Middle East.

One of the leitmotivs of this book is that media play a role in the preservation of social order by declaring a crisis where one does not necessarily exist, while denying a state of crisis that is in the interests of elites to obscure. There can be no better example of this than the experience of eastern Europe from 1945 to 1989, where media were seen as strictly instrumentalist. As Karol Jakubowicz shows with special emphasis on Poland, the forced concordance of media performance and state policy in a situation of recurring, if not quite perpetual, crisis, resulted simply in the alienation of mainstream media from any democratic function.

Reading Jakubowicz, one can distinguish a curious parallelism between the soviet totalitarianism he describes (after Kolakowski, 1989) and Kellner's 'crisis-of-democracy' America. At the risk of appearing unfashionable, we would suggest it useful to read his rich study of eastern bloc media as applicable to 'western' media as well. In both systems, information is/was used as a form of political power; in both systems, the ground rules governing media operations have been mastered by political authorities anxious to deliver a message. In both systems, situations of crisis provide a vulnerable and fertile ground for the sowing of a political crop. One of the key distinctions between the two systems, in fact, is the relative success of the media in the west vis-a-vis their counterparts in the east, instrumentally speaking.

The subsequent two chapters argue that crisis is essentially a media construct. Drawing on more than 20 years of research into the mediatization of violence in its different forms, George Gerbner argues forcefully that this phenomenon reinforces social power through a variety of means, notably by fostering feelings of insecurity among the powerless and legitimating the mobilization of state violence against often marginal opposition groups. Labelling a situation as one of crisis, Gerbner reminds us, is a means of social control.

What does exposure to violence and terror do to different groups' conception of their own vulnerability, to society's approach to conflict, to the distribution of power and the likelihood of its abuse, Gerbner asks? As the Cold War turns into a new Holy Alliance (whose first mission was in the Gulf), media violence will tend increasingly to encourage audience passivity. Meanwhile, few countries appear willing to invest in a cultural policy that does not surrender the socialization of its children to market forces. Gerbner concludes with a call for a new 'international cultural environmental movement' dedicated to media reform – echoing the implied conclusions of other contributors.

Peter Bruck also makes a convincing argument for crisis as a strictly media-constructed phenomenon. Crises, Bruck argues, do not exist in the real world, but only in discourse. Bruck illustrates the role of sensationalist tabloid news formats in the spectacularization of social life, and the resulting disempowerment of individual members of society, who are led to consume the various aspects of their own social reality rather than act to change it.

Spectacularization, to Bruck, is a media technique for focusing a crisis in such a way as to achieve a discursive distance between the spectators and the observed. The spectacle, in this framework, is the pay-off to the consuming reader/viewer. Successive crises provide the material with which to describe a world in turmoil. As in Gerbner's analysis, the logical upshot is that media consumers will tend to make loyal subjects. And since media need crises, their news-diffusing codes and routines will tend to create them. The implication is that defining a crisis undermines the democratic function of media.

On the other hand, we would argue that there are actually existing crises in the real world and in history. One could go even further and claim that denying the crisis that exists can be a strategic political choice in an attempt to preserve social order. To the extent that media follow the lead of political authorities, their role can be to attenuate the crisis, rather than exacerbate it. In such cases, the full contradictory nature of mass media emerges – one can almost say that it is in times of crisis that the media reveal themselves, their workings and their motivations.

The chapters by Bernard Dagenais, Marc Raboy and Lorna Roth provide examples of the contradictory role of media in three radically different types of crisis situation: one directly challenging the political authority of a national government; one involving a profound crisis in social relations; and one concerning a stand-off between a distinct social group and the rest of the society of which it is a part. The three are all drawn from the editors' home context, Canada, but the phenomena they inform are, we feel, universal, rather than local.

Quebec's October Crisis of 1970, discussed by Dagenais, marked the transfer of the politics inspired by the 'urban guerilla' movements of Latin America to the advanced industrial north. Later overshadowed by the spectacular activities of groups like the Red Brigades and Baader-Meinhof in Europe, the October 1970 kidnappings of public officials by the Front de Libération du Québec (FLQ) were actually the first of the kind in a highly industrialized and highly mediatized society. Exacerbating a prevailing climate of general social unrest, the FLQ action led the Canadian government to declare a state of 'apprehended insurrection' and suspend civil liberties. This type of confrontation, perceived by authorities as being greatly threatening to the legitimacy of the state and the preservation of social order, characterized the crisis politics of the west in the 1970s and well into the 1980s. Dagenais' study illustrates the richly ambiguous nature of media involvement in such a crisis, the multi-layered texture of the media's role in a crisis situation. As he shows, it is too facile to pigeon-hole media into a single role: they are both observers *and* actors.

Far from the high politics that surround such notions as legitimation of the state, are the multiple manifestations of continuity and change as they are played out in the activities of everyday life. These rarely find their way into the media spotlight – until some spectacular event exposes the crisis. But, as Raboy shows, even then there can be strong pressure to deny the existence of a crisis situation, especially when the crisis is as deep-rooted and ultimately threatening as the one provoked by the profound change in male–female relations over the past 20 years.

The extraordinary event Raboy analyses – the mass murder in Montreal of 14 women by an avowedly 'anti-feminist' gunman – revealed the media's great difficulty in rendering meaningful the most fundamental crises of everyday life. Raboy sees the media as a site of 'discursive struggle', where naming the crisis for what it is can become a decisive battle. This analysis can be applied, on a macro-social scale, to treatment of such questions as famine and poverty, chronic unemployment and generational welfare, or the unequal distribution of wealth and resources. In all of these cases, media attention is generally event-driven, and attempts to politicize the discussions tend to be dismissed as ideological.

The modern saga described by Roth – an episode in the centuries-old struggle of North American native peoples for self-determination and sovereignty – has a singularity of form and content which removes it to a plane beyond that of a simple case study. By trying to capture the 'structure of feeling' of the 1990 confrontation between the Mohawk communities and the non-native authorities in Canada, Roth demonstrates the profound cultural bias (in the anthropological sense) of the media of communication developed by and associated with Euro-American society. Notwithstanding the sympathies of individual media workers, however important, the media as institutions remain part of the colonial apparatus from which indigenous peoples in the Americas are trying to shake free. The mediatization of Canada's 'Mohawk crisis' of 1990 helped place the issue of native self-government on the public agenda – but ironically, as Roth shows, this was accompanied by a commodification effect which made a grotesque caricature of even the most high-minded critique of media commercialization. The result, here, of what she calls the commodification of crisis is nothing less than the commodification of culture.

In the final chapter, French scholars Armand and Michèle Mattelart seek to present an overall picture of the media–crisis relationship. They are ideally suited for this task, having published an important book on the role of media in time of crisis in 1979. Here (in a text first presented as the inaugural lecture of the 'Media and Crisis' conference held at Laval University in October 1990; Mattelart and Mattelart, 1990) they update their earlier thesis.

'A certain idea of crisis is in crisis', write the Mattelarts at the start of their contribution, referring to what they see as a major distinction between two periods: the late 1960s–early 1970s, and the late 1980s–early 1990s. Their chapter presents aspects of the changing role of media in time of crisis, from 1968 to 1990. Placing media function in a framework of national, international and global crisis management, the Mattelarts cover the changes in the relationship between media and social movements, communications development in north–south relations, and the role of technological innovation in the new social context where capitalism appears to have emerged, at least for the time being, 'as the best of regimes for lack of a better one, the only one capable not only of managing crisis but of managing itself through crisis'.

This approach provides fascinating and illuminating insight – not only into the period concerned, but into the historic nature of the media–crisis relationship and its impact on democracy. In itself, this study demonstrates what we meant above when we suggested that crisis could be a paradigm for understanding the tensions between social continuity and social change.

## Notes

The authors wish to thank Doug Kellner for his helpful and constructive comments on this introduction.

1 Chantal de Rudder (1991) reports that US military strategists began planning 'special operations' to counter the persistence of anti-militarist sentiment in the United States, and 'especially in the media', as early as 1983. This is consistent with the well-publicized view of the Trilateral Commission (Crozier et al., 1975), that media freedom by the mid-1970s constituted a 'crisis of democracy' (see chapters by Kellner and Mattelart and Mattelart in this volume).

2 '"CNN owned Baghdad", said John MacFarlane, managing director of news programming for CTV (the Canadian private sector network) . . . "At the reporting end, they're not always slick, it could almost have been your sister or grandmother reporting from that hotel room. But when you look at Wednesday night, it doesn't really matter. *What matters is being there and being able to disseminate information* . . . What's a Herculean effort for the rest of us, is just business as usual for them . . ."' (cited in Harris, 1991, emphasis added).

The Canadian Broadcasting Corporation had a crew in Baghdad but, like most of the foreign reporters in town, they could not find a working telephone line. This prompted the CBC's national news editor, Tony Burman, to describe the CNN effort 'as more a telecommunications achievement than a journalistic one' (Harris, 1991).

According to Peter Rehak, executive producer of CTV's flagship current affairs programme *W5*: 'CNN has forced everybody (in broadcasting) to re-evaluate the way they cover news. You don't have to wait for the Cronkite show or the Brokaw show anymore. You just turn on CNN. We all have to react to that' (Harris, 1991).

3 Media academics were among those to cash in on the commodification of the Gulf media crisis – in France, a spate of instant books was off the press and in the shops by early May (*L'Evénement du jeudi*, 1991). Leading the way was the irrepressible Jean Baudrillard, with a steamy pamphlet entitled: *La guerre du Golfe n'a pas eu lieu* ('The Gulf War did not take place') (Baudrillard, 1991).

4 The cultural framework that has marked western media reporting on the Middle East in general has been well characterized in the work of Edward Said (1979, 1981), as 'orientalism'. Gulf War coverage abounded with examples of television anchors speaking about the 'anti-Arab' (instead of anti-Iraqi) coalition, asking their studio expert guests to 'Try and take us inside the Arab mind', or to explain to the audience 'In ten seconds, what is an Arab?' (all observed on newscasts of the relatively unjingoistic Canadian Broadcasting Corporation).

# 1

# The Crisis of the Sovereign State

## *John Keane*

Modern states, remarked Robert Southey in the early nineteenth century, can no more stand without pens than without bayonets (cited in Jerdan, 1866: 413). This maxim might well have been phrased as a long-term prognosis, for all western democracies are today faced by a gathering problem: the long-term drift, largely unplanned, towards a loose community of interlocking states, whose undemocratic structures of decision making are multi-layered, quasi-supranational and equipped with various mechanisms for powerfully regulating and distorting the exchange of information and opinion among their citizens. The symptoms of this long-term trend are already quite evident. The flow of opinions among citizens is hindered by the executive use of old-fashioned prerogative powers and new techniques of official information management. It is obstructed by the resort to secrecy and dissimulation and the recurrent appeal to the principle of the sovereignty of the state ('national security'). And, since the First World War, the cause of political censorship has been furthered by the steady spread of unsupervised corporatist mechanisms and by 'invisible' forms of local, national and supranational government – departments, commissions, agencies and intergovernmental conferences which are normally neither accountable to citizens or their mass media, nor subject to the rule of law.

It is curious that researchers in the fields of communications and political science have paid little attention to these trends, despite their profoundly disturbing implications for our understanding of democracy. Unaccountable power has always been regarded as scandalous in democratic countries, and yet those countries are now faced by a permanent scandal. The core of all democratic regimes today contain the seeds of despotism. The historic (if never completed) transformation of early modern absolutist states into late modern constitutional states governed by parliaments is over. We are entering a new era of political censorship, the age of the democratic Leviathan, in which key parts of life are structured by unaccountable political institutions equipped – as Southey might have observed – with old and new pens of various shapes and sizes.

A revised theory of freedom and equality of communication must come to terms with these forms of state interference in the process of publicly defining and circulating opinions. Five interlocking types of political censorship warrant particular attention. They are described as ideal types and examined below in order of their familiarity:

*Emergency Powers.* Time-honoured attempts by governments to bully parts of the media into submitting directly to their wishes by means of instructions, threats, bans and arrests continue to make their presence felt in western democracies. Such techniques of political repression come in two forms. *Prior restraint* (as it was known originally in constitutional circles in the United States) includes all those informal and formal procedures – from the friendly chat and cocktails with a government spokesperson and simple requests or warnings delivered by telephone to the issuing of mandatory and discretionary guidelines – whereby the publication of matter (be it oral, visual or print) is vetted by the state authorities. *Post-publication censorship* operates from the time of the initial publication of material to its dissemination. It may include legal action taken against material already available in civil society. It normally leads to the banning, shredding, burning, reclassification or confiscation of books or visual material (photographs or paintings, films or videos), or the confiscation of the technical means by which that material has been produced. Post-publication censorship may also extend to the closure of newspapers, printing houses, radio and television stations. It may encompass the banning of particular 'anti-state' organizations and the censoring and punishing of journalists for 'condoning terrorism' by expressing their sympathies for such organizations.

Especially in times of (alleged) crisis, these two sub-types of political repression of the media are often combined. The media are seen by the political authorities to have no useful or legitimate function unless as accessories to the armoury of the state. The media thus come to play a distinctive political role. They ensure that a latent crisis becomes manifest by rendering collective the feeling of crisis among citizens, and by amplifying the claim of state officials that drastic action is required to remedy the crisis, which they have defined as such through the media.

*Armed Secrecy.* Modern state power thrives on police and military organs which are shrouded in secrecy. The reason is obvious: there is no better way in which state officials can outmanoeuvre their domestic or foreign opponents than to learn about them by monitoring their activities, without being monitored in turn. This dynamic underpinning the growth of invisible 'repressive state apparatuses' is certainly evident in twentieth-century western democracies. Police and military apparatuses marked by secrecy, cunning, and the insistence on compulsory unanimity within the organization are normal features of democratic states. They are also deeply antithetical to political democracy and to freedom of communication.

The problem of armed secrecy, Kant and others observed, was evident within the operations of early modern governments, which appreciated, for example, the value of planting informers in opposition groups at times of crisis (see Meinecke, 1957). Wars and revolutions were typical breeding grounds for armed secrecy. Yet until the late nineteenth century these systems of shadowy armed power were improvised and transient, being built around the capabilities of specific groups of officers and linked to individual government ministers and particular threats or sudden crises. Or (as in America) secretive armed power remained in private hands; the surreptitious gathering of information about social groups was conducted by private policing agencies, such as the union-bashing Pinkertons, who hired themselves out to businesses and other organizations of civil society. All this changed in the early years of the twentieth century. Between the summer of 1909 and the autumn of 1911 in Britain – whose permanent institutions of armed secrecy were among the first to develop – MI5 and MI6 were born, and the modern Official Secrets Act was passed. The 'D-Notice' system for vetting newspaper stories bearing on 'national security' was devised. A register of aliens living in Britain was established, blanket interceptions of certain categories of mail at the Post Office began, and the Special Branch was transformed into a domestic counter-subversion agency.

After this time, the bureaucratic instinct for survival ensured the permanence of secret police and secretive military organizations within the state. Their continuity was guaranteed less by dangers to the state and more by budgetary allocations and such mundane concerns as offices, desks, telephones, files and pension plans. This trend in western democracies was greatly strengthened by the onset of the Cold War, and by attempts to portray domestic dissent as linked to dangerous international enemies. This has resulted in a well-organized form of permanent political censorship at the heart of state power. Governments regularly control official press releases and authorize briefings in matters of 'national security'. Information is classified or reclassified as 'secret'. Dirty tricks are covered up. Selected citizens have their phones tapped, their homes bugged and their offices broken into without the benefit of a judicial warrant. Government officials in the intelligence, military and police are subjected to a duty of 'lifetime' confidentiality.

The growth of armed secrecy has recently produced bizarre effects. Parts of the elected executive branch of the state have snooped on their potential rivals and systematically disinformed legislatures (Watergate). The police have conducted clandestine paramilitary operations against either their peaceful opponents (the Rainbow Warrior bombing) or their violent enemies (as in the bombing campaigns and assassinations in Spain conducted by the shadowy Anti-terrorist Liberation Groups, or GAL, whose function was to terrorize Basque terrorists and their sympathisers). Extensive junta-like operations (such as the Iran-Contra affair) have been conducted behind the backs of elected authorities. And state paramilitary secrecy has been used to protect secretive anti-state organizations employing paramilitary tactics (the Piazza Fontana massacre and the Gladio affair). Finally, the phenomenon of secret armed power has spread into the realm of intergovernmental negotiations. The routine conduct of NATO and WEU affairs, for example, involves the integration of national defence bureaucracies with transnational defence organizations; these in turn create centres of power which escape the control of any single member state, government or parliament. Supranational military organizations shift decision-making power away from legislatures. They increase the level of electoral unaccountability and secrecy of government operations. And, since the growth of supranational organs encourages particular govern-ments to allege the necessity of political compromise with other govern-ments, it leads governments everywhere to formulate 'flexible' negotiating positions, thereby discouraging legislatures from 'interfering' in suprana-tional negotiations.

*Lying.*   The nasty business of lying in politics is a characteristic feature of democratic (and other) regimes. The belief of politicians that half of politics is image making and the other half the art of making people believe the imagery, whatever 'the facts', is rampant; the old maxim that politicians can be understood only by watching their feet and not their mouths remains true. The practice of lying is partly an inheritance from the early modern period. During the phase of state building and the formation of nation-state politics, truthfulness was rarely counted among the political virtues. Kant's insistence that lying is never justified, not even to save a friend from probable murder – a thesis he directed against Benjamin Constant during the Thermidorean phase of the French Revolution (Pozzo di Borgo, 1964) – is a cry in the wilderness of modern political power. Outright lies and calculated secrecy, as Hugo de Grotius pointed out in *De jure belli ac pacis* (1625), were always regarded as legitimate means of achieving political ends.

In recent decades the commitment to the 'methods of defactualization' (Arendt) has assumed new forms. For example the art of political lying has adopted the tough charm, parrying 'good will' and slick-tongued tactics of the Madison Avenue public relations person. This is the art practised by government press officers: throwing critics off the trail, calming nerves, keeping journalists happy, preparing stories for public consumption with a careful eye to making them credible. This art of lying through public relations is most fully developed in the United States, where White House staff regularly seek to shape the media's portrayal of the president. Administration is viewed as a continuous public relations effort. State-ments from various government departments are vetted and tightly coordinated. Press conferences are used to project the opinions of the presidency. Certain reporters are accredited; questions are planted; follow-up questions are disallowed; 'cream puff' topics are given priority; and, since Truman, carefully prepared opening statements help set the agenda for reporters in attendance. The administration provides a range of 'services' to the media, such as interviews, photo opportunities, back-ground sessions, travel accommodations and daily handouts. Briefings are especially important occasions for gentle lying. Briefings may be 'off the record' (the information reporters receive may not be used in a story); 'on the record' (remarks may be attributed to the speaker); 'on background' (a specific source cannot be identified although general descriptions of its position and status – such as a 'White House source' – are permitted); or they may be 'deep background' (in which case no attribution is allowed). When these (potentially) mendacious methods fail, the administration attempts to punish the media for coverage perceived as unfair, unfavourable or both. Particular journalists are asked to choose between their career interests and their critical opinions of the government. In extreme cases, media hostile to the administration are denied access to official sources.

*State Advertising.*  The rulers of the early modern state, especially during its absolutist phase, regarded themselves as the source and principle of unity in a particularistic society of orders and estates. These executives of state power sought to protect and legitimate themselves by taking counsel from others – through parliaments, individual and corporate petitions, personal networks of informants – and by peddling their own opinion among the clients of state power. Southey's remark about bayonets and pens drew attention to this latter mechanism. In Europe, the *London Gazette*, which first appeared under the title of the *Oxford Gazette* in 1665, was among the most famous and influential of these organs of government advertising. It channelled officially sanctioned interpretations of foreign news. 'What came in the foreign mails is in the *Gazette*' was a constantly recurring phrase. Its single folio sheet reported the sovereign's speeches to Parliament, and found space for royal proclamations and resolutions of the Privy Council. Promotions at court were also reported to the public: to be 'gazetted' is still the formula of career advancement. In addition, the *Gazette* printed information provided by informers, published the numbers of winning tickets in government lotteries and made space available for those advertisements for bear-grease for baldness and other quack remedies which were so prominent a feature of eighteenth-century journalism.

Today, the methods of the *London Gazette* have become more sophisticated and a regular feature of all western democratic governments. Government advertising is big and serious business. The self-promotion of state power absorbs a budget of nearly £200 million a year in Britain – where the state is the second largest advertiser, behind only Unilever – covering 'campaigns' on every conceivable policy matter. The steady growth of state advertising gives all democratically elected governments enormous powers of blackmail. Since most independent newspapers, radio and television stations rely heavily on revenue from advertising for their survival, threats by governments to withdraw such funding tends to produce compliance with pressures or even the collapse of such ventures. The growing ability of governments to use parts of the mass media strengthens this trend (and reinforces the patterns of lying through public relations work, mentioned above). Media reporting based on unattributed back-door leaks, and the authorized and informal briefings of the 'lobby system' are well-known examples. Other examples include government campaign advertising (backed by professional consultants, actors, actresses, film directors and hiring agencies), official press releases and kite-flying – the unacknowledged spreading of rumours or disinformation by governments to test the waters of public opinion. The official accreditation of experts with pro-government views also serves to legitimate (or increase the level of visibility of) official sources, thereby coat-tailing the media to the management of opinion by governments,

The positively-slanted coverage of political leaders through television and radio interviews is a less obvious but no less important example of state advertising. In recent years, intimate links have developed between broadcasting journalists, with their firm views of what the audience has the right as citizens to know about the actions of government, and the executive, backed by phalanxes of government information officers, press officers and other minders arguing almost legalistically with producers about the rules of engagement and appearance. Political interviews tend to become vehicles for political persuasion and veiled party-political broadcasts. The outward form of the journalistic interview is preserved, but the story is framed by the ground rules (concerning transmission duration, the timing of an interview, and the importance of having 'the last word') laid down by the interviewees. Questions designed to make politicians answerable to publics are replaced by questions intended to please politicians and to let them say what they like. Journalists climb into the pockets of politicians. Government statements become 'noble lies'. This trend is summarized by a leading British broadcaster:

As television has become a medium of marketing more than of broadcasting, so the advertising cast of mind manifest by government has caught journalists by surprise. In the past press officers have wanted to channel and control the journalists' understanding of the story. Today, they see us as another outlet, more volatile but not dissimilar to an advertising slot. A newspaper can talk to a politician and there is no supposition that every word uttered will be reported. On television, there are demands for effective control of the editing. It is as if the appearance belongs to the interviewee. (cited in Tusa, 1989; see also Heritage, 1985)

*Corporatism.* During the twentieth century, networks of private sector organizations performing functions for the government through the devices of negotiations, grants and contracts have become commonplace. A substantial number of decisions of public consequence are taken, not in executives, legislatures or markets, but in bargains struck between the 'representatives' of social groups, or between these groups of civil society and the state itself.

Corporatist procedures of this kind have resulted from the offloading by the state of a considerable number of its functions to the non-state organizations of civil society, whose key power groups have demanded a share of political power. Consequently, the boundaries of state and civil society intertwine. They are mediated by the bargaining, jostling and shifting compromises of 'public' officials and state machinery and private 'non-state' agencies. Corporatism is a process of state intervention which contracts out official status to interest groups and organizations, which are charged to a greater or lesser degree with the formulation and/or implementation of public policy. Corporatism brings strategically important functional groups inside the state – 'politicizing' parts of civil society – while at the same time extending the state sphere into civil society, thereby 'socializing' certain state functions. This process is patterned and tiered in complex and dynamic ways. It operates at different levels of decision making, and appears to broaden the general franchise by supplementing territorial forms of political representation with functional modes of decision making. Trade unions, businesses, professional associations and other organizations become integral and indispensable components of public policy making because they have a monopoly of information relevant for government. They also often exercise a substantial measure of control over their respective constituencies. But none of this guarantees the 'openness' or 'representativeness' of corporatist procedures. They tend to be highly elitist. Government personnel are not directly subject to parliamentary election or control. The 'private' bargaining organizations are also structured bureaucratically. Their negotiators tend to instrumentalize the rank and file membership, who are relegated to the role of policy takers. Negotiators tend to define agendas from the viewpoint of the corporate body. The costs of decisions are passed off on to the less powerful and poorly organized groups of civil society.

Corporatist procedures have also developed behind a veil of confidentiality and extra-legality. Although permanent features of the political landscape, such procedures are rarely given legal form and not often subjected to the requirements of public accountability. They constitute a form of government by moonlight. Corporatist procedures are not obliged publicly to reveal, to explain or to justify their activities. Decision makers are under no *ex ante* legal obligations to consult widely on the range of choices available to them. Nor are they subject to *post hoc* obligations, for example, to justify publicly either their patterns of expenditure or the degree of success or failure in achieving the goals which they have set themselves.

These five interlocking trends in western democracies are worrying. They indicate the growing quantity of political power which is normally accountable neither to citizens or to the mass media nor subject to the rule of law. If the rule of law (Dicey's phrase (1885)) means the systematic elimination of arbitrary state power from political life, where arbitrary power is power immune from public evaluation and criticism and insensitive to and incapable of learning from its environment, then without exaggeration we can speak of a growing lawlessness in western democracies.

Within these regimes, there is a surprisingly large number of observers who are defensive of these trends and unsympathetic or hostile to citizens' attempts to extend the rule of law, to reduce the arbitrariness and secrecy of political power. Democracy is seen to require a powerful, authoritative state which acts as an overlord of the private sphere. The sinews of a 'free' society, it is claimed, are provided by coherent administrative power, by the bold, decisive action of statesmanlike politicians, and by governments' willingness to enforce national traditions and the laws of the land – against the internal and external enemies of the state and civil society.

Such observers succour the old doctrine of sovereignty of the state. This doctrine originally had no meaning at all apart from the system of absolute monarchy in which it was born. According to the various theories of sovereignty of early modern writers such as Bodin, Althusius and Hobbes, the people are a body crying out for a head. This head is ultimately indivisible and absolute. Especially in times of public calamity and (threatened) crises of the body politic, it has the exclusive rght to silence its subjects and to speak on their behalf. The sovereign is an earthly god whose power resembles the master who issues commands to his slave, or the father who disciplines his children. Guided by the principle *salus rei publicae suprema lex* (the safety of the state is the supreme law), the sovereign, whether by divine right, natural law or the fact of conquest, is duty bound to govern as cunningly as possible. Sovereignty requires the *arcana imperii*, that is, it feeds upon the mysteries and aura of state power. It is constantly on the lookout for enemies at home and abroad. It must perforce be a form of rule which is both secretive and deceptive. Arcane dealings and noisy and pompous displays of power are the two sides of the sovereign state coin. Those who rule must not only *dissimulate* their power, which is most effective when they know and see without being seen by their subjects. Subjects must know that there are some who watch over them without knowing the location of the watchtower. Subjects must also live in awe of the magnificence of the state. Sovereign state power requires *simulation*, visible signs of its supremacy: escorts of soldiers, splendid clothing, sparkling crowns and sceptres, elaborate rites of passage, obelisks, arches, columns, fountains and a beautiful palace in the heart of the leading city.

## Government in the Sunshine

Both this old imagery of sovereignty and the unaccountable power which it harbours are incompatible with the open and flexible government specified by the principles and procedures of representative democracy. Democracy is a form of public decision making conducted in public. Democratic procedures are unique – and superior to all other types of decision making – not because they guarantee both consensus and 'good' decisions, but because they provide the citizens who are affected by certain decisions with the possibility of reconsidering their judgements about the quality and unintended consequences of these decisions. Democratic procedures increase the level of 'flexibility' and 'reversibility' of decision making. They encourage incremental learning and trial-and-error modification (or 'muddling through'), and that is why attempts to expose and publicly control the democratic Leviathan are slowly becoming more common in western democracies.

The agenda for 'government in the sunshine' is admittedly inchoate at present.

One priority is the exposure and repeal of the censorial methods of contemporary state power. In view of the growth of lawless and invisible government, the onus must be placed on governments everywhere to justify publicly *any* interference with *any* part of the circulation of opinions. Government must not be considered the legitimate trustee of information.

This principle, when brought to bear upon the forms of political censorship outlined above, points to the need for a new constitutional settlement in all western democracies (and in the regimes of central-eastern Europe, presently preoccupied with the difficult business of constitution making and dismantling totalitarian structures). Freedom and equality of communication requires legal protection and, where necessary, a written constitution. A great variety of legal means can help to promote freedom of expression and access to information among transacting citizens. Where a country has a written constitution, freedom of expression and of the media should be protected within it as well as within other national legislation. The principle that freedom is the rule and limitation the exception should be adhered to.

The US First Amendment ('Congress shall make no law . . . abridging the freedom of speech or of the press') still serves as the prototype of such legislation. It certainly contains several troubling conceptual flaws, which have become the subject of intense controversy and which must be addressed by a revised democratic theory of the media. Two centuries of constitutional adjudication have clouded an Amendment whose wording appeared to be shiningly clear. As Alexander Hamilton and others predicted, it has become buried under piles of antecedent case law which confronts each new justice with the awkward task of stepping lightly through fine distinctions and picayune details, and of accounting for prior decisions, rather than of interpreting and applying the Amendment directly. Many examples leap to mind. Whether 'freedom of the press' and 'freedom of speech', both of which are protected by the Amendment, imply separate systems of differing constitutional protection or are simply reiterations of one indivisible freedom, has been a continuing source of debate. Another dispute revolves around the *kind* of speech referred to within the Amendment – obscene or religious, commercial or political, private or public.

The adoption of a *corporate* view of press freedom, applying the press clause of the First Amendment to justify special privileges for the 'institution' of the media, has been resisted on the grounds that freedom of the press arose historically as an *individual* liberty, and that freedom of speech and of the press remain 'fundamental personal rights' (Chief Justice Hughes). Further arguments have been sparked by the problem of compulsory disclosures, for example, whether journalists can be threatened with fines or prison terms and made to disclose the information which was entrusted to them in confidence in their professional capacity as journalists. And there has been continuing controversy about whether the First Amendment was intended as a *defence* against government, that is, as a shield to defend citizens and the media against prior restraints on their power of expression, or whether the clause can also be invoked as a weapon for ensuring 'freedom of information', that is, as a means of *attacking* state censorship.

The path-breaking case of *Richmond Inc v. Virginia* (448 US 555 [1980]) settled this last controversy in favour of the view that the principle of freedom of communication can be used as a sword against state power. It pointed to the vital need, in any democracy, for legislation enforcing citizens' right of reply in the media against their governments. Suing governments for damages is prohibitively expensive for the majority of citizens. Legal backing is required which allows anyone injured by offensive or inaccurate statements the right of reply in the same communications outlet in which such statements have been made.

Freedom of expression among citizens supposes not only the power to impart points of view against government, in addition it requires the power to *seek* points of view. This 'right to know' requires solid institutional support. Of special importance would be the abolition of 'lobby systems', various forms of which presently function to limit publicity surrounding potentially controversial events in favour of selected journalists and current government policies. The (further) development of independently minded and publicly accessible standing committees – of the legislative, investigatory or advisory kind anticipated in the Bundestag and the US Congress – could ensure more effective scrutiny and control of both the executive and the invisible branches of the democratic Leviathan.

The 'right to know' also requires firm legal recognition and protection, since it is fundamental to ensuring open and publicly accountable government. Among the path-breaking efforts to do this is the hard look doctrine, first articulated in the United States in the case of *Greater Boston Television Co. v. FCC* (1970), and later moulded into the 1977 Government in the Sunshine Act (see Welborn et al., 1984; Harden and Lewis, 1986). The doctrine grew out of widespread complaints that parts of the state were not compelled to speak openly to the relationship between their own and wider interests. Hard look doctrine is suspicious of closed bargaining and *ex parte* negotiations. It aims to make state institutions accountable to their citizens without producing administrative overload.

The doctrine seeks a path between so-called 'substantial evidence' rules, which require policy makers to explain and justify their every move, and more lenient 'kid gloves' standards, which oblige decision makers to explain only the logic underpinning the decisions they reach. Hard look doctrine circumscribes what can be dealt with collectively when citizens cannot be present at hearings. It provides that all other meetings of an agency be open to public observation unless the matter is statutorily exempted. It specifies the procedures for closing meetings, and requires that records of such meetings be kept. The doctrine lays down procedures for guaranteeing public access to these records, and specifies the ground rules for judicial review of alleged violations of the doctrine itself.

Finally, legislation covering data protection is also an important means of preventing political censorship. The principle of data protection was first enshrined in West German and Scandinavian legislation in the early 1970s. It developed out of concerns over the growing power of computer systems to manipulate information without individuals and groups knowing what data is filed and the purposes for which it is used. The European Convention on Data Protection, which came into force in October 1985, provides an international legal framework for individual countries to adopt. Most national data protection legislation deals only with information stored in computers – in some countries the law extends to records kept manually – and it often excludes rights of access to the records of government departments dealing with such matters as social security, taxation, police and immigration. The point underpinning data protection legislation is nevertheless serious and important, if paradoxical: individual citizens require guaranteed access to their personal files held by state (and civil) 'data users' in order to ensure the *privacy* of that information. Such legislation aims to prevent unauthorized access to personal information as well as to enable individuals to certify that their personal data is accurate, up to date and actually relevant for the purpose for which it is filed. These points are well summarized in Article 1 of the French Law on Informatics and Liberty (France, 1978): 'Computer science must be at the service of each citizen; its development has to operate within the framework of international co-operation; it should not damage human identity, human rights, private life or individual and public liberties.'

**Rethinking Sovereignty**

There remains the vexed question of how to deal with the unaccountability of supranational political institutions. Their expanding power could be rendered more accountable by subjecting them to various forms of parliamentary supervision. These could include strengthened standing committees, closer cooperation among national legislatures and, in turn, their coordination with supranational legislatures – such as the European Parliament – whose strengthening, contrary to some expressed doubts, might well contribute to the revitalization of their national counterparts.

Another potentially fruitful option is suggested by proposals for developing an international civil society.[1] The fullest possible implementation of high international standards governing citizens' rights of communication is clearly important. Article 19 of the Universal Declaration of Human Rights is an example: 'Everyone has the right to freedom of opinion and expression; this right includes the freedom to hold opinions without interference and to seek, receive and impart information and ideas through any media and regardless of frontiers' (United Nations, 1988: 4).

Declarations of this kind are fuelled by the ideal of a new global information and communication order – a concept mentioned for the first time in a UN General Assembly resolution in 1978 and voiced in documents such as the MacBride Commission's *Many Voices. One World* (UNESCO, 1980). It also tends to be supported by the development, since the 1960s, of electronic and satellite technologies, which feed upon the economies of scale inherent in broadcasting, where the marginal cost of an extra viewer is zero. Satellite communications enable users to fly over and around the walls of the nation-state. They are able to transfer voices, data, texts and images swiftly over long distances and to large geographical areas. The relayed information can take the form of television or radio broadcasts, fax messages and telephone conversations, or it can be specific data, related to financial markets, professional conferences, sporting events or weather information, often collected by computer databases at both ends of the link.

Such developments in global communications media, in theory at least, make the world smaller and more open. These media operate to an extent as a global Fourth Estate – as during the recent 'velvet revolutions' in central-eastern Europe. Telephones, fax machines, photocopiers, electronic bulletin boards, video and audio recordings, especially when linked to global telecommunications networks, are now used worldwide to subvert repressive governments. Developments in global communications theoretically ensure that events anywhere can be reported anywhere else on radio within minutes; on television within hours. But theory and practice are often far apart. Government regulation, combined with the high costs of installing telecommunications equipment and providing publicly accessible terminals, prevents citizens of most countries from accessing such global telecommunications networks as teleconferencing and electronic mail systems. Meanwhile, private broadcast news has become a global business, almost like the music industry, with its own 'Top Ten' and an inevitable streamlining of opinions and tastes. A few major organizations control the newsflow. Syndicators guarantee that wider and wider audiences get to read, see or hear the same stories.

Other problems concerning the ownership and operation of satellite communications are emerging. A few wealthy countries monopolize the ownership, launching and control of satellites due to the high costs incurred in purchasing and maintaining the technology. There is an absence of common technical standards which would ensure the easy exchange of information between different satellite communication channels. Problems also arise from the limited number of satellites that can be launched into a geostationary orbit, from which they operate as transmitters for certain geographical areas; at present, satellite orbit slots and frequencies are the subject of intense international dispute between those who consider that space belongs to the earth in common and those governments which assume that their more powerful number should decide. And there are emerging controversies about whether satellites should be used for secret intelligence gathering, military photography and telephone tapping.

For these reasons, the development of an international civil society cannot be left to legislators or technologies alone. It also requires militant efforts to enrich *from below* the flows of information among communicating citizens, regardless of the nation states within which they live. To some degree, this requirement can be satisfied by intelligent, public-spirited forms of journalism, which have emerged in recent years as a separate and specialized branch of the media. So-called quality investigative journalism came to the fore during the Watergate scandal, but it has long been a feature of the type of cosmopolitan journalism exemplified by *Der Spiegel* and the *New Statesman*.

Quality journalism rejects tabloid newspaper tactics, whose golden rules are: please the news desk; get front page coverage and stay in front of everyone else; reflect the prejudices of readers; defend nationalist hype and page three pin-ups; fight for 'the scandal of gay vicar' and other sensational exclusives with as little legal comeback as possible; remain emotionally uninvolved in any and every story; if necessary, invade privacy on a scale that would impress a burglar; all the while explaining to the interviewees that their willingness to cooperate will help others in a similar plight. High quality investigative journalism lives by different rules. It seeks to counteract the secretive and noisy arrogance of the democratic Leviathan. It involves the patient investigation and exposure of political corruption, misconduct and mismanagement. It clings to the old maxim of American muck-rakers – 'the news is what someone, somewhere, *doesn't* want to see printed'. It aims to sting political power, to tame its arrogance by extending the limits of public controversy and widening citizens' informed involvement in the public spheres of civil society.

An international civil society of freely communicating citizens can develop if public encouragement and material support is also given to a wide variety of non-governmental associations working to combat political censorship. In recent years, such organisations have become a feature of the 'globalization' of power. Most of them are little known and struggle for survival under harsh financial and political pressures. Such organizations are of two types: those which are nationally-based, such as the Index on Censorship, Wolnosc i Pokój and the Alliance for Justice, which strive to monitor and document the performance of governments and to mobilize public opinion in support of their findings; and those with affiliated bodies or memberships in several countries, such as International PEN, Greenpeace, Amnesty International, Ecoropa, the Helsinki Citizens' Assembly, the International Federation of Actors, and the International Commission of Jurists.

Ultimately, this bundle of proposals can be plausible only if the thorny old *problématique* of sovereignty of the state is confronted head-on, and displaced. Defenders of political censorship react sharply to such proposals. They are adamant that the state must always be empowered to eliminate the 'worms within the entrails' of the body politic (Hobbes). Under emergency conditions, citizens must confront the state in awe and fear. The presumption in resistance must always be against them: 'When the final absolute authority of the state executive is threatened, and when push comes to shove', a defender of nation-state sovereignty might insist, 'freedom of communication is a dispensable luxury. Freedom of expression can produce disorder and even civil war.'

Here the argument traps itself within the chain of reasoning of Joseph de Maistre's *Du Pape* (1830): 'There can be no human society without government, no government without sovereignty, no sovereignty without infallibility.' Those who still assert such cynical views need to be answered in the toughest terms. The defence of state censorship is a nonsense, because it rests upon the obsolete principle of executive sovereignty. The 'sovereign state' is today under siege from two sides. At home it is subject to important centrifugal tendencies, bearing especially on the shifting boundaries between civil society and the state. In foreign affairs states are even more intermeshed in transnational frameworks of decision making. Ever more executive decisions are limited or foreclosed by the membership of states in military arrangements and intergovernmental organizations such as the IMF, GATT, the UN and the EC, as well as by the investment decisions of transnational corporations. Both trends are in a real sense synthesized by the invention and deployment of nuclear weapons. Their capacity to annihilate both attacker and defender under battle conditions arguably puts an end to the independence abroad and exclusive jurisdiction at home of all nation states.

These forces working against unlimited and indivisible executive state power should certainly not be exaggerated. The end of the modern nation state is not nigh. The so-called 'globalization' process is highly uneven. The extent to which the 'sovereignty' of a particular nation state is presently eroding depends not only on its past history (eg whether and to what extent it ever enjoyed 'sovereign status'). It also depends on such contemporary factors as its position in the force-fields of global power politics, its place in the world economy, its implication in international agencies and legal systems, and the strength and effervescence of the domestic and international civil societies underpinning its power structures.

Nevertheless the argument that sovereignty does not and cannot reside in the hands of state executives must now be taken seriously. The modern idea of the centralized, sovereign nation-state which is both independent of any external authority and capable of governing the territory and population it monopolizes is in deep trouble. The governmental bodies of nation-state communities no longer (if they ever fully did) exclusively determine the lives of their citizens. Our globe is beginning to resemble the *form* of the medieval world, in which the political powers of the monarch or prince were forced to share authority with a variety of subordinate and higher powers. 'Sovereignty' is becoming a fiction – if still a most useful fiction in the hands of undemocratic forces, who insist that there are times when the state be granted the plenitude of power, and who cry, with Dante, that the *maxime unum* is the *maxime bonum*.

The 'decline of sovereignty' has profound implications for a democratic theory of the media. It forces a fundamental rethinking of the classical theory of 'liberty of the press', which viewed communications systems only within the framework of the system of single nation states. It highlights the distance between the early modern period and today's world. It forces consideration of the rise of globally organized media companies, whose operations routinely break the straitjacket of the nation state and its domestic markets. And it reminds us of the importance of the growing impact of supranational legal and political arrangements, and of the slow and delicate growth of an international civil society.

The decline of sovereignty also has profound implications for radical strategies of enhancing media freedom at the end of the twentieth century. The traditional twentieth-century view of radical opposition – the revolutionary strategy of seizing state power, if need be through the use of violence – thought in terms of 'capturing' the General Post Office, 'seizing' radio and television stations and other 'centres' of state power and influence. The aim was to prevent counter-revolution and to plant the seeds of the future society. This thought informed the Soviet government decree of mid-November 1917, curtailing freedom of the press. 'The state is only a transitional institution which we are obliged to use in the revolutionary struggle in order to crush our opponents forcibly' (cited in Bunyan and Fisher, 1934: 221).

The decline of state sovereignty renders *implausible* this strategy of 'capturing' the 'centres' of power and communication which – as the labyrinthine structures of political censorship discussed above indicate – are in fact tending to become more dispersed. The highly differentiated and disunified character of democratic regimes provides the reminder that there is simply no single centre of state power which could be 'occupied' and used to transform radically civil society with the help of the means of communication. Not only that, but insofar as 'the state' is insufficiently in one place to be 'seized', the strategy of monopolizing the means of communication for radical purposes is rendered *unnecessary*. The uncoordinated and dispersed character of state power makes it more susceptible to the initiatives of social movements and citizens' groups, backed by countervailing networks of communication, which challenge prevailing codes and practise the art of *divide et impera* from below. Dispersed networks of communication can more easily penetrate the pores of civil society and build networks of meaning among various groups of citizens. These networks are important because they explicitly recognize the urgent need to deal with the various forms of political censorship which have grown enormously in recent decades. They are important for another reason: they indicate ways in which new forms of social solidarity, especially among the less powerful citizenry, can be developed against the atomizing effects of modern life. Communicative networks can help to offset the tendency of the mass media to pile discontinuity on to us, to wash away memories, to dissolve and fast-cut, to throw away yesterday's papers. Decentralized networks of communication address the dangers of 'up-rootedness', and the felt need of many citizens to put down roots within civil society through forms of association which preserve particular memories of the past, a measure of stability in the present, and particular expectations for the future. Finally, communications networks developed 'underneath' and 'beyond' the structures of state power – so-called bush telegraphs – have important potential for empowering citizens. They weaken the tendency (as Virginia Woolf put it) for a dozen censors to rush in, whenever we express our opinions, telling us what to say or not to say. They cultivate the virtues of democratic citizenship: prudence, judgement, eloquence, resourcefulness, courage, self-reliance, sensitivity to power and common sense. Communications networks renew the old insight that the decentralization of power is sometimes the most effective cure for an undue parochialism; that through involvement in local organizations citizens overcome their localism. And these networks stimulate awareness of an important new insight about power. They recognize that large-scale organizations, such as state bureaucracies and capitalist corporations, rest upon complex, molecular networks of everyday power relations – and that the strengthening and transformation of these molecular powers necessarily induces effects upon these large-scale organizations.

These considerations on the decline of sovereignty lead some observers to the conclusion that the principle of seditious libel – the principle brought to bear on Thomas Paine at the end of the eighteenth century – must now be rejected as dangerous and obsolete.[2] It is argued that public discussion must never be made dependent upon government sufferance.

Political freedom ends when government can use its various discretionary powers to silence its critics. The point is not the tepidly conventional liberal view that there should be room for public criticism of the government. It is rather that defamation of government is a contradiction in terms in a democracy. The right publicly to burn the national flag should be absolute, and therefore unchallengeable.

This species of libertarianism correctly spots the dangers inherent in restrictions on communications media in the name of preserving 'sovereignty'. As the leading German journalist August Ludwig von Schlözer noted prior to the French Revolution, enlightened rulers might permit wide-ranging press freedom, but where freedom of the press depended on a sovereign power, it could be taken away just as easily as it was granted (cited in Schneider, 1966). The deployment of the state's executive powers against dissenters in the name of 'preserving the integrity of the state' usually magnifies the attraction of anti-democratic propaganda and authoritarian movements and parties railing against the existing order, which is portrayed (plausibly) as authoritarian. Besides, temporary clampdowns on the flow of opinion have a nasty habit of becoming permanent. The silencing of public criticism of political power, to borrow a phrase from Bismarck, is often the 'early fruit' or precursor of more prolonged clampdowns on communication. It greatly strengthens the military and police bases of state power. It accustoms citizens to dictatorial conditions, encouraging them to turn a blind eye to disinformation and demagogy, and to act in self-serving and toadyish ways.

Libertarianism is right about all this. Yet it contains a serious blind spot. This is its failure to deal with the problem, raised in Milton's *Areopagitica*, that in matters of 'liberty of the press' the toleration of the intolerant is often a self-defeating position. The troubling fact is that freedom of communication is never a self-stabilizing process. A pluralistic civil society marked by a multitude of opinions will never resemble one big happy family. It will always tend to paralyse itself. 'Visionaries and crackpots, maniacs and saints, monks and libertines, capitalists and communists and participatory democrats' (Nozick) cannot build their visions and set alluring examples without crossing each others' paths. Precisely because of its pluralism, and its lack of a guiding centre, a tongue-wagging and sign-waving, fully democratic civil society would be dogged permanently by poor coordination, disagreement, niggardliness and open conflict among its constituents. Its self-critical self-destabilizing tendencies would also make it prey to morbid attempts to put a stop to pluralism and to enforce Order. It is often true that 'conflict is a form of socialization' (Simmel). But freedom of communication can be used to destroy freedom of communication: it gives freedom to despots and libertarians alike. The sound and fury over Islamic blasphemy and apostasy generated by Salman Rushdie's *Satanic Verses* reminds us, if the point needed accentuation, that an open and tolerant civil society can degenerate into a battlefield, in which, thanks to the existence of certain civil liberties such as 'media freedom', lions can roar and foxes can come to enjoy the freedom to hunt down chickens. Under extreme conditions, a quarrelling civil society can even bludgeon itself to death.

That is why freedom of communication among citizens within civil society requires a vigorous *political* and *constitutional* defence. As I have argued (in Keane, 1988) democratically elected and internationally coordinated parliaments are indispensable means of aggregating, coordinating and representing diverse social interests and opinions. There is of course no guarantee that they will succeed in this. The strongest legislature cannot rise above a deeply hostile society or state. But there is no other democratic alternative. Since there is no 'natural' harmony either among social opinions or between civil society and the state, democratic parliaments are an indispensable mechanism for anticipating and alleviating the constant pressure exerted by opinionated social groups upon each other, and upon the state itself. And, when faced with recalcitrant or power-hungry organizations in crisis situations, legislatures become an indispensable – but still publicly recallable – means of ordering the arrest and punishment of those individuals who cry fire, for fun, in crowded theatres, or the suppression of those groups which worship the 'divine right of the gun' (Wole Soyinka), and which therefore consider it their duty to snarl at their 'enemies', to arm themselves to the teeth, and to destroy freedom of communication in a hail of bullets and a puff of smoke.

## Notes

An earlier version of this chapter appeared in Keane (1991).

1 Compare the constitutionalist (neo-Kantian) interpretation of Dahrendorf (1988) with that of Keane (1990); Keane (1988) with Ougaard (1990). There are also stimulating remarks on the possibility of an international public sphere in Garnham (1989); and Hallin and Mancini (1991).

2 See the remarks of Levy (1985: viii–xix), and the conclusion of Chafee (1942: 21) that the central minimum intention of the drafters and ratifiers of the First Amendment was 'to wipe out the common law of sedition, and make further prosecutions for criticism of the government, without any incitement to law-breaking, forever impossible in the United States of America'.

# 2

# Media and the State in Periods of Crisis

*Mustapha Masmoudi*
*translated by Anna Fudakowska*

In democratic regimes, media are increasingly like the mirror which
reflects the general orientation of political life and the microscope which
allows citizens to pay attention to different national activities and, by
expressing their opinion, contribute to the progress of the nation. A
modern state, therefore, cannot ensure its durability except by permanent
communication between its citizens and the different wheels of power.
Much has been written on this theme (eg Le Net, 1981, 1985) and
numerous study groups looking into this issue have recognized the right of
the state to use media in all of their forms.

In this way, state use of media towards political goals, hotly contested in
the past by certain schools, may today be considered, with certain
reservations, as indispensable and well justified. But can the same
approach be justified both in normal periods and in times of crisis? As we
know, a terrorist act, a shake-up in a government crisis, economic
difficulties and social upheavals are always of such a nature as to give rise
to specific behaviour on the part of public powers and, at the same time, on
the part of the media.

Is such a change of behaviour legitimate? Are there limits to its
justification? Are there nuances to correlate with the nature of the crisis or
with that of the tension? Can the same hypotheses apply indiscriminately in
developed countries and in developing countries?

We wish to reply to these questions by examining them from the
following angles:

1  The relationship between freedom of expression and a certain degree of
   development.
2  The range and limits of journalistic information (according to UN-
   ESCO's International Commission for the Study of Communication
   Problems – the MacBride Commission (UNESCO, 1980)).
3  Media ethics in time of crisis (a preliminary reflection on the case of the
   Persian Gulf).

## Freedom of Expression, Democracy and a Certain Degree of Development

Nowadays no one can deny the media's role in consolidating social cohesion and development action. State information is therefore legitimate in a developed society where individual freedoms are guaranteed. But may we apply this thesis to developing countries? Some may even ask if freedom of expression can have a real meaning without economic and social development. Here are three different attempts at an answer.

First, referring to the events in China in 1989, the French Minister of Cooperation and Development, Jacques Pelletier, declared 'there can be no democracy without development' (*Le Monde*, 16/12/89). The Chinese events, he stated, demonstrate how difficult it is to reconcile the demands for freedom and the satisfaction of urgent material needs, giving rise to the temptation of concluding that a certain level of economic development must be attained in order to introduce democracy.

On the other hand, he went on, there is no country in the world where growth has not, from a certain stage onwards, brought about democratization of political life, while lack of democracy has always paralysed and rendered initiatives for development sterile.

Secondly, in an exposé at the Tunis international symposium on democratic transition in today's world (4 November 1989), the French Prime Minister, Michel Rocard, considered democracy to be the best answer to the social transformation brought about by development, while maintaining that democratic liberties are of such a nature as to perturb the development of the poorest countries (*La Presse*, 1989).

An accumulation of constraints paralyses government and increases the risk of confrontation, he said – hence the fear of seeing national consensus suffer from political openness, the authorization of new parties or the appearance of a suddenly free press in a developing country. All of history shows us, he specifies, that situations in which one brutally passes from a state of silence to the right to speak out are difficult to manage – but no developing country can afford to economize on democracy.

Thirdly, the President of Tunisia, Zine El Abidine Ben Ali, in his opening speech at the same international symposium, stated the liberal point of view of developing countries: 'Freedom is part of the human struggle wherever it occurs, and democracy is a need for all nations'. Confirming his position before the Tunisian Parliament three days later, President Ben Ali declared: 'Democracy is also the most dependable instrument for managing the affairs of the collectivity in such a way as to carry out the objectives of development and to guarantee political stability and the well-being of the citizenry' (*Le Temps*, 1989).

In any case, all those who have studied the problem closely have been unanimous in their conclusions: citizen participation through the media is indispensable in order to carry out coherently the economic and cultural development of a society. Because, although communication cannot by itself engender development, inadequate communication slows development and makes it more difficult. This function of communication comes from the fact that it constitutes an instrument of change for a society's collective psychology as well as for its living conditions, in addition to being a fundamental element for development.

In effect, the integral or even sectoral development of a society cannot take place without real democratization of communication which can help to raise the individual to the rank of active partner, to increase the diversity of information and to improve the quality of participation and representation in social life.

It is commonly admitted that democracy in its largest sense rests on intangible principles such as, notably, freedom and responsibility: freedom of opinion and expression and responsibility of leaders as well as of those who are ruled. Power-holders claiming to be democratic have a duty to guarantee liberties and accept that government actions, or even those of local administrations, can be criticized and even popularly sanctioned by the press or by parliamentary and municipal representatives.

Power which does not respect these principles cuts itself off from public opinion and can no longer follow society's evolution. It ends up losing its authority because it loses its legitimacy.

Those who exercise power in democratic regimes commonly admit this point of view, but they are not opposed to the use of media by state-controlled services. Like Michel Le Net (1981), they consider that the use of information allows them to 'sell regulation'. It bypasses the difficulties of incomprehension arising from the 'boomerang' phenomenon one observes when state information mechanisms have not functioned appropriately. Authorities recognize that information is not sufficient to modify public habits with respect to social behaviour that has developed without restriction over a long period of state permissiveness. Regulatory measures are, in such cases, necessary. (It is sufficient to make a measure compulsory for an important proportion of the public for it to be respected right away.)

Regulation supposes application. If a law is not applied, its effect is more prejudicial for the authorities than if it did not exist, as it diminishes their power, and this explains recourse to permanent controls and to sanctions. Yet non-respect is not always a refusal of the measure, it can also be the result of ignorance or mere negligence.

This is why the adage 'no one is wise to ignore the law' remains a theoretical notion, while in practice, the state makes increasing use of media, in order to recall the scope of the law and to make sure that public opinion is largely informed of its decisions.

These rules are, in principle, as valid in a developed society as in a developing one, even if the degree of receptivity varies depending on the intellectual level of individual citizens.

**The Range and Limits of Journalistic Information According to the MacBride Commission**

The problem of institutionalized state-controlled information has been analysed in the final report of the International Commission for the Study of Communication Problems, created in 1977 by UNESCO and headed by the Irish jurist Sean MacBride (UNESCO, 1980), as well as in parallel studies by individual commission members.

The question was considered both in general terms and in specific conditions, that is to say with respect to periods of crisis or tension.

*The MacBride Report*

In its report, the UNESCO commission considered that no government should be the sole judge of what people need to know and even less of what they have to say. No form of indoctrination is without fault and experience shows that a permanent monologue ends up by obliterating critique and abolishing all free judgement. The commission recommended going beyond the traditional distribution of roles, where media send and the public receives, and founding a more equitable dialogue between equals, by integrating citizens into the decision-making process. In this way public opinion could become a form of consciousness transformed by an understanding of public affairs and the experience of social practice.

The main point is to encourage the creative use of communication in developing the public's critical sense. The MacBride Commission considered that with all the means at governments' disposal, institutional communication has become a very powerful force developing at a growing pace. The importance of this form of communication also translates the increasing role of public authorities and institutions in general, in the resolution of socioeconomic problems and the promotion of society's development in all countries. It attests to the fact that those responsible for activities that aim to improve the quality of life have the duty to inform the people concerned in order to secure their agreement and to generate a favourable public opinion.

The field that we designate, rather imprecisely, as public relations, also aims to form and influence public opinion. During the last few decades, it has become a real communication industry with an annual budget amounting to billions of dollars. Its various operations are not clearly defined. They were not totally accepted in the past due to the dubious nature of certain alleged public relations activities. Today it is an area of rapid growth, the role of which is to provide information deemed pertinent to the media and public. In practice, public relations are used to transmit a favourable image of the organizations concerned, to respond to criticism and sometimes to see to it that embarrassing pieces of information are not disclosed. While finally recognizing a justifiable role for institutional communication, the MacBride report also warned against its dangers.

While institutional communication may be necessary, the report concluded, it can be used to manipulate opinion, to give information an official character, to monopolize the sources of information; it can also abuse the principles of government secrecy or state 'security' by concealing basic facts. Too numerous are those who, occupying positions of power and influence, consider information an asset which they can dispose of at will and not a right for all who need it. The use made of institutional communication depends on the objectives which are assigned to it: it can aim at persuading individuals and at forming critical minds; it can reinforce narrow individual interests or favour interest in collective problems; it can contribute to the subjection of those who are dominated by the dominators, or create the will and the opportunity for real participation; it can humanize or bureaucratize social relations. Communication practices are not an end in themselves, they are only a part of a much larger whole.

### Thesis of Hubert Beuve-Méry, founder of Le Monde and member of the MacBride Commission

The conclusion of the MacBride report on the subject of institutional communication can neither faithfully translate nor summarize to perfection the different analyses appearing in the report, which relate to media conditions under different circumstances.

The point of view presented by the late Hubert Beuve-Méry to his colleagues (1980) largely inspired the text of the sections dealing with the role of communicators in periods of crises or during perilous situations. Given its importance, we will summarize his point of view in the following paragraphs.

Beuve-Méry begins with Article 19 of the United Nations' Universal Declaration of Human Rights (10 December 1948): 'Everyone has the right to freedom of opinion and expression; this right includes freedom to hold opinions without interference and to seek, receive and impart information and ideas through any media and regardless of frontiers' (United Nations, 1988: 4). This declaration was later seen to be too rigid, as it did not take into account often inescapable contingencies.

Thus, in 1966, the UN's International Covenant on Civil and Political Rights interpreted Article 19 of the 1948 charter in this way: 'the exercise of (freedom of expression) carries with it special duties and responsibilities. It may therefore be subject to certain restrictions . . . :

– For respect of the rights or reputations of others.

– For the protection of national security, or of public order, or of public health or morals' (United Nations, 1988: 26).

Here the problem of limits to the freedom of information emerges in a legal framework. This freedom cannot in effect be without limits – limits which are not easy to specify because they vary necessarily with the times, customs and circumstances. This may mean refusing journalists, whose role is to provide public information, the right to place a priority on the principle of freedom of information in the face of established powers whatever they may be. To illustrate his point of view, Beuve-Méry quotes Albert Camus: 'The press, when it is free, can be good or bad, but assuredly, without freedom, it can only be bad'.

The press has had many occasions to intervene in such cases, specifies Beuve-Méry. He quotes the example of the Dreyfus affair when, at the beginning of the twentieth century, the writer Emile Zola took the risk of denouncing military, judiciary and political authorities in the journal *L'Aurore*, against the advice of numerous patriots who preferred 'injustice to disorder'. He then recalls revelations in the press which, during France's war in Algeria, compelled the governments in office to cease their official denials that 'torture was, alas, quite current practice in both camps' (Beuve-Méry, 1980).

If the press is in a position to control, impede or interfere with established powers, these, without necessarily going beyond the framework of the law, have many means of defending themselves, even imposing their solutions, and at this they often succeed. It is up to the press to be able to resist all of these pressures.

'Liberty, even when recognized, is never altogether a free gift; we must be willing to pay the price for it. It can also, alas, be abused', by giving priority to commercial exploitation or harmful intentions (cited in UNESCO, 1980: 23, n. 2). Under the French socialist regime of the Popular Front, Beuve-Méry recalls, opposition weekly papers led such a violent and slanderous campaign against one minister that he ended up by committing suicide. In 1979 another French minister's suicide was in the news, Minister of Labour, Robert Boulin, the tragic outcome of an embroiled affair whose pettiness brought to the fore 'the unhappy reverse side of liberty'.

Even if we consider only countries where the constitution and the law are based on human rights, and where these are in fact more or less respected, the question is not fully resolved. Can information professionals 'feel justified, whatever they do, by virtue of the principle: "The law, the whole law, but nothing but the law"? Or must they, on the contrary, themselves extend the scope of their responsibilities and consider the possible or probable consequences of publishing information which they nevertheless know to be true?' (Beuve-Méry, 1980). Put differently, must all truth be stated at any time, anywhere, to anyone? More precisely, should the journalistic profession admit that there exist, beyond the codified law, what may be called 'unwritten laws' that can impose themselves on a professional's conscience in certain cases?

Hubert Beuve-Méry does not himself reply to this question but refers to other journalists; he quotes Katherine Graham, publisher of the *Washington Post*, who thinks that a journalist should not be concerned about the possible consequences of disclosure, for fear that undue prudence can lead to a fatal pitfall of self-censorship that goes against the very spirit of the profession. 'If any limits on the disclosure of information are to be imposed, it is for the law-makers to say so and not for us. Journalists are not elected by the people; their only job in the public arena is to tell what is happening . . . in any society, ignorance of the facts is always harmful' (cited in UNESCO, 1980: 19, n. 1). Beuve-Méry then quotes *L'Express* editor Françoise Giroud, who declared in turn: 'From the moment one asks oneself the question: is it really necessary to speak of this? one should not be practising journalism.'

Beuve-Méry finally relates the opinion of an executive of a great international press agency (which he does not name) who admits an exception to this rule, but only in extremely serious cases, and, consequently, extremely rare. But he questions: are these cases then so rare that they cannot be of very unequal gravity?

## Media Ethics in a Period of Crisis: The Case of the Persian Gulf

Never before in an international crisis have mass media played as important a role as they did in the Persian Gulf crisis.

### Live Television Diplomacy

In the early stages of the crisis, the mass media became real channels between the parties in conflict. The American cable television network, CNN (Cable News Network), carved out the lion's share of this process for itself. Numerous competitive networks with an international dimension were remarkable because of the interest they gave to this crisis. On the whole, public authorities in all countries of the world used the press and television to a far greater extent than in the past, and certain politicians did not hesitate to point out the merits of live television diplomacy. In effect, major news agencies and television networks replaced embassy telexes as the main sources of information for heads of state about their opponents' or allies' actions and reactions.

### Commendable Objectivity

Prior to the actual outbreak of war, these measures, to some extent, appeared equitable with respect to the belligerents, and avoided taking abusive positions. According to Duja Turki (1990), a Tunisian journalist out of Washington who analysed the American press reaction, in the shuffle of reports on the Gulf crisis and its consequences, articles could be found which, without losing sight of American interests and support for government policy, allowed themselves to criticize certain aspects of this policy and to propose solutions in order to prevent the Iraqi regime from resorting to desperate acts.

Certain media even went further to bring out the origin of the crisis and explained it by mass Arab frustrations in the face of their leaders' failure to contain Israeli extremism, supported by American public power. This was greeted with enthusiasm from seasoned observers who still remember the position of the major media in 1973, during the Yom Kippur War. It was the excessively hostile attitude towards orientals at that time which was at the origin of the appeal to found a New World Information and Communication Order (NWICO).

## Annoyance and Irritation

This new media approach which appeared in western countries seemed to irritate politicians and gave rise to hostile reactions in diplomatic quarters.

Thus, for example, President Bush sought to achieve parity, demanding equal time for American images and expressions: 'I would very much like for my part to have the same opportunity to appear on Iraqi television', he declared, after having noted the interest accorded to the Iraqi leader by CNN. The right to reply was granted to him on Iraqi networks, an important first in a psychological war.

Unsatisfied, France's Prime Minister Michel Rocard warned journalists against the risk of serving a foreign power's propaganda interests (*Le Monde*, 23/8/90). For his part, French opposition critic and former foreign affairs minister François Poncet, on a television broadcast (*Antenne 2*, 2/9/90), reproached the media for demobilizing public opinion by emphasizing the issue of western hostages and raising questions of a humanitarian nature. Some journalists who shared this point of view warned against the 'concern about stardom and the taste for the spectacular taking precedence over the concerns for information'. According to them, the question was to know how to distinguish between information and a show, between providing readers and viewers with a service and racing after the sensational, between journalism and the star system.

## Excessive Use of the Media

Besides articles of moderate tendency and objective analyses could also be found, in the same newspapers and among the most prestigious, a large grandstand in favour of the everyday well-being of the western citizen and a disparagement of all Arabs, including those the west had come to support. Racist campaigns and caricatures of Arabs in turbans were reproduced in some newspapers in total confusion.

The objective of restoring international legality and the right of a society to have its independence respected was quickly forgotten; it was replaced by support for strategic interests above and beyond the will of sovereign countries which had, it is true, solicited help – but of a different nature.

Countries which did not share this way of looking at things were considered pro-Iraqi and therefore qualified as anti-American, in spite of the links of friendship which had united them with the American people for decades.

And so whatever the economic repercussions of this grave situation, countries like Tunisia, Algeria and Jordan must pay their dues and not be compensated like others for having taken into consideration the tenor of their public opinion. The paradox was that these same countries had been hailed as a whole by the western press several months earlier for having made progress on the road to democracy and respect for human rights.

This hostile media reaction affected even those European countries which had expressed a neutral stance; and so, for example, Austrian public opinion was accused of blindness because it supported by 90 per cent its President's efforts to obtain the release of hostages.

In Arab countries, that is to say in those countries most affected by the occupation of Kuwait, contrary to previous confrontations with the west, media confusion was almost total. With the exception of a few well-known editorialists who observed their usual moderation and avoided the pitfalls of subjective preconceptions, the majority of the media went beyond the will of the governing authorities at times, aligning themselves systematically with the position of one of the belligerents – thus overheating spirits and stirring up resentment without any consideration for the ideals of freedom, wider national interests or the human lives directly threatened by the crisis.

Publicity was disguised as information and commercial exploitation was evident. Pro-Iraqi newspapers held the advantage in terms of circulation while the pro-Saudi ones were more solicited by the holders of financial and economic power. But the Gulf countries most affected realized that in spite of their technological capacity for audiovisual and print communication, their media had not committed the necessary effort in terms of content and political information.

### Conclusion – Towards a Code of Conduct

It is in such dramatic moments for the entire society and for the media in particular that the need for an ethic makes itself felt; yet, until now, there has been no codified ethic to guide the act of informing the public in periods of crisis. It is, however, a legitimate objective which ought to be realized on the basis of sound reflection and long experience.

We referred earlier to the international attempts to define the limits to freedom of information, but is it possible to define limits which vary necessarily with the times, customs and circumstances?

Is it appropriate to refuse to journalists who ensure a public information task the priority of freedom in the face of established powers?

Should these journalists worry about the possible or probable consequences of information which they know to be factually correct?

Should the whole truth be told at any time, anywhere and to anyone?

Should the profession admit that unwritten laws exist which can take precedence at certain times in the conscience of the communicators?

The journalist's mission is to inform wtihout reservation, without preconception and without harmful intention; ignorance generally being harmful, journalists should not resort to self-censorship except for a major cause and in extremely serious cases. They should especially seek to avoid the abuses of commercial exploitation.

Free, moderate and well-thought-out commentary would enlighten public opinion on all aspects of any crisis. The most useful are those which have as their major preoccupation the safeguarding of peace, the protection of lives and, consequently, vital human interests.

From all of these observations, we can see a number of constants capable of being the foundations of the relationship between media and the state in periods of crisis. These are the following:

1 It is no longer possible to exercise power without permanent communication between citizens and political authorities. Thus, the use of media by state information services, contested in the past, is acknowledged today, despite certain reservations as a most legitimate recourse.

2 Public opinion's high degree of maturity and its capacity for adherence to this interactive communication model favours the consolidation of democracy and socioeconomic development.

3 If this model is more difficult to establish in a developing society than in a developed one, it is fitting to acknowledge that freedom of expression is part of human struggle everywhere, and that democracy is a fundamental need for all nations regardless of their degree of development.

4 If state information is recognized as an indispensable enterprise for better understanding between citizen and government and for the resolution of socioeconomic problems, it is strongly recommended to undertake such activity with discretion, without abuse and with well-defined objectives.

5 Working with a view to associating the citizen with the administration of public affairs in critical moments of a nation's life, should remain the main objective of political information at every level of power.

6 When communicators feel that public opinion is not well informed or insufficiently forewarned of a potential danger, their mission is evident even if this means upsetting the majority of their readers, listeners and viewers.

7 The mission of journalists and of communicators in general is to inform without reservation and without preconception; they should not self-censor or attribute to themselves a role of exercising public power.

8 Departure from this rule can, however, take place in extremely serious and rare situations; one must also keep in mind a major preoccupation: the safeguarding of human lives and, consequently, of vital human interests; in this context the protection of journalists in their difficult and dangerous missions should particularly be taken into consideration.

# 3

# Television, the Crisis of Democracy and the Persian Gulf War

*Douglas Kellner*

A democratic social order, as was conceived in the United States, requires a separation of powers so that no one institution or social force dominates the society and polity. The US Constitution separated the political system into the Presidency, Congress, and the Judiciary so that there would be a division and balance of powers between the major political institutions. Yet democracy also requires an informed electorate that can participate in political affairs. Genuine democracy consists of the sovereignty of the people and thus government by, for and of the people. In order for a free people to govern themselves, they must be adequately informed and able to participate in public debate, elections and political activity. Freedom of the press was therefore guaranteed by the Bill of Rights in order to ensure that the press would be free from domination by any political force so that it could criticize the government and promote vigorous debate on issues of public concern, thus enabling the public to participate in political affairs.

Consequently, the dual democratic functions of the press were to provide a check against excessive power and to inform the people concerning the major issues of public interest. A free press was thus vitally necessary to maintain a democratic society and it is often claimed by champions of democracy that freedom of the press is one of the features that defines the superiority of democratic societies over competing social systems. This concept of a free press was also extended to the broadcast media which were assigned a whole series of democratic responsibilities in the Federal Communications Act of 1934 and subsequent legislation and court decisions (Kellner, 1990). The democratic functions of the press and then the broadcast media were to provide information, ideas and debate concerning issues of public significance in order to promote a democratic public sphere. Broadcasting was conceived as a public utility, with the airwaves established as part of the public domain, subject to regulation by the government to ensure that broadcasting would meet its democratic responsibilities. During the Reagan and Bush administrations much of this regulatory apparatus was dismantled and giant corporations took over the major broadcast media, while mainstream print media also became increasingly corporatized in an age of mergers and conglomerates which profoundly changed the nature and social functions of the mainstream media (see Bagdikian, 1990; Schiller, 1989).

I described the deregulation of television, the takeover of the major TV networks by corporate conglomerates, their ensuing turn to the right and their active support of the Reagan and Bush administrations in *Television and the Crisis of Democracy* (Kellner, 1990). Against the Trilateral Commission which argued that the media were fostering a 'democratic distemper' and 'adversary culture' that undermined leadership, challenged authority and delegitimated established institutions (Crozier et al., 1975), I argued that the media have been undermining the foundations of democratic government. My argument is that the very existence of democracy in the United States is threatened by the dual process through which television is assuming growing power in elections and the manufacturing of public opinion, while conservative forces have taken control of the state and media and systematically used these institutions to further their own interests. In this situation, the mainstream media literally became corporate media, owned and controlled by giant corporations and used to advance their agendas.[1]

My presupposition is that democracy requires a balance of power and an informed electorate and that democracy is now in profound crisis to the extent that its very survival is threatened. I am using the term 'crisis' here in the medical sense in which 'it refers to the phase of an illness in which it is decided whether or not the organism's self-healing powers are sufficient for recovery' (Habermas, 1975: 1). A crisis is a disruption of a state of affairs that threatens to produce a decisive change. A 'crisis of capitalism', in Marx's classic theory, describes a situation in which the survival of capitalism is threatened and a 'crisis of democracy' in my analysis describes a state of affairs in which the very existence of genuine democracy is at issue.

From this perspective, US democracy is now at a crisis point from which it may or may not recover because the separation of powers and sovereignty of the people are threatened by excessive corporate power – in which corporate elites use the state and media to advance their interests and to manipulate and pacify rather than to inform and empower the public. In this chapter, I argue that the mainstream media coverage of the Persian Gulf has further exacerbated the crisis of democracy by failing to assume its democratic responsibilities and instead by uncritically promoting the policies of the United States government and military, thus strengthening the power of the National Security State. My argument is that rather than debating the issues involved and informing the public, the mainstream media, especially television, simply promoted the agenda of the Bush administration and Pentagon, and manufactured consent to their war policies. First, however, I suggest how corporate control of television has greatly increased the power of the dominant conservative and corporate forces and has used this power to undermine democracy. Then I shall analyse the form that the corporatization of television assumed during the crisis in the Persian Gulf and the ensuing war.

**US Television in the Corporate Power Structure**

The story of the last decade in the United States is that corporate capital has tightened its control of both the state and the media in the interests of aggressively promoting a pro-business agenda at the expense of other social groups.[2] The consequences of the Reagan/Bush programme of deregulation, tax breaks for the wealthy, military build-up, cut-back of social programmes and the widening of class divisions, is constituting the narrative of the 1990s. As the next century approaches, we are thus facing the spectre of ever-increasing corporate power, worsening social conditions for the vast majority, and sporadic mixtures of massive apathy and explosive conflict. In this conjuncture, the corporate media, especially television, will continue to play a major role in managing consumer demand, producing thought and behaviour congruent with the system of corporate capitalism, and arbitrating political reality. Since television is likely to become an ever greater political power and social force, it is all the more important to continue carrying out sustained theoretical reflections on the social functions and effects of television and the corporate media.

The corporate media constitute a system which interacts and overlaps with each other (see Horkheimer and Adorno, 1972; Negt and Kluge, 1972). The major corporate newspapers in the US – above all *The New York Times, The Washington Post,* and *The Wall Street Journal* – provide the daily news which cues the national television networks (ABC, CBS, NBC and CNN) and weekly news magazines (*Time, Newsweek* and *US News and World Report*) as to what is important and newsworthy. The television networks and news magazines also draw on each other and the national newspapers attend closely to and draw on both, as well as on the national wire services (AP and UPI). These mainstream corporate media are supplemented by a wide variety of investigative, special interest, entertainment and opinion media which pursue a wide range of interests and issues, and which present a tremendous spectrum of news, entertainment and ideas. The mainstream corporate media are rather self-contained, however, and usually feed upon each other. They are timid and conformist, often ignoring investigative efforts in the alternative media which question dominant views and policies, or which pursue views out of the main stream. There are very few examples in recent years of corporate media breaking with the prevailing consensus and pursuing with any depth or tenacity issues or positions that are not part of the mainstream discourse and focus. Thus, if there is a prevailing conservative ethos, the corporate media will reinforce it.

During the 1980s and early 1990s, there was indeed a widespread conservative hegemony and the corporate media were a major part of the production of the conservative consensus. Immediately after Reagan's election, television entertainment shows featured conservative law-and-order patriarchs from the television past, while liberal programmes like *Lou Grant* were cancelled (Gitlin, 1983). Television news and information were basically uncritical of Reagan and his policies (Hertsgaard, 1988; Kellner, 1990) and the Reagan administration gave them undreamed-of benefits and favours. For example, the Reagan programme of deregulation significantly increased corporate control of television and gave the television networks unparalleled advantages that greatly strengthened their wealth and power. In line with Reagan's attack on all regulatory agencies (Horowitz, 1989), his Federal Communications Commission (FCC) did everything possible to take apart the regulatory structure which had been built up over the previous few decades.[3]

Reagan's FCC Commissioner, Mark Fowler, undertook a systematic deregulation of broadcasting. By the end of 1984, the FCC had: (1) increased the number of radio and television stations that a company could own nationally from seven (AM and FM) radio and TV stations to twelve of each; (2) exempted radio and television stations from government-imposed limitations on the number and extent of commercials during a given hour; (3) eliminated requirements that broadcasters must carry a certain amount of public service broadcasting and that they should provide a minimum amount of educational material for children; (4) extended licence renewal periods from three to five years while eliminating requirements to keep programming logs and financial records for public inspection or FCC ascertainment for licence renewal, which would presumably be automatic in the future; (5) exempted broadcasters from the requirement that they own a television station for three years before selling it, thus triggering mergers, takeovers and heavy traffic in television stations; and (6) promoted the deregulation of cable. The FCC later eliminated the Fairness Doctrine which mandated that television networks present a diversity of controversial issues of public importance. Also eliminated was the 'equal time rule' which stipulated that opposing sides would be fairly treated, with representatives of different positions allowed to express their opinion, or with qualified candidates for public office permitted to answer opponents.[4]

The Reagan administration's deregulation agenda attempted both to remove all major structural constraints on the broadcasting business in terms of ownerships, licences and business practices, and to eliminate all public service requirements and many restraints on advertising and programming, thus allowing the television networks to broadcast pretty much what they wanted to (Fowler's FCC did, however, follow the right-wing agenda of the day in attempting to regulate obscenity; and Fowler himself once sternly lectured broadcasters to 'get it right' when they meekly criticized Reagan for his lax 'management style'). Consequently, the Reagan FCC dramatically redefined the relationships between government and television and attempted to undo decades of regulatory guidelines and programmes.

Deregulation also led to dramatic conglomerate takeovers of radio stations and curtailment of radio news operations. Research in Florida revealed that there was an average 30 per cent decrease in weekday public affairs programming, and a 24 per cent decrease in the number of locally prepared newscasts (Edwardson, 1986). In practice, this meant major curtailment of local news, thus depriving communities that did not have a local daily newspaper of news concerning their area. Previously, it had been radio that was the voice of these communities, but with the takeover of local radio stations by corporate conglomerates, local news and public affairs were often cut back significantly and sometimes even eliminated completely.

The deregulatory policies of the Fowler FCC were continued by his successors Dennis Patrick and Alfred Sikes, who became FCC commissioner in the Bush administration. The consequences for democracy of the Reagan/Bush deregulation programme have been extremely destructive. The mergers allowed by the Reagan/Bush pro-business administrators enabled major corporations such as General Electric to tighten corporate control of the media, and provided them with new sources of wealth and power. The decline of documentaries, public affairs programming and political discussion on the three major television networks helped produce a less informed electorate, more susceptible to political manipulation. Corporate control of the media meant that corporations could use the media to promote their own interests aggressively, and need not fear as much the exposure and criticism that had begun to intensify in the 1970s (Kellner, 1981).

In addition, the Democratic Party became more subservient to corporate interests during this period. The enormous amount of money required for successful political campaigns in the age of television forced politicians to depend for financing on wealthy contributors and corporations. The Savings and Loans (S&L) crisis, especially the plight of the 'Keating Five', who accepted giant contributions from S&L crook Charles Keating, and who allegedly did favours for him, has dramatized the dependency of Congress on big business and big campaign contributions. In this climate, most Democrats went along with the Reagan deregulation programme, strongly favoured by big business, and failed to speak out against the excesses and failures of the Reagan administration. This sad situation testified to a growing crisis of liberalism in the United States and deprived the mainstream media of critical voices to oppose the Reagan/Bush policies.

Thus Congress went along with the Reagan/Bush deregulation of television and helped promote the growing power of corporate media to pursue corporate interests. In 1985, ABC merged with Capital Cities Communications, and RCA merged with GE. CBS fought off a hostile takeover in 1985 and merged with the Tisch corporation in 1986, producing another mega-communications giant. In March 1989, Time Inc. proposed a merger with Warner Communications Inc. to form the largest media conglomerate in the world. The combined company, Time Warner Inc., had a total value of $18 billion and a projected yearly revenue of $10 billion from its magazine and book publishing empire, its film and television production companies, its cable systems and networks, and subsidiary businesses.

The communications industry was thus marked by growing concentration during the 1980s; as Ben Bagdikian has documented (1990), 23 major communications corporations dominated the market in 1989 (down from the 46 which dominated it in 1981 when he surveyed the field for the first edition of his book). This corporate control of information and entertainment provides what Bagdikian calls 'a new Private Ministry of Information and Culture'. The television networks are part of this conglomerate structure with ties to the other major entertainment and information industries (film, publishing, music, radio, cable TV, etc), as well as to other major corporate and financial powers. NBC's ties to defence industries are particularly close, while they and other networks are also connected with the space and satellite industry, health care and management concerns, housing, crime and surveillance, education and manufacturing (Bunce, 1977). The networks' ties to banks and major financial institutions are close, while interlocking ownership and shared boards of directors link them with other major corporations as well (Morrow, 1985; Herman and Chomsky, 1988: 10ff; Henson in *Left Business Observer*, 25, 27 and 31: 1988/1989).

The merger between GE and RCA/NBC allied NBC with one of the major transnational conglomerates and signalled the centrality of communications within the multinational corporate power structure. RCA and GE had been among the largest defence contractors and their merger would make them the second largest contractor to sell electronics to the Defense Department (*Business Week*, 27/1/86: 117). GE produces crucial components of nuclear weapons, aircraft engines and guidance systems for ICBMs, and has close relations with the Air Force. RCA specializes in advanced radar, satellites and electronic equipment for missile-launching cruisers and has close relations with the Navy. Together, they would presumably play a central role in the development of the Star Wars technology proposed by the Reagan administration. GE also plays a key role in the nuclear power industry, as well as manufacturing. Both corporations have a diverse portfolio of businesses in electronics, advertising, financial services, transportation and a variety of other enterprises.

Since the acquisition, GE/RCA have consolidated their holdings in broadcasting with GE capital 'providing more than $2.7 billion for 19 deals spread across cable, broadcast TV, radio and publishing' (*Channels*, 11/88: 65). In 1988, GE/RCA became part of the cable industry purchasing Cablevision's sports, news and entertainment programming (*Broadcasting*, 26/12/88: 27ff; *Variety*, 28/12/88: 1–2). This enabled the conglomerate to acquire six sports channel networks and the Rainbow Network which includes Bravo, American Movie Classics, Long Island News 12, and the Consumer News and Business Channel. It has also entered the world of entertainment production by contributing to a restructuring of New World

Entertainment.

The mid-1980s network mergers have thus contributed mightily to trends towards concentration in the broadcasting industry and merger of the television networks with other major corporate enterprises. ABC, for instance, owns eight TV stations, 18 radio stations, a satellite music network, several cable channels, many newspapers and magazines and various database concerns. Consequently, the television networks are big businesses interconnected in significant ways with other big businesses in the system of transnational capitalism.

This trend towards merger, concentration and corporatization of the broadcast media reverses 50 years of broadcast history which featured more vigorous regulation and utilization of anti-trust laws. In 1932, for instance, GE was forced to divest itself of NBC/RCA and in 1966 when communications giant ITT wanted to take over ABC, the anti-trust laws were used to prevent this merger (see Kellner, 1990: 35, 82). Under the Reagan and Bush administrations, however, the corporations were allowed to do more or less exactly as they wished, including takeover of the most powerful communications media.

**Television and Democracy**

Giant transnational corporations now control the three television networks in the United States. The consequences for democracy of this development are menacing. Previously, the history of congressional decisions on the media, the regulation of broadcasting, and a variety of court decisions have generally at least paid lip service to the stipulation that the air waves are owned by the people, and that broadcasting should be regulated as a public utility which should serve democratic and not solely capitalist imperatives.[5] Consequently, although the 1934 Communications Act mandated that the airwaves belonged to the public as a public good and that broadcasting was to serve the 'public interest, convenience, and necessity', the Reagan and Bush deregulation policies subverted the notion that broadcasters were public trustees and, in effect, stipulated that they were simply businesses which would benefit from deregulation, and provide more and better programming for the public. The whole notion of broadcasters as public trustees who must serve the public interest was thrown out, along with accountability to the public. The result was a drastic reduction of news, documentary and public affairs broadcasting. A survey by a Ralph Nader-affiliated public interest group, Essential Information, carried out a study that indicated that in comparison with 1979, programming in 1988 carried 39 per cent less local public affairs programming, while 15 per cent of all stations carried no news at all; programme-length commercials, prohibited until the 1980s, constituted about 2.6 per cent of airtime (Donahue, 1989).

There was also a demonstrable decline of documentaries produced by the television networks in the 1980s. Whereas each network broadcast around 20 documentaries a year during the 1960s, by 1985 all three networks together were broadcasting a mere 14 hours worth. Instead, news magazines such as ABC's '20/20' and CBS' 'West 57th Street' appeared, along with 'reality programming' (sensationalistic tabloid journalism of the sort found in the New York *Daily News* or *Post*), including Geraldo Rivera's 'exposés' of satanism and live drug busts. In this way, political journalism turned towards a tabloid style of journalism and away from analysis and criticism.

Other studies indicated an increased amount of commercial interruptions, causing a dramatic deterioration in children's television, large cutbacks in news and public affairs programming, and a more conservative corporate climate at the networks where individuals feared for their jobs in a period of 'bottom-line' corporate firing. Furthermore, right-wing pressure groups used a variety of strategies to push and keep network news coverage on the right track. For instance, the 'Accuracy in Media' group conducted campaigns against programmes with a perceived 'liberal bias' and demanded, and sometimes received, free time to answer supposedly 'liberal' programmes.[6] Lawsuits by US General William Westmoreland against a CBS Vietnam documentary, and by Israeli General Ariel Sharon against *Time* magazine, pressured the media against criticizing conservative politicians who were taking up libel lawsuits to keep the media in check. Both Westmoreland and Sharon lost their lawsuits, but these highly publicized media events had a chilling effect on the mainstream media, no doubt checking critical discourse.

Not only are the news programmes slanted towards the hegemonic positions of corporate and government elites, but discussion shows that they are also dominated by conservative discourses. Political discussion and debate on the three major networks is almost exclusively limited on commercial television to Sunday morning talk shows and ABC's *Nightline*, which features late-night debate of issues of topical interest. Yet one wonders if the public interest is served by the composition of these network talk shows, which are almost always limited to mainstream representatives of the two major political parties, or other white male, establishment figures. A study of ABC's nightly talk show, *Nightline*, hosted by Ted Koppel, for example, indicates that over a six-month period Koppel's guests were almost always white, male, conservative spokespeople with Henry Kissinger, Alexander Haig, Jerry Falwell and Elliot Abrams the most frequent guests (FAIR, 1989). A later FAIR study of Public Television's *The MacNeil/Lehrer News Hour* (1990) showed that it was even more conservative in its biases, and a 1991 FAIR study of the Persian Gulf War coverage indicated that almost no anti-war spokespeople turned up on network news and discussion programming dedicated to the war.

Furthermore, the era not only saw a sharp turn to the right in television entertainment, but television actively helped forge the conservative hegemony of the period. Television not only went down 'on bended knee' to the Reagan administration, failing to criticize its policies with any vigour (Hertsgaard, 1988), but actively promoted the Reagan programme of tax breaks for the rich and corporations, deregulation, union-busting, a massive military build-up, chauvinistic patriotism and aggressive foreign intervention. There were limits, of course, beyond which the media did not allow the zealous Reaganites to tread and the Iran/Contra coverage forced extremists out of the administration, forced Reagan to negotiate an arms reduction treaty with Gorbachev, lessened Cold War tensions, and created the climate for the flourishing of the more centrist, conservative politics which helped elect George Bush.[7]

The mainstream television networks in the United States have long promoted the major trends of US foreign policy and have generally failed to criticize US interventions or policies (Parenti, 1986; Herman and Chomsky, 1988; Chomsky, 1989). This trend was particularly striking in network coverage of the Panama Invasion (see chapter by Armand and Michèle Mattelart in this volume – ed.) and the Persian Gulf crisis and then war from August 1990 until March 1991. Coverage of the Iraqi invasion of Kuwait and Bush's immediate despatching of troops to Saudi Arabia as the only natural response tended to support Bush's military policy, making it appear that war in the Middle East was inevitable. Media coverage of the Persian Gulf crisis from August 1990 till January 1991, followed by coverage of the war itself, indicates how the corporate media promoted the agenda of the Bush administration and the military–industrial complex, and just how far corporate control of the media constitutes a crisis of democracy.

### The Persian Gulf Crisis: The Media Beat the War Drums

In response to the Iraqi invasion of Kuwait in early August 1990, the political and media establishment in the United States immediately began whipping up war hysteria and promoting a military solution to the crisis. When the Bush administration quickly sent a massive troop deployment to the region, the media applauded these actions and became a conduit for mobilizing support for US policy. For weeks, no dissenting voices whatsoever were heard in the mainstream media, and TV reports, commentary and discussion strongly privileged a military solution to the crisis, serving as a propaganda vehicle for the US military and national security apparatus which was facing severe budget cutbacks and loss of public prestige on the very eve of the invasion. No significant debate took place over the dangerous consequences of the massive US military response to the Iraqi invasion and the interests and policies which the military intervention served. Critics of US policy were largely absent from the mainstream media coverage of the crisis, and little real analysis of the Gulf crisis was presented which departed from issues presented by the Bush administration.

For the first months of the crisis, the dominant media discourse was overwhelmingly in favour of a military solution, to the benefit of the Bush administration and its corporate supporters. This pronounced bias points to the effects of ownership of the media by corporations like GE which are heavily invested in the military industries, and which have been strongly supporting the conservative and pro-business Republican administrations for the past decade.

From the beginning, the media vilified Saddam Hussein as a madman, a Hitler, and worse, and whipped up anti-Arab war fever. Saddam was characteristically described as a 'dictator', a 'military strongman' and a menace to world peace and the American way of life. Mary McGrory described him as a 'beast' (*Washington Post*, 8/8/90) and a 'monster' that 'Bush may have to destroy' (*Newsweek*, 20/10/90; 3/9/90). *The New Republic* doctored a *Time* magazine cover story on Saddam to make him appear more like Hitler by shortening his moustache. Cartoonists had a field-day presenting images of the demon Saddam Hussein, and television resorted to cartoon techniques itself as when an NBC 'war game' simulation on 8 August 1990 had a US colonel pretending to be Saddam, stating 'I'll hang a hostage every day!' The media eagerly reported all of Saddam's alleged and actual crimes (suddenly focusing on actions and events which had gone unreported when Saddam was a US ally, such as his use of chemical weapons against Kurdish rebels in his own country). There was even speculation on Iraq's plans for future terrorism when no current atrocities were on hand (see *Christian Science Monitor*, 21/9/90).

Saddam Hussein is, of course, a dictator with imperial ambitions who is ruthless, repressive and inclined towards military solutions and actions. Yet his vilification was so extreme that it ruled out diplomatic solutions in advance and reduced any possible Iraqi initiative to resolve the crisis diplomatically to mere propaganda and deception. Week after week, report after report, Saddam was described in purely negative terms with commentators stressing his brutality, irrationality and duplicity. It is significant, however, that the media characteristically describe similar foreign tyrants who are sympathetic to US interests merely as 'military leaders' or 'presidents' and regularly portray them in positive or neutral frames – this was the case with repressive Vietnamese leaders who the US supported, as well as the Shah of Iran, Chile's Pinochet, the Philippines' Marcos, and even Panama's Noriega, until he fell out of favour with US policy makers.

Saddam, by contrast, is constantly demonized as the absolutely evil 'foreign other'. In this way, the frames of popular culture entertainment, which are structured by a Manichean opposition between good and evil, are deployed in the discourse on Saddam Hussein as the absolute villain, the evil demon who is so threatening and violent that he must be destroyed and eradicated. One cannot talk sensibly with such a villain, nor seek common ground nor a diplomatic solution; instead, one must totally eliminate such evil to restore stability and order in the universe. Such is the fable of Hollywood movies and popular television entertainment, and such are the politics and dominant media frames of the US intervention into the complex politics of the Middle East.

The effect of the demonization of Saddam Hussein was to promote a climate in which the necessity to take decisive military action to eliminate him was privileged. Against the 'evil' Saddam, the media posed images of the 'good' American soldier. In the nightly repetition of these positive images of American troops valiantly protecting a foreign country from aggression, the need for a strong military was repeatedly dramatized and pounded into the public's psyche. The US military could not have asked for better advertisements or PR. Capital's 'private Ministry of Information and Culture' (Bagdikian, 1990) became a cheerleader for militarism. While the military prepared for all-out war in the Middle East, urged on by hawks like Henry Kissinger, William Safire and editorialists in *The Wall Street Journal, The New York Times*, and *National Review*, the media whipped up war fever and built a consensus for administration positions, no matter how dangerous and potentially catastrophic.

The images of Arabs during the first weeks of the crisis were overwhelmingly racist. Repeated images of a negatively-coded Saddam Hussein, of mobs of Arabs demonstrating and shouting anti-US slogans, and repeated associations of rich, corrupt Arabs with oil – and other Arab leaders with terrorism – provided an extremely negative set of anti-Arab images. Television coverage of the frequent Arab conferences during September and October, which sought Arab solutions to the problem, almost always focused on the more radical Arab leaders and almost always featured scenes of Arab anti-American demonstrations where US flags were ritualistically burned. When Secretary of State Baker visited Syria, for instance, to recruit Syrian support and troops for the anti-Iraq mobilization, television coverage stressed the links between Syria and terrorism and utilized negative stereotypes of Arabs.

The few images of anti-war demonstrators in the US that appeared during the first months of the US intervention utilized the same frames, coding anti-war demonstrators as irrational opponents of US policies. US demonstrators were portrayed as an unruly mob, as long-haired outsiders, as Arabs; their discourse was rarely shown and coverage focused instead on slogans, or images of marching crowds, with media voice-overs supplying the context; major newspapers and news magazines also failed to cover the burgeoning new anti-war movement. Thus, just as the media symbolically constructed a negative image in the 1960s of anti-war protesters as irrational, anti-American and unruly, so did the networks frame the emerging anti-war movement of the 1990s in predominantly negative frames.

The media coverage of the Iraqi invasion of Kuwait and US intervention in Saudi Arabia during the early months confirmed the analysis of Herman and Chomsky (1988) that the corporate media tend to picture 'enemies' of the US as evil while overlooking the crimes of US allies. When Saddam

Hussein was a US ally against Iran and the recipient of US aid and arms sales, he was presented positively and his crimes were ignored; when he became US enemy number one, then his every evil deed was magnified. Likewise, when the US invaded Panama, its actions were defended by the same corporate media that later attacked Iraq for similar aggression.

In their coverage of the largest US military intervention since Vietnam, the media mainly focused on the logistics of the operation and its impact on the home front. Night after night, details of the US military deployment were presented; desert manoeuvres were shown; troops were interviewed and allowed to send greetings to the folks at home (images that ultimately forged strong bonds between the troops and the TV viewers on the home front); and shiny and powerful new high-tech weapons were displayed, punctuated by frequent news reports warning against Iraqi chemical weapons and the one-million-strong, well-armed and highly trained and experienced Iraqi military forces.

In general, television and the rest of the mainstream media repeated endlessly the legitimations given by the Bush administration for their successive military intervention and actions. In the early days, they dramatized the dangers to Saudi and other Gulf State oil-fields if the Iraqi invasion was not stemmed by the US military presence and the economic blockade of Iraq. When US policy turned from a defensive posture to an aggressive one, after Bush doubled the number of troops in Saudi Arabia in mid-November 1990, the media dramatized Iraqi brutality towards Kuwait and alleged mistreatment of US and foreign hostages. Indeed, the hostages and their periodic release became a major focus of mainstream news coverage of the crisis. For months, almost every television report contained ritualistic segments depicting the plight of the hostages, negotiations for their release, the suffering of hostages' relatives, and the happy homecoming of those released. In this way, too, the media presented morality tales depicting the Iraqis as evil hostage takers and the Americans and other foreign hostages as innocent victims.[8]

The gender construction of TV images of the military and their families pointed to the cohabitation of conservative and traditionalist images of gender and the family with more liberal images. On one hand, the construction of gender of US military families is extremely conventional with the male soldiers going off to war, while the wife and children stay behind. This frame reproduces the conservative division between the public sphere as the domain of male activity with the private sphere reserved for women. The frame also privileged the sexist picture of men as active and virile and women as passive and helpless; constant pictures of tearful wives breaking down as their men went off to war in a manly fashion reinforced this traditional picture, as did the juxtapositions of the men active in the desert, while the women at home were seeking help from psychiatric counsellors or support groups. Image after image of stoic men marching off to war and tearful women staying at home thus reinforced a traditional concept of gender differences between men and women to the detriment of women.

Yet there were also women in the military being sent to the desert and from the beginning the media were fascinated with these new 'women warriors'. *Newsweek* featured a cover story on women and the military (10/9/90), as did *People* magazine (10/9/90). As the crisis proceeded, images of women troops appeared ever more frequently in the TV news coverage as well. These images, which have been popularized in film and television since the volunteer army allowed women to join, are also functional for the US military machine. They provide free advertisements for a military desperate to recruit new men and women as enlistment dramatically plunges in response to the dangers of war.

In addition, images of US women in the desert were often juxtaposed with pictures of Arab women in veils, thus presenting pictures of 'modern', 'progressive' US society contrasted to 'backward', 'reactionary' Arab regimes that continue to oppress women, further legitimating US intervention in the region as a progressive force. This was highlighted in mid-November, when Saudi women protested against a ban on driving cars with a 'drive-in' during which they defiantly drove round Saudi cities. The Saudi women were harshly criticized by the regime and in some cases fired from their jobs; the US media dwelt on this story for several days, contrasting the plight of Saudi women with US women soldiers driving jeeps and participating actively in military life – presenting the message that the US was bringing a progressive 'modern' influence into backward Saudi Arabia.

Frequent TV network presentations of possible scenarios for a US invasion of Iraq and all-out war in the region indeed previewed the actual war that broke out in January 1991. During the weekend of 15–16 September 1990, there were reports on Air Force General Dugan's claim that only an all-out air war against Iraq would succeed in getting Saddam Hussein out of Kuwait; *Time* magazine published a report in the same period citing a State Department official saying: 'If we are serious about going beyond getting Saddam out of Kuwait – and we are damn serious about it – then war is just about inevitable' (cited in *In These Times*, 26/9/90: 4).

General Dugan, then, merely said in public what administration officials were saying in private and even ultra-hawk Pat Buchanan attacked the 'clowns' who were calling for bombing Iraq (CNN *Crossfire*, 13/9/90). War scenarios, however, continued to be leaked to the media and the television networks willingly broadcast them: during the weekend of 22–3 September, there were other reports, with diagrams, charting the course of a US invasion and all-out war, and such reports continued to be broadcast for months. These reports induced war hysteria, created the impression that war was inevitable, and prepared the public for the actual war itself – indeed, such reports may create a desire for war to resolve the situation or to relieve the tension built up by the hysterical reporting.

The key point is that the extremely propagandistic and militaristic tone of TV and mainstream print media coverage of the Gulf crisis helped push the country into war with all of its destruction, potential destabilizing effects, and promotion of militarism as the way to solve political problems. There was no significant visible opposition to Bush's policies, with the exception of coverage of congressional hearings and debate on the eve of the war, and most media commentators presented the sending of US troops to the Gulf and the subsequent war positively, building a consensus for US military presence and action.

## The Media Propaganda War

When the war itself broke out, television and the mainstream media became a conduit for Bush administration and Pentagon policies and rarely criticized any of its positions, disinformation or atrocities. Television served primarily as a propaganda apparatus for the multinational forces arrayed against Iraq and as a cheerleader for their every victory. Anchors like Dan Rather of CBS and Tom Brokaw of NBC went to Saudi Arabia and, along with the network correspondents there, seemed to identify totally with the military point of view. Whenever peace proposals were floated by the Iraqis or the Soviet Union, the networks quickly shot them down (for systematic analysis and critique see Kellner, forthcoming).

The media repeated endlessly the Big Lie of the Bush administration concerning its efforts to seek a diplomatic solution to the crisis. In fact, the US never sought to develop any dialogue with Iraq, to respond to any Iraqi offers for negotiations, or seriously to discuss any diplomatic solutions. Instead, they continually delivered ultimata and insults to Saddam Hussein, making the possibility of a peaceful solution increasingly remote. Every expert on crisis resolution indicates that to resolve a crisis one must be ready to make concessions, compromises, and to give one's adversary a dignified way out of the crisis. The Bush administration failed for months, however, to take any diplomatic steps to resolve the crisis peacefully, and once the war started blocked every attempt at a negotiated settlement proposed by Iraq or the Soviet Union.

Anti-Iraqi propaganda was so developed in the mainstream media that even Saddam Hussein's willingness to negotiate with the US and his surprising offer to release all foreign hostages in early December was portrayed negatively. The 1 December NBC newscast used soldiers and the mother of a soldier about to go to the Middle East to express scepticism about whether Saddam Hussein could be trusted and whether one could negotiate with him.

Although the corporate media presented the diplomatic moves towards a peaceful resolution of the crisis in early December positively, they failed to criticize the unwillingness of both sides to undertake a peaceful diplomatic solution. There was no major analysis of the reluctance of the

Bush administration to negotiate a peaceful solution which would probe into why Bush might favour the military option. Instead, the mainstream media favoured the Bush administration's rationale for its policies, and thus primarily served as a propaganda organ for the administration while failing to promote a genuine debate of alternatives to war.

The lack of significant critical voices during the crisis in the Gulf and then the Gulf War disclosed the timidity, narrowness and fundamental subservience of the mainstream media in the United States, especially the television networks. The broadcast media are afraid to go against a perceived popular consensus, to alienate people, to take unpopular stands, and since US military actions have characteristically been supported by the majority of the people, at least in their early stages, television is extremely reluctant to criticize what might turn out to be popular military actions. The broadcast media also characteristically rely on a narrow range of established and safe commentators and are not likely to reach out to new and controversial voices in a period of national crisis.

The media are prone to wait until a major political figure or established 'expert' speaks against a specific policy and that view gains certain credibility as marked by opinion polls or publication in 'respected' newspapers or journals. Unfortunately, the crisis of democracy in the United States is such that the Democratic Party has largely supported the conservative policies of the past decade and so the party leaders are extremely cautious and slow to criticize foreign policy actions, especially potentially popular military actions. The crisis of liberalism is so deep in the US that establishment liberals are afraid of being called 'wimps', or 'soft' on foreign aggression, and thus often support policies that their better instincts should lead them to oppose. Thus, the only criticisms that appeared in the mainstream media during the first weeks of the US intervention in the Gulf came from hawks like Jeanne Kirkpatrick and Zbigniew Brzezinski, and far right conservatives like Pat Buchanan, thus signalling once more the crisis of liberalism and the bankruptcy of the Democratic Party. (On the other hand, it is not certain if no mainstream opposition was to be found, or whether television simply ignored any voices that would interrupt the manufacture of war hysteria and public support for the US intervention.[9])

In some ways, what was not shown or discussed in the mainstream media is as significant as what was portrayed. There was almost nothing in the mainstream media on the geopolitical history of the Middle East region where the confrontation was occurring: there was little discussion of the history of the borders in the region, or of the complex relations between colonial powers and Arab states, between Israel and the Arab states, or between the Arab states themselves. The media avoided analysis of the history of US involvement in the region, the precise nature of US interests in oil production, the political economy of oil, and the relations between US oil companies and the governments of the region. Nor was the question raised as to why the US reacted so aggressively to the Iraqi invasion, while accepting the Israeli invasion of Lebanon, the Syrian and Israeli occupations of Lebanon, and the Israeli occupation of land claimed by the Palestinians and others. And there was no serious discussion of the interesting parallels between the US invasion of Panama and the Iraqi invasion of Kuwait.

The only attempt to contextualize the crisis in the Gulf by the three dominant US commercial networks during the first several months was the ABC Special *A Line in the Sand* (11/9/90).[10] The programme glossed over the complex geopolitical history of the Middle East in moments, without addressing the issues noted above. Peter Jennings mentioned in passing that the borders of the states involved in the crisis were imposed by Great Britain earlier in the century, but provided no further historical analysis. Jennings constantly mentioned that 'geography is important' as he walked on a simulated map from one country to another, but seemed oblivious to the fact that history is also important.

Jennings ended his Special, however, on a disturbingly hawkish note. After mentioning the spectrum of possible resolutions to the crisis, ranging from US air strikes to peaceful negotiations, he indicated that the 'worst option of all' might be for Saddam Hussein to withdraw intact to Iraq, preserving his military machine, chemical weapons and potential nuclear weapons for future mischief in the area. Jennings' implication was that it would be better to take the route of eliminating him completely, thus implicitly presenting the argument for US military attack on Iraq.

There was little on the history of US dependency on Middle East oil; how during the Carter administration, the US drastically reduced dependency and attempted to develop a coherent energy policy; and how under Reagan and Bush the US increased dependency and abandoned developing an energy policy – thus continuing the blatant bias towards the Republican Party that Entman (1989) has demonstrated, and that I have documented in different contexts (in Kellner, 1990). There was no analysis of how the Republican administrations first sought cheap oil prices at the expense of oil dependency, leaving price and supply to the 'magic of the marketplace', and then sought higher oil prices (see Cleaver, 1991). Nor was there much discussion of the fact that the US now gets about 25 per cent of its oil from the Middle East, while the figure was down to about 7 per cent when Reagan took over as president.

There was little discussion pointing out that it is mostly Western Europe and Japan which are directly dependent on Iraqi and Kuwaiti oil (the US only gets about 3 per cent of its oil from these two countries), or that the US has been reduced to a mercenary force supplying troops and weapons to intervene on behalf of its capitalist allies. There was little on the need to develop sane energy alternatives, and what discussion of this issue there was focused on the need to rethink the nuclear energy option and to loosen restrictions on oil-drilling in environmentally sensitive areas (rather than on the need to develop solar energy or renewable and ecologically safe energy alternatives). Instead the corporate media took advantage of the crisis to promote the failing nuclear energy industry and to urge the loosening of environmental restrictions on oil production (*The New York Times* repeatedly took this line, as did NBC).

Before the war broke out, there was almost no discussion of the economic consequences and environmental holocaust that would ensue if the Kuwaiti, Iraqi or Saudi oil fields were bombed and set on fire, or if there were massive oil spills in the Persian Gulf. The Iraqis mined the Kuwaiti oil-fields and threatened to set them on fire, and indeed did during the war itself, while US-led bombing caused many oil fires in Iraq and at least 36 which the allies admitted to in Kuwait. In early January 1991, ecology experts at an environmental conference in London warned that a Persian Gulf war would be an environmental holocaust due to the likelihood of major oil spills and fires, but television and the mainstream media paid no attention to these reports; *The New York Times* published an article on 16 January, the day that Bush began bombing Baghdad, indicating that there was no great danger of ecological crisis from a Persian Gulf war, and television simply ignored the issue until the war broke out and it was too late. Ecologists also warned about the dangers of bombing Iraqi nuclear, chemical and biological weapons facilities, and while the alternative press published articles describing serious contamination from allied bombing, this issue was never explored on television or in the other mainstream media.

There was also little discussion of the political instability of the Middle East that might result after an all-out war. While there was some criticism of Bush's visit to Syria's Assad and some speculation that Syria or Iran might invade and take over Iraq after an all-out war, there was little discussion of the complex politics of the region or the impact of the war on the various Arab regimes. Such discussion focused mainly on 'winners' and 'losers', claiming that all Arab regimes that allied themselves with the United States would benefit, while those, like Jordan and Yemen who failed to join, would be 'losers'.

Thus, the mainstream media failed to raise serious questions concerning the political and ecological significance of a Gulf war and generally presented every position and action by the Bush administration and its multinational coalition positively. There were few voices raised against the slaughter of more than 100,000 Iraqis, including many civilian deaths, or the destruction of the Iraqi economic and social infrastructure by coalition bombing. Even the slaughter of tens of thousands of fleeing Iraqis, after their government formally announced withdrawal from Kuwait and sought a cease-fire in the United Nations, was ignored or quickly passed over in favour of joyous images of the liberation of Kuwait, or a replay of Iraqi atrocities against Kuwaitis. The issue of the Bush administration coalition's responsibility for much of the ecological crisis in the Gulf was not raised, even though part of the oil spills, some of the oil fires in Kuwait, and all of the ecological destruction in Iraq was caused by the US-led coalition bombing.

## Conclusion

And so democracy in the United States is imperilled because the mainstream media are controlled by conservative corporate forces that use television especially to further their own interests and agenda. The democratic imperative that broadcasting provide a range of views on issues of public interest and controversy has been increasingly sacrificed, as have been media's responsibilities to serve as a check against excessive government or corporate corruption or power. In the case of the crisis in the Persian Gulf and subsequent Gulf War, the media served as a conduit for state and military positions and did not raise a whole range of issues, or question military and state propaganda and disinformation.

Thus, once again, we see the need for alternative media to promote genuine democracy and to provide essential information. During the Gulf War crisis, those of us who opposed the war got information from computer databases, like PeaceNet, or progressive publications like *The Nation, In These Times* or *Zeta Magazine*. Locally, in addition to holding daily teach-ins at the University of Texas, we attempted to make use of public access television and radio to promote criticisms of the Bush administration's war policy and refusal to negotiate. The limitations of this strategy were evident in the overwhelming consensus for the war managed by the mainstream media. Yet the very limitations of the mainstream media in times of acute crisis show the need to develop independent alternative media.

## Notes

1 See Entman (1989) and Kellner (1990), where I document how network television in the 1980s advanced the interests of the conservative Republican political regimes of the epoch. I argue that the conjunction of the growing power of television in elections and the manufacturing of public opinion with the capture of the state and media by big business, which relentlessly used these institutions to further their own interests, constitutes a crisis of democracy. I refer to the mainstream media as corporate media because they are owned by big corporations like GE, ABC/Capital Communications, and CBS/Tisch Financial Group and express the corporate point of view; corporate media in the US include the three major television networks, national news magazines like *Time* and *Newsweek*, and national newspapers like *The New York Times* and *Wall Street Journal*. While my argument focuses on the United States, there have been trends throughout the capitalist world over the last decade towards increased corporate control and less public control of television. This has resulted from the hegemony of conservative governments in many countries and the introduction of cable and satellite television, which have proliferated commercial channels.

2 On changes in the capitalist system see Lash and Urry (1987), Kellner (1989), Harvey (1989) and Schiller (1989).

3 On broadcasting and regulation, see Horowitz (1989).

4 On the Fairness Doctrine, see Rowan (1984).

5 On the tensions between capitalism and democracy as one of the main constitutive forces within US history, see Wolfe (1973, 1977), Cohen and Rogers (1983), Bowles and Gintis (1986) and Kellner (1990).

6 After the right-wing attacks on its nuclear holocaust film *The Day After*, ABC bowed to

right-wing pressures and allowed a conservative-dominated panel to discuss nuclear policy after the film and then agreed to produce an anti-communist mini-series, *Amerika*, which depicted a communist takeover of the United States; PBS financed a right-wing 'answer' to its series on Vietnam and allowed conservative commentary after several allegedly 'liberal' programmes; as far as I know, no network has allowed any 'liberal' responses to conservative programming.

7 This story is told in Ch. 4 and the appendixes of Kellner (1990).

8 This scenario replayed the primal captivity drama, one of the mainstays of American popular literature which began with Indian captivity narratives and continued through media coverage of the Iran hostage crisis.

9 Jesse Jackson managed to get to Iraq for an interview with Saddam Hussein, which won him a few minutes of airtime to criticize the US intervention, and the only Congressperson whose critique I encountered during the first month of the crisis was San Antonio representative Henry B. Gonzalez who blamed the US government and banks for funding much of Saddam's military build-up and who called for immediate withdrawal of US troops from the Middle East (*Austin American-Statesman*, 4/8/90: 1A, 4A). Later, Gonzalez initiated an impeachment proceeding against George Bush, which was also ignored by the mainstream media.

10 The title of this programme parroted Bush's own phrase denoting his resolve that US forces would draw 'a line in the sand' to protect US interests in the region.

# 4

# Framing the Crisis in Eastern Europe

*Julian Halliday, Sue Curry Jansen and James Schneider*

## Prologue

This chapter was originally written during a brief period of hegemonic rupture, crisis and opportunity in the United States that extended from the fall of the Berlin Wall to the beginning of the Persian Gulf War. It has been substantially revised twice to take into account the shifts in power relations produced by the war and more recently by the attempted coup in the Soviet Union and its aftermath. These developments not only confirm the acuity of the quotation from E.P. Thompson that we use below, they also underscore some of the hazards of the genre that George Gerbner (personal communication, 10 September 1991) describes as 'instant history'. Our analysis spotlights an extraordinary time when the masks of power slipped and the struggle among US elites for control over the language and logics of representing political reality became visible in mass media; it also dramatically displays the void in the mythic structures of US power-knowledge that Saddam Hussein was, for a time, recruited to fill. Subsequent events have not only demonstrated the failure of US elites imaginatively to meet the ideological and practical challenges that departure from Cold War ruling strategies pose, they also illustrate the soundness of what we call the operations of hegemonic processes within US media.

## 'The New Hinge of History'

History is, in the words of E.P. Thompson (1990: 117), now turning 'on a new hinge'. Events in Eastern Europe are rendering familiar languages and categories for political analysis obsolete. As a result, constructions of social reality secured by Cold War mythologies are losing their resonance. Claims encoded in the old categories of western power-knowledge now invite, sometimes even solicit, ironic decodings. In the US, political cartoonists, headline writers, editorial commentators – even advertisers seeking to marshal support for medicines that fight the Cold War on other fronts – have been quick to exploit the opportunities for comedic mischief produced by this profound categorical rupture. Thus, for example, a header for an editorial in *The Washington Post* (10/12/89) announces, 'The loss of an enemy is a frightful thing', and a header for *The New York Times*

(3/12/89) provides the precis for 'Three European views on the risks of peace'.

In contrast, American administrative spokespeople, conservative political pundits, defence intellectuals and intelligence bureaucrats do not appear to be amused by the ironies that lubricate the new hinge of history. On the contrary, they are engaged in a deadly serious struggle to reclaim face, preserve and advance existing structures of power and re-establish their position as authors and mediators of global events.

This chapter explores the rhetorical and ideological problems/*crises*, that events in Eastern Europe pose for US power and information brokers. We do not analyse events in Eastern Europe *per se*. Rather we direct our attention to one of the sideshows in the carnival of history. That is, we look at how the changes in Eastern Europe have been 'framed' and interpreted in US electronic and print media. We use these frames and interpretations to examine crises *within* US power structures.[1]

Attending to this sideshow offers access to an historically significant struggle for the control of reality. The ritual view of communication (Carey, 1989a), as structured interaction that produces, maintains, repairs and transforms reality, guides our approach to this struggle.

We treat the definition of crisis and thus its status as *real* as the specific terrain upon which this struggle is engaged. We access this terrain through an examination of the mythic elements US media and their official sources mobilize to secure their definitions of crises. Following Barthes (1972: 114), we conceive of myth as a 'second-order semiological system' which appropriates language (the first order) for its own peculiar purposes. One of the distinctive features of myth is its 'imperative, buttonholing character': myth tells me, its addressee, as much about myself as it tells me about the world. It is speech with a pronounced subjective character despite its usual lack of specific marks of personal or direct address. In short, it tells me who I am and how I fit into the scheme of history.

Metaphor is a particularly telling agent of mythic thought. Metaphors bridge the gaps between the known and the unknown. They allow people to experience and understand one kind of thing in terms of another; metaphoric thinking expands human horizons and thereby facilitates adjustment to change (Hesse, 1966; Lakoff and Johnson, 1980; Rorty, 1986). The kinds of things people use to achieve understanding of other things are not merely promiscuous couplings; they are not just fortuitous slips of the tongue. These things embody, display, preserve and police the 'faded mythology' (Schelling, cited in Jansen, 1988: 5) that creates order and makes community and communication possible. They are culturally patterned, purposive, and sociologically significant. In short, metaphors are rich preserves for cultural analysis.

This form of cultural analysis is, however, a speculative venture. Metaphors are, by definition, ambiguous. Indeed ambiguity is what makes them work; their polysemic character allows them to create and colonize sizeable communities of meaning. They can simultaneously house, heal and conceal unresolved contradictions. When metaphors settle down into apparent literalness, they lose their capacity for invention (Rorty, 1986). Consequently all attempts to pin down their full meanings are destined to fail. The best we can do is freeze some metaphoric frames, chart some shifting ensembles of meaning, and identify some 'preferred readings' of terms and phrases. For this reason, all exercises in metaphoric analysis are works-in-progress. Nevertheless we believe they are valuable exercises for the following reasons: (a) they offer some access to (subjective) 'vocabularies of motive' (Gerth and Mills, 1953; Burke, 1962) which guide the vision and colour the language of US 'defense intellectuals';[2] (b) analyses of elite responses to the rapid breakdown in established codes and conventions for representing the *other* – 'the enemy', 'the Red Menace', 'Godless Communists', 'the evil empire', etc, – allow access to processes of reality construction and repair normally hidden from public view; and (c) these constructive and repair efforts, in turn, locate portals to emerging forms of power-knowledge at an historical moment or juncture when they are still open to critical interventions and revisions.

In the following pages we attempt to display the promise of this mode of analysis in three ways. First, we briefly examine the use of mythological thinking in a much publicized essay by Francis Fukuyama, 'The End of History' (1989). Secondly, we identify some patterns of metaphoric usage that figure prominently in US media representations of events in Eastern Europe, and track some of the changes in these conventions that have occurred since September 1989. In this section, we pay particular attention to the role of *The New York Times* – sometimes referred to as 'the newspaper of record' in the US – in mediating the ideas of defence intellectuals and policy makers. Thirdly, we briefly explore some of the dynamics of these representations within popular culture, specifically in advertising.

The architecture of our argument permits us to examine some of the ways these events are being framed in three forms of media: an esoteric text of limited circulation addressed primarily to conservative academics, policy makers, and defence intellectuals; news reports from major/elite media addressed primarily to well-educated, affluent, lay people; and advertisements, visual and print texts, addressed to the population at large, as consumers. Tracking framing processes at different levels strengthens our claims about the operation of hegemonic processes, since the processes for production of meaning become increasingly organized and, in a sense, collectivized as they move from esoteric to exoteric media.

While our analysis suggests that some of the moves in this process are top-down – a particularly strong case for the trickle-down position is made when we trace migration of the evolutionary metaphor as it is represented in *The New York Times* – we nevertheless recognize that there is also significant flow in the other direction. Elite intellectuals and policy makers are, of course, also members of the larger culture and subject to its influences; moreover, in developing their formulations, they consciously try to anticipate and accommodate to, as well as influence and rally, what they conceive of as popular ideas. Like the creators of advertisements, they look for images that will sell their positions. Moreover, some of the most compelling images of our time originate within popular culture. Indeed, our analysis suggests that those who have conceived and developed ads using post-Cold War imagery have been far more innovative, imaginative and potentially subversive in exploring its possibilities and limits than their counterparts in the policy think-tanks, newsrooms and editorial offices.

### Framing the Crises: From Disintegration to Evolution

The word *crisis* derives from the Greek, *krisis*; it literally means decision. In its early incarnations, the word implied human agency. The agency is retained in some modern uses of the term, eg actions of a 'terrorist' may produce a crisis, public officials may formulate policies to avert crisis, etc. However, human agency is usually lost when the term enters the vocabularies of the natural and physical sciences, as when a disease reaches a crisis, the eruption of a volcano produces a crisis, etc.

Within the story-telling routines of US media, framing an event as a crisis generally denotes a dramatic disturbance of order; it usually connotes threat or danger. Crisis frames are used in reporting events initiated by human agents as well as events set in motion by impersonal forces (natural disasters); however, when human agency precipitates crisis, pejorative adjectives are frequently used to describe the agent: he/she is portrayed as transgressing boundaries – as a law-breaker, terrorist, demagogue, dictator, etc (Gitlin, 1980). In reportage of natural events, floods, earthquakes, hurricanes, etc, human agency is absent; in these scenarios human interest stories focus on the suffering of victims, the luck of survivors, and the selflessness of heroic rescuers (Erikson, 1977).

### *'Cold War' as a Controlling Metaphor: Crisis and Binary Logics*

The metaphors that colour the mythology and news coverage of the Cold War emphasize the evil designs of human agents. Winston Churchill fired the opening shot on 5 March 1946 in Fulton, Missouri, when he announced that an 'iron curtain' had descended upon Europe; the Soviets were, of course, portrayed as the aggressors in the new hostilities. Walter Lippmann coined the term, 'the Cold War', in response to Churchill's initiative.

The metaphors introduced by Churchill and Lippmann hung the hinge of history on a very narrow frame. They restricted exercise of political imagination and rhetoric to the reductive parameters of a binary code. According to Thompson (1990: 120), the ideologies this code supported 'nourished and reproduced reciprocal paranoias' and 'deadend imagination with a language of worst-case analysis and a definition of half of the human race as an Enemy Other'.

Binary patterns have been a hallmark of western thought at least since the emergence of Platonic dualism: they have been a prominent constituent of modern power-knowledge since the first appearance of a 'red' menace during the French Revolution; but they acquired a new urgency and a quasi-official status in 1919 with the Palmer Raids, a series of violent attacks on the headquarters of dissident groups led by US Attorney General A. Mitchell Palmer. With the advent of the Cold War, anti-communism became the template for all political and cultural life in the US; moreover, conformity to the configurations of this template has been enforced by military actions, security measures, intelligence networks and congressional inquiries.

The existence of what former President Ronald Reagan called an 'evil empire' – a common enemy – produced unparalleled levels of social cohesion (albeit coerced cohesion) in the US, a nation with a history of violent internal class/labour, race and ethnic conflict. As ruling strategy, the Cold War was an enormous success. Consequently its end poses a profound crisis for US defence intellectuals and policy makers.

For them, the good news is also bad news: in the words of Defense Department analyst Francis Fukuyama, the end of the Cold War is a 'very sad time'. This sadness appears to explain the recurrent imagery of 'nostalgia' in US media coverage of changes in Eastern Europe. Consider, for example, the opening paragraph of a 92-column-inch article by Larry Eichel in *The Philadelphia Inquirer* (9/11/89) entitled, 'Wall kept things simple':

> The Cold War in Europe may or may not be over yet. But it seems to be ending. And some experts miss it already. They say the day may come when the world looks back on the 40 years after World War II as the good old days – when life was simple, people knew which side they were on and a standoff between superpowers kept the peace.

Without the excuse of the Cold War, the centre of US strategic policy and mythology no longer holds. Established categorical interdictions lose their force, and the polarized patterns that inflect all its terms no longer make sense. The threat of peace radically subverts the narrative structures, languages and logics that have provided the auspices for global expansion of the US empire for nearly half a century.

As a result, policy makers and journalists cannot practise business as usual. Conventional story-telling routines no longer work. This historical twist forces those who would preserve the simplicity, predictability and hierarchies of the old order to innovate: to search for new narrative frames to explain and contain events that are, by definition, impossible within the world order secured by Cold War mythology.

## Framing the Crisis: The Discourse of Defence Intellectuals

Francis Fukuyama has been one of the most successful innovators within Reagan–Bush strategic planning circles. In an article published in an obscure but well-funded conservative journal, *The National Interest*, during the summer of 1989, he offered a eulogy for 'The End of History?' and laid the ideological and mythic groundwork for articulation of the concept of 'a New World Order' which later became the centrepiece of President Bush's Persian Gulf War rhetoric (Fukuyama, 1989). Fukuyama's ideas were widely disseminated and became something of an intellectual *cause célèbre* following the appearance of a long article about him in *The New York Times Sunday Magazine* (27/10/89).

Three facets of Fukuyama's perspective warrant detailed analysis: (a) his embrace of a Hegelian concept of evolution, (b) his treatment of agency, and (c) his conflation of the 'end' of history and the ends of free market economism. Fukuyama attempts to clear away the wreckage wrought by the communist menace by returning to the conceptual roots of the problem: Karl Marx's inversion of Hegelian idealism. Marx, it has often been said, turned Hegel on his head; Fukuyama returns the philosopher to an upright position. He tries to restore ideas, particularly the Hegelian concept of evolution, to the centre of the historical process. Within Fukuyama's reconstruction of the principles of historical immanence, communists are no longer the gravediggers of capitalism. On the contrary, communism is conceived as a regressive move in the march of historical progress: a march that is set in motion by the quest for individual and commercial freedom, a quest that reaches its highest expression in free market economies.

Fukuyama's concept of evolution is profoundly ambivalent about who/what drives the engine of history. On the one hand, he embraces historical immanence: human freedom/consumer-based capitalism triumphs over all other ways of being in the world because of its *natural* superiority. Yet his apologia for freedom makes it difficult for him to entirely surrender the concept of human agency; hence the question mark in his title, and the shift in mood that occurs within his essay from bold assertion of the triumph of liberal democracy to a more provisional assessment. Thus, for example, Fukuyama describes the sadness of a future at the end of history, but also suggests, in his closing sentence, that, 'Perhaps this very prospect of centuries of boredom at the end of history will serve to get history started once again'. Since boredom is a human reaction, Fukuyama seems to imply that human agents could intervene and once more jump-start the engine of history.

It is this ambiguity which gives Fukuyama's essay both its claim to objective authority and its mythic dimensions. According to Barthes (1972: 143), myth transforms history into nature: 'In passing from history to nature, myth . . . abolishes the complexity of human acts, it gives them the simplicity of essences, it does away with all dialectics, it organizes a world which is without contradictions because it is without depth. . . . History becomes an impersonal process: the present contains the seeds of the future.'

For Fukuyama, the triumph of good (capitalism) over evil (communism) as a result of victory in the Cold War will deliver us to a future, 'a universal homogeneous state', characterized by 'liberal democracy in the political sphere combined with easy access to VCRs and stereos in the economic' (Fukuyama, 1989: 8).

Before publication of this essay, Fukuyama was virtually unknown outside the relatively closed circle of defence intellectuals. He achieved his 'fifteen minutes of fame' by effectively evoking the crisis that the terminal point of Cold War mythology posed for western elites. The 'end' he describes does not simply mean the transition from one state of affairs to another. Rather it marks the end of a mythic structure that has worked very well and movement towards another which needs to be able to consolidate the 'victory' without losing the adventure and the legitimation associated with moral conflict. Analysis of Fukuyama's hesitations and ambiguities reveals the gaps around which those with other goals might gather to intervene and redefine the future of the 'New World Order'.

## Framing the Crisis: Coverage in Elite US Newspapers

This section considers US media strategies and conventions for defining and framing crises. It examines the play of these conventions in coverage of events in Eastern Europe by major US news media.[3] It places special emphasis upon the analysis of metaphors used in this coverage because metaphor is a vehicle of mythological thinking as well as 'an agent of ideological transfer' (Bloor, 1977: 70).

Metaphors bridge the gap between the known and the unknown, the familiar and the exotic, what is secure and what poses a threat. Metaphor is a medium that the reluctant innovators who seek to preserve the simplicity and hierarchies of the Cold War must use to create a new world order.

The language of crisis is, predictably, invoked to describe the dramatic changes in the 'evil empire'. However, crisis frames pose some serious problems for these recuperative efforts. The mythology of the evil empire is secured in a teleology which sees a communist 'plot', 'conspiracy', or 'master plan for world domination' as a prime mover of world history. This teleology produces a double-bind. To impute agency to the events is to suggest either: (a) a dramatic change in the enemy's intentions – within the terms of binary logic, a change from evil to good; or (b) deception, a trick, the evil empire is using the pretence of change to set a trap for 'the free world'.

Both of these frames are risky; those who try them discover they can boomerang. Nevertheless, both *The New York Times* (10/12/89) and *The Christian Science Monitor* (12/12/89) managed to craft frames that cast Mikhail Gorbachev in the role of an agent of positive change without sacrificing credibility. A brief *Times* editorial, 'A Precious Moment', described, without qualification, Gorbachev as 'remaking history'. More commonly this approach is tempered by adjectival equivocations that carry anti-democratic connotations. Thus, for example, in framing Gorbachev as an agent of positive change, the *Monitor* describes him as 'the Kremlin *boss*' and characterizes him as moving in the *right* direction almost by accident as he 'slip-slides toward a "corporate state"'. Option (b) has proved more hazardous. Thus, for example, former US Defense Secretary Casper Weinberger's claim that the end of the Cold War is a communist trick to lull America into a false sense of security made him an easy target for caricature. Conservative columnist Louis Rukeseyer ('Hold Berlin Wall euphoria; make a reality check', Tribune Media Services, 11/89) and Jeanne Kirkpatrick ('A Safer World?', *The Washington Post*, 28/5/90) negotiated this route more successfully by invoking the unpredictable nature of history and the virtue of caution.

In the early weeks of the dramatic transformations of Eastern Europe, some major media employed crisis frames but were able to massage the question of agency effectively by using metaphors normally reserved for reportage of natural disasters. Consider, for example, the opening sentence of an editorial in *The New York Times* (3/12/89): 'A political *earthquake* sends East Europeans *surging* into the streets to shake off oppression'. The *Times* also used the heading, '*Watershed* for Europe' (22/11/89). Similarly, the producers of *USA Today* news, a television programme (18/11/89), used the running logo, '*Winds* of Change', to frame its Eastern European coverage; while *The Washington Post* (10/12/89), and *The Wall Street Journal* (12/12/89), invoked the metaphor of '*disintegration*'.

Perhaps the most interesting and systematic source of documentation for tracking metaphoric frames is provided by the heading *The New York Times* has used to frame its running coverage of Eastern European events. Since November 1989 the *Times* has carried at least one full page of analysis of Eastern European events each Sunday; some Sunday editions have carried as many as three full pages of coverage, and the *Times* has sometimes extended its running coverage to weekday editions. This special coverage is bracketed by running heads which are used repeatedly. In the early issues, there was considerable experimentation with headers. Some initial offerings were 'Clamor in the East' (11/11/89) and 'The New Europe' (19/11/89). 'The New Europe' ran recurrently through December. By spring 1990, however, the *Times* had introduced a new running head, 'Evolution in Europe'. Printed in bold print, it was followed by subtitles in lighter type such as 'Seeds of Unity and Confusion' (6/5/90); 'Moving Slowly, but Planning a Bankroll' (6/5/90); 'Free to Travel, Free to Politick' (3/6/90), etc.

Serial use of such running heads is a dramatic departure from the *Times'* routine practice for framing international news; the usual frame is predictably 'international news'. This departure not only signals events in crisis, it also signals a crisis in conventions for covering these events. It marks an occasion of overt editorial intervention in the selection of frames.

The *Times'* editors' decision to embrace and retain the evolutionary metaphor followed temporally and perhaps causally the appearance of the long article in the *Times Sunday Magazine* in October 1989 showcasing Francis Fukuyama's neo-Hegelian evolutionary interpretation of the current transformations in international politics.

The *Times'* heavy investment in the evolutionary metaphor was a curious move, especially for a publication that prides itself on its commitment to fact. The term is, of course, borrowed from biology; it has, however, also had a long and particularly undistinguished career in western social theory. Indeed, Charles Darwin borrowed it from the sociologist, Herbert Spencer. Critique of the teleological, tautological, and racialist assumptions of social evolutionary theory has been part of the 'canon' of sociology for over 60 years.[4] The role social evolutionary assumptions have played in US conservative thought, as well as in the advance of racist and imperialist ideologies, has been carefully documented by mainstream historians like Richard Hofstadter (1944; see also White, 1976; Gould, 1981). In short, the wheel that both Fukuyama and *The New York Times* have reinvented and licensed as the prime mover of history is, in fact, a familiar and, in some of its previous incarnations, very dangerous one.

How can we explain this move at a time when even President Bush claims, reform in Eastern Europe 'absolutely mandates new thinking' in the west (Associated Press, Brussels, 5/12/89)? It may simply indicate that the conservative think-tanks, always more heavily endowed by capital than imagination, have run out of fuel. There is some evidence to support this view. Defence intellectuals at the Rand Corporation frankly admit that events in Eastern Europe caught them by surprise. Michael Rich, vice president of Rand's National Security Research Division, acknowledges that, 'In no way can you say that any piece of work predicted what would happen in 1989': and Stephen Drezner, vice president of Rand's army division, asserts, 'The truth . . . is that we don't understand where the main thrusts of the world are' (cited in Dionne, 1990).

Kirkpatrick, Rukeseyer and Weinberger all tie their suspicions of the changes in Eastern Europe, at least in part, to the fact that the Cold War models failed to predict them. Fukuyama, by contrast, is singular among defence intellectuals in claiming to apprehend agency in contemporary history or, more accurately, in 'the end of history'. And, as Albert Camus (1955: 5), pointed out, 'A world that can be explained even with bad reasons is a familiar world'.

The evolutionary trope imputes a reason which allows the American empire to remain on the crest of history. The spotlight is removed from Gorbachev and Yeltsin and from the streets of Timisoara and Vilnius. Events in Eastern Europe are hijacked and transformed into logical outcomes of US policy. Moreover, necessity is imputed to the (*evolutionary*) move towards marked-based consumer economies; these economies – economies just like those of the west – are conceived as the end, the *telos*, of historical development.

The efficacy of evolution as a media frame is displayed in a header for a column by conservative columnist George Will, which valorizes a familiar

Fukuyamian theme, 'Markets are key to Europe's unity' (Washington Post Writers Group, 11/89). Embedding his discourse in references to the 'unity' of Europe under pre-Reformation Christendom (what we call metaphors of salvation), Will invokes the evolutionary concept of 'progress', albeit with a double edge, when he suggests: 'Perhaps peace-through-enervation, the peace of the satiated consumer, will prevail. If not, Europe's future conflicts will start with all watches synchronized. Call it progress.'

Although the solution to the crisis that the evolutionary metaphor offers is very neat, some defence intellectuals are not buying it. Indeed, Kirkpatrick explicitly rejects it when she asserts, 'In truth we have not discerned the "laws" of historical development, probably because there are none' (*The Washington Post*, 28/5/90).

When we prepared our initial draft of this chapter (June 1990), we pointed out that the representational crisis plaguing US power-structures and media organizations had not been resolved. As we revise (February 1991), this is no longer the case: the regressive retreat of the Bush administration to militarism seems to have resolved (or deferred) the framing crisis. In what is perhaps the most telling quotation of the earlier draft, this fateful move was anticipated by Jeremy Azrael, a Rand Corporation Soviet specialist in May 1990 when he asserted: 'There is a terrible danger that defense intellectuals will have to go whoring. Folks in the services will go looking for threats out there' (cited in Dionne, 1990).

There was some evidence at the time that Azrael articulated his concern that this 'whoring' had already begun. Thus, for example, John Benson of the American Institute of Aeronautics and Astrophysics argued (National Public Radio, 17/5/90) that development of the Strategic Defense Initiative weapon system (Star Wars) needed to be continued in order to provide a defensive shield to protect humans against falling asteroids. However, some defence intellectuals were, in the words of Azrael, accepting 'the disappearance of the Cold War world that had been very good to them' (Dionne, 1990). John Andrews, a weapons lobbyist for Rockwell International, is among this group; in what has to be one of the more daring assaults in the metaphoric wars, he co-opted Thompson's 'hinge of history' metaphor and used it to advise his compatriots to get into the peace business, for example by selling printing presses and other non-military technologies to countries like Czechoslovakia (PBS Radio interview, 10/6/90).

Andrews' advice was not heeded. The war business is now flourishing in the US. The value of stocks in Raytheon Company, the defence contractor that manufactures the Patriot missile, is increasing. In the carefully staged and controlled media presentations of the war in the Persian Gulf by the US military, the Patriot was used as a public relations representative for the Star Wars missile system. Although the Patriot is actually an upgraded version of an earlier missile technology, the military and the defense department was *re-presenting* it as a mini-prototype of the Star Wars defence system. Its successes have been videotaped and beamed throughout the world via CNN, and its failures and misfires shielded by US and Israeli censorships. The Star Wars system, which had been targeted for elimination from the US defence budget as part of the 'Peace Dividend' the end of the Cold War was supposed to produce, is now scheduled for refunding in President Bush's 1992 military budget proposal.

The framing crisis that the end of the Cold War posed for US elites has apparently been repaired. President Bush's 1991 'State of the Union Address' was a seamless performance. Within its rhetoric, the evil empire, scaled down to more manageable proportions, has been restored as the centrepiece of a renovated and recharged version of a familiar mythological system. It casts Saddam Hussein as Adolph Hitler redux, and introduces the 'New World Order' as a trope which reclaims and repositions the expansionist objectives of the American empire.

## Framing the Crisis: The Logics of Advertising

Advertising is also rich in mythic discourse. In Barthes' terms (1972: 142–50), it is the 'depoliticized' speech where a culture's common-sense constructions of the world are articulated and reconfigured. Within it, we can find some very revealing traces of the representational crisis posed by the end of the Cold War. These traces are significant because they operate outside official channels for dissemination and analysis of political information. Consequently they naturalize emerging mythic images and conventions at the level of the popular where they can be recalled and remobilized when they are needed to do other work within hegemonic processes.

Advertisements provide ongoing translations between different systems of value and meaning. Judith Williamson (1978: 25) describes the advertisement as 'a system of systems or "metasystem"', its purpose is 'not to invent a meaning' for the product it advertises, but 'to translate a meaning for it by means of a sign system we already know'. This description helps make visible the logic by which advertisements connect 'current affairs' to their own, commercial, agendas.

In the immediate aftermath of the Cold War, advertisements made elliptical connections between advertising and politics. In place of 'history' (Fukuyama), ads offered an abstracted threat or an equally disembodied triumph. In a number of ads, the Berlin Wall did an elegant semantic slide within the advertisement's metasystem, coming to stand, immediately and efficiently, for the new order of things: a new order where advertising is at once the hypostasis, and the 'proper' and 'natural' signifier of that order.

Centrality is perhaps the most salient feature of advertising, in terms of its response to changes in east–west relations. This is often manifest as an effort to be as all-embracing – as generic – as possible. When popular forms take up material that is so clearly positioned between an old and a new sense of the world, they tend to be cautious. This caution keeps the semiological system intact by drawing renegade meanings back to the centre: it sets into motion what Fiske and Hartley (1978: 87) call 'clawback', a mechanism of cultural systems which preserves the intelligibility of the text and the reader's sense that his/her culture's response to crisis is adequate. In this way, the mythic speech of advertisements posits stable *termini* where there is a great deal of evidence pointing to unstable *transits*.

A familiar strategy is to celebrate the changes while positioning them in a familiar framework of meaning, usually the market. Representation of 'the market' carries multiple charges as a crucial issue in redefinition of Eastern European societies and as the key component both in US concepts of 'democracy' and in what the west has to offer the east. In this way, ads work as a forum where these issues are addressed and elaborated, but also as a metonym for the system towards which those societies are commonly assumed to be 'evolving'. Sanka uses this strategy in a television advertisement presented against a backdrop of news headlines. In the Sanka ad, the narrator announces, 'In the rush of events that ushered in the new decade, you may have missed the news about Sanka . . .'. This ad is significant because it does not simply drag down momentous events into the banal world of the commodity; on the contrary, it performs a breath-taking act of translation between what in other logical systems might appear incommensurable, and succeeds in referring the novel to the familiar in a common-sensical manner.

The frames these responses create to contain the crisis are similar to those used by both Fukuyama and the elite news media. These framing devices embody a series of assumptions about the *telos* of political change, imposing an evolutionary frame that normalizes and naturalizes it. The sociocentric transit of the Sanka ad places us at the terminus of historical change – at its point of arrival – or, in Fukuyama's terms, at its 'end'.

A series of advertisements for *US News and World Report*, which appeared in *The New York Times Sunday Magazine* on 11 and 14 November and 2 December 1990, also build upon this convention; but these ads overtly use the language and logic of a 'Darwinian' evolutionary theory of society to frame their response to the crisis. Each of the ads is formally similar: three coloured frames appear across the top of a largely white page, each frame part of a narrative that demonstrates the beneficent intervention of the magazine. A stylized hand directs the eye of the reader across the page from left to right. At the bottom of the page, the magazine's logo is placed beneath a simple message, 'News you can use'.

The first ad features three hominid forms against a background that suggests crumbling parchment, connoting the passage of a great span of time. The first frame depicts a stooped, hirsute, simian creature; the next a more erect humanoid, clutching a magazine; and the third presents an upright figure, fully human, still naked but neatly coiffed. The second and, for our purposes, the most interesting ad in the series shows a series of panels depicting Karl Marx metamorphosing, under the influence of *US*

*News and World Report*, from the wild, bearded prophet of socialism to a well-groomed, grandfatherly icon of capitalism in a pin-striped shirt. The third ad in the series invokes religious imagery to suggest that without the useful news in *US News and World Report*, Noah would have stocked the ark with unpaired animals.

These ads make sense by pushing hubris over the edge into ironic self-congratulation. Substituting the magazine for the voice of God in Noah's case, and for the complex process of genetic mutation in the ape's case, and then juxtaposing those dynamics with Karl Marx's emancipation from communism, presents a fully articulated instance of the evolutionary metaphor at work assimilating the crisis and normalizing the mythic rupture it has created. These ads do not merely naturalize the changes in the world order, they position their product, *US News and World Report* – and by extension the US and its news industry – as the agent(s) of all definitive transformations in mythic principles, whether these are biological, political or religious.

These examples are obviously selected for their relevance to our argument. A more fully developed analysis of the hegemonic work advertising does would, of course, be far more subtle, qualified, dialectical and rigorous. Nevertheless, these examples illustrate some of the ways advertising translates images and meanings between different value systems, attempting to harness the power of one discourse in order to further an agenda within another (and quite different) discourse. Advertising's attempt to re-present privileged discourses – like policy analysis and news which, dealing explicitly with political issues, are generally acknowledged to be 'serious' and 'important' – is accompanied by an unusually open polysemy. Ambiguity, generality and rich ironies provide the ground for advertising's responses to the crises and rupture in the narrative structures of Cold War mythology. These reassure us that our roles as consumers will be safe, under the terms of the new semiological and social orders.

**Conclusion**

Our examination of the representational crisis the new hinge of history poses for US media and their official sources supports some tentative conclusions about hegemonic processes.

First, some images and explanatory structures for framing the crisis seem to be cultivated in all three mediated channels, specifically the evolutionary image and its requisite explanatory structures. This point is made especially salient when *The New York Times* is treated as a case study: Fukuyama's neo-Hegelian evolutionary theory received detailed explication in a feature story in its *Sunday Magazine* in October 1989; news of changes in Eastern Europe was systematically presented under the header, 'Evolution in Eastern Europe', during most of 1990; and the series of *US*

*News and World Report* advertisements, using explicitly evolutionary images, appeared in the *Times Sunday Magazine* over a four-week period in late 1990.

Secondly, the process of cultivation appears to be a hierarchical operation involving some top-down moves. Thus, for example, the evolutionary metaphor made its initial appearance in the most esoteric/elite channel, an obscure conservative academic journal. This channel, policy analysis, is a site of overt hegemonic work. Fukuyama and other defence intellectuals and members of policy think-tanks are overtly commissioned to generate evidence and explanatory structures which can serve as the raw material for developing policy and securing official positions.

Thirdly, the second channel for mediation of the crisis, news production, appears to be both more and less autonomous than hegemonic theory might predict. Early in the representational crisis, major news mediators such as *The New York Times* appeared to experiment freely with metaphoric images for framing the changes in Eastern Europe. After the *Times* editors featured a story on Fukuyama's perspective, however, the play of experimentation constricted. Beginning in early spring 1990, most news and all news analysis appeared under the 'Evolution in Europe' header. Something more than Louis Althusser's 'authorless theater' (cited in Jansen, 1990: 245) seems to be at work here since serial use of innovative editorial headers would appear to require overt intervention or, at least, approval at the highest decision-making levels within the *Times'* organization. Moreover, the header survived a change in the editorship of the international news section which suggests that the *Times* had more than a casual investment in the longevity of this framing device.

Fourthly, within popular culture, particularly advertising, the hinge of history appears to turn on a particularly interesting axis. Since popular dissemination of images and explanations of the changes in Europe – particularly images and explanations mobilized to sell products – must be secured within broadly accessible languages and logics, it is here that we would expect to apprehend the emergence of viable solutions to the representational crisis. That is, it is within these popular forms that we would expect to discover the emergence of new (post-Cold War) conventions for mediating and framing events, and to find these new frames essentialized, naturalized and reified. For these reasons, the presence of the evolutionary metaphor in this channel is particularly significant. Where one might expect evidence of rupture, one finds frames which suggest seamless continuity; in place of forced adaptation, what looks like comfortable assimilation. Is this because the New World Order is merely an expanded (and expansionist) rearticulation of the familiar icon of Cold War mythology, the 'free' market? Does it simply marshal support for further acceleration of the long process of replacing democracy with capitalism? In short, is the emerging mythology merely a celebration of the *raison d'être* of advertising?

It is still too early to offer any definitive predictions regarding the outcome of this fateful sideshow of history. Events in Eastern Europe may undermine or render irrelevant the hegemonic work being carried out in US media. Or will the experience of the Persian Gulf War lead the US to recover its national identity by returning to its Cold War persona as 'policeman of the world', albeit without the ideological cover the mission of preserving democracy once provided? The new hinge of history may still turn in directions that will expose cultivation of evolutionary narrative structures as the ultimate irony of the post-modern age. Indeed, the failed coup in the Soviet Union and its aftermath has heralded yet another such turn.

### Epilogue

A particularly telling play on the evolutionary trope appeared in a political cartoon by David Levine (*The New York Times*, 1/2/91). The six-by-thirteen inch cartoon, entitled 'The Descent of Man', shows a succession of figures, following the same format as the *US News and World Report* advertisement already discussed. The first and largest figure (five inches in height) presents a finely turned out image of the debonair American film star of the 1940s, Clark Gable. Gable is followed by a large and powerful looking baboon; it, in turn is followed by a smaller and rather stupid looking monkey, scratching its head; in the next frame, there is a coiled snake positioned with mouth opened and ready to attack; and, in the final position, a tiny (two-and-a-half inch) figure of Saddam Hussein is presented surrounded by flies and sinking into an ambiguous pool of liquid which could be oil, blood or primordial slime.

The evolutionary scheme that secures the New World Order is a totalizing perspective which consolidates semiological resources into the categories of a crudely essential doctrine. If this resolution of the framing crisis prevails, it will hang history on a hinge that is even narrower than the one secured by the mythology of the Cold War. Within the mythic code that secures the vision of the New World Order, the enemy other is a lower form of life rather than a powerful and menacing counterpart. The world secured by this code is far less stable than its antecedent. Exterminating a lower form of life is much easier to justify and accomplish with impunity than taking on a powerful enemy – an enemy that can also exterminate its foe. It makes genocide plausible and perhaps possible.

### Notes

1 We borrow the concept, 'media frame', from Gitlin (1980: 6–7), who borrowed it from Goffman (1974). According to Gitlin, 'What makes the world beyond direct experience look natural is a media frame . . . Media frames, largely unspoken and unacknowledged, organize the world both for journalists who report it and, in some important degree, for us who rely on

their reports. Media frames are persistent patterns of cognition, interpretation, and presentation, of selection, emphasis, and exclusion, by which symbol-handlers routinely organize discourse, whether verbal or visual. Frames enable journalists to process large amounts of information quickly and routinely: to recognize it as information, to assign it to cognitive categories and to package it for efficient relay to their audiences. Thus, for organizational reasons alone, frames are unavoidable, and journalism is organized to regulate their production.' See also Tuchman (1978) and Hall (1980).

2 The term, 'defense intellectual', is borrowed from Cohen (1987) and Dionne (1990).

3 By major media, we mean the so-called 'elite media': the premier papers of the large newspaper chains which have national circulation and/or syndicated news services, e.g. *The New York Times, The Washington Post*, The Tribune News Service, etc, large circulation news magazines, e.g. *Time, Newsweek*, etc, as well as national (and in the case of Cable News Network (CNN) international) broadcast networks, e.g. CBS, PBS, World Monitor News Service, etc.

4 This critique was already well developed by 1927 when Sorokin completed *Contemporary Sociological Theories: Through the First Quarter of the Twentieth Century* (1928). It was part of the taken-for-granted assumptions of the field by the time standard theoretical reference works appeared at mid-century. See, for example, Timasheff (1955), Gross (1959) and Martindale (1960). In the wake of the horrors social evolution-based theories of Aryan racial supremacy had wrought during the Second World War, the term had very limited currency in social theory during the peak of the Cold War although its stepchild, modernization theory, retained many of its assumptions. The leading figure behind modernization theory, Talcott Parsons, did, however, reclaim the term in *Societies: Evolutionary and Comparative Perspectives* (1966); in Parsons' version, cybernetic metaphors replaced their biological antecedents. There has been a renewal of interest in neo-Parsonian incarnations of evolutionary theory among some social scientists in recent years. See, for example, Beniger (1986).

# 5

# Media and the Terminal Crisis of Communism in Poland

*Karol Jakubowicz*

The collapse of communism in Central and Eastern Europe has been widely regarded as a sudden and abrupt process. In Poland, at least, it was nothing of the sort: 'the [whole] history of the Polish People's Republic was one of a gradual dismantling of totalitarianism' (Walicki, 1990).

Elemér Hankiss (1990) uses the concept of the 'organizational principle' as an analytical tool for studying social organization. Following Habermas, he says that the formation of a society is always determined by a basic organizational principle that delimits the space within which society may change without losing its identity – the space within which the system of the productive forces, the system of steering mechanisms, and the system of values securing social identity may change and develop.

In various historical and socioeconomic contexts, organizational principles tend to cluster into more or less stable configurations. In Eastern Europe, the configuration communist regimes sought to impose involved the streamlining and control of society in all its aspects by a unique and strong central system, by the logic of the one-party state, in which there is the unity of power and ownership or, in other words, of absolute power: political, economic, military, ideological, police and judiciary powers are all subordinated to a single centre and controlled by a single power body (cf. Selucky, 1972).

Socialist countries have been described accordingly with the use of such terms as 'Leninist monisms', as 'mono-archies' or 'mono-organizational societies', or, in Kolakowski's (1989: 65) words, 'a total power . . . intended to attain the unattainable goal: total destruction of civil society, and total replacement of all human bonds by artificial state-imposed mechanisms'.

Of course, the drive to impose one all-encompassing organizational principle on communist societies was far from successful. The highly centralized, dirigist one-party systems struggled with serious dysfunctions from the very beginning. Their rigid and hierarchical institutional systems were unable to cope with the problems of governing complex modern societies. Hence the penetration of other organizational principles through the cracks and gaps of the system, especially into social and economic domains not directly controlled by the official institutional system. This was promoted by the passive resistance of the population which sought, wherever possible, to adapt and adjust the institutions of the communist state to what it thought right or at least acceptable.

Elements of other organizational principles were also periodically introduced because the leadership realized that the system was inhumane and unworkable (eg Khrushchev's 'thaw' in the mid-1950s). Gorbachev's perestroika may be seen in precisely those terms.

More importantly, however, Central and Eastern European countries were repeatedly the scenes of fundamental socio-political crises, often triggered by anger over unsatisfactory living standards and quickly erupting into open defiance of the system as a whole, as in East Germany in 1953, Poland and Hungary in 1956, Czechoslovakia in 1968, Poland in 1970, 1976 and 1980. The goal in all cases was clearly that of substantially modifying the organizational principle of communism into, for example, that of 'socialism with a human face', or of wholly eliminating it. One may say that the demands grew more and more radical with the passage of time, as experience showed that mere modification or evolution of the system did not lead to real change.

Half-hearted or partial reforms and other factors providing for interference and conflict of dominant and alternative organizational principles led to their 'hybridization' (cf. Hankiss, 1990: 192), producing chaos, confusion and still greater inefficiency, and thus sowing the seeds of continued tension and new crises.

The cumulative effect of this protracted and faltering process of change was far from negligible, at least in some cases. First, it promoted transition in some countries from outright totalitarianism to authoritarianism. Differences between them include the following.

1   In the totalitarian system, the party has a clearly articulated and distinct political identity; in the authoritarian one the party is more polymorphous and blends, through the *nomenklatura* system, with various segments of the state and economic administration often at odds with one another.
2   Under totalitarianism, ideology plays a major role and there is a clear distinction between official and private language; under authoritarianism, ideology is progressively ritualized and semantic differences between official and private discourse are diminished, with differences of meaning resulting from the context.
3   Under totalitarianism, the emphasis is on mobilization, with society seen as a 'resource' to be used by the power structure; differences between that structure and society at large are blurred; under authoritarianism there comes demobilization and a clear distinction between the authorities and society appears (an authoritarian–bureaucratic system).
4   In one system there is lawless terror, while in the other, quasi-legalism, which nonetheless views the law as an instrument of power.

Authoritarianism was then successively corroded and weakened by continued opposition. Zbigniew Brzezinski (1989) distinguishes three stages of the 'retreat from Communist totalitarianism' which are clearly distinguishable also in Poland's post-war history: communist totalitarianism – 1949–56; communist authoritarianism – 1957–70; post-communist authoritarianism – 1971–89; post-communist pluralism – 1989– .[1]

The first three stages correspond to what is popularly known as 'the communist system', and only the fourth stage marks a clear break from it.


## Communism in Poland: Still-born and Crisis-ridden

If we disregard the initial years of 1944–8, we may say that the death throes of the system actually began at the point when communist totalitarianism was introduced in 1948–9. By the manner of their takeover of power, and because of the terror they unleashed to consolidate their hold on it, communists forfeited any chance of winning legitimacy for the system at that stage, even if the fast pace of post-war reconstruction and industrial development – made possible by mobilization of society under a virtual war economy system – did seem to offer real promise that the goals of communism would be attained. When it became obvious that the system was incapable of delivering its promises of social equality and democracy – or indeed prosperity – there was an explosion of popular discontent in 1956 which ushered in communist authoritarianism. For all intents and purposes it also sounded the death knell for the communist system in Poland, even if originally the manner of the conflict's resolution gave the system the only brief period of true popular support and legitimacy it was ever to have. The energy propelling its earlier dynamic expansion had been spent, however; since the promises of democratization made in 1956 were never seriously meant, the system soon entered a stage of retrenchment and gradual decay. The system also lost its nerve, as it were, and began its long and forlorn quest to win popular support for, or at least acquiescence in, the system, while at the same time continuing to rule by fear, and thereby to condemn its own quest for legitimacy to failure. This quest for popular support, together with a desperate effort on the part of some parts of the power elite to be recognized as 'civilized', introduced 'an embarrassment factor' into Polish politics, whose importance in weakening the power structure's resolve to crush opposition by whatever means necessary is not yet fully recognized (much more important, of course, was society's unity in actively or passively opposing the system).

After the crisis of 1970 the loss of nerve was even more noticeable: the change of political and ideological course it brought about signified the arrival of post-communist authoritarianism, involving in part the 'effective de-Communization of the party' (Walicki, 1990). Class struggle was replaced with a quest for 'the moral and political unity of the nation', material prosperity, consumerism and an opening to the world (including freedom to travel), seen as a sop to the population and a way to win its support for the system. The strategy failed for reasons of economic mismanagement and lack of comprehensive economic reform.

The strikes of 1980 which gave the impetus for the birth of 'Solidarity' might, but for martial law, have initiated the introduction of post-communist pluralism. Martial law did not lead to solving any of the problems inherent in the system. As a quirk in the consistent and steady process of the dismantling of totalitarianism, it merely delayed the inevitable. Around 1987 the communist government launched an effort to remodel the system in recognition of the effective existence of pluralism in society. It hoped to be able to stay in control by adapting to existing circumstances and introducing what amounted to its own version of post-communist pluralism. However, a new wave of strikes in 1988 revealed its final and irreversible bankruptcy, making transition to genuine post-communist (ie non-communist) pluralism unavoidable: 'Communism ha[d] suffered many defeats in Poland over the years; now . . . it . . . capitulated' (Michnik, 1990: 7).

Thus, each successive stage of the 'retreat from Communist totalitarianism' was initiated by a social crisis of great magnitude and produced a greater tangle of contradictions: the hybrids became more and more curious until the system lost all coherence and collapsed under the weight of those contradictions and its inability to deliver on its own promises – and to provide a satisfactory explanation for that inability.

A special committee appointed in 1981 by the Central Committee of the Polish United Workers' Party to study the social conflicts found that most of them were all-encompassing crises touched off by widespread anger against deficiencies in the operation of social, economic and political aspects of the system, in most cases involving strikes, street demonstrations, violence and bloodshed. In each case, initial liberalization and democratization resulting from the crisis was followed by a return to many of the same old policies, eventually provoking new outbursts.[2]

### Communism and Communication

#### Communist Totalitarianism

In pursuit of its goals, communist totalitarianism sought to impose genuine and full thought control. In order to subsume and assimilate the totality of culture, the communist power structure sought, in part, to gain mastery over interpersonal, group and mass communication: all communications between people and all forms of community were to be filtered through the state machinery. The communist totalitarian regime was constructed on the clear realization of the fact that the mechanisms whereby information is handed over and distributed in society fundamentally define the functioning of that society (Kolakowski, 1989; Meyrowitz, 1985). By the same token, it was the first truly modern political system: 'It worked on the self-evident axiom: "The more control of information, the more power"' (Kolakowski, 1989: 65). Hence in part the imposition of a monocentric system of uniformization on mass communication (Jakubowicz, 1990a), and particularly broadcasting.[3] In addition to their other functions, the media were given the task of creating a symbolic environment supporting and bearing out as 'true' the propaganda line of the communist government.

When communist totalitarianism was introduced in Poland, direct political supervision of the news media was established and the Soviet model of 'the press of a new type' was zealously copied, with the news media (except those published outside the direct control of the Communist Party) seen as a part and direct extension of the party apparatus and as an 'ideological weapon' of the party (with journalists defined as 'officers of the ideological front'). The view of the press as a collective propagandist, agitator and organizer was prevalent (cf. eg Pisarek, 1978).

As a result, practically the entire media content was strongly propagandistic and designed directly to serve the strengthening of the political system and the ideological education of the masses: 'In the years 1950–1955, pride of place in press content was taken by production issues (fulfilment of the six-year plan!) and political and social subjects' (Pisarek, 1978: 117). The same was true of broadcasting, where all, even seemingly quite apolitical, subjects (eg Easter holidays) were used to drive home an ideological or political message. One case in point are programmes on historical subjects broadcast for schools in 1951–53:[4]

> They had two basic features. First, an antagonistic view of the world of values . . . values are contrasted with antivalues [there is] no place for neutral attitudes . . . The deeds of the heroes of radio shows are unambiguous – absolutely good or absolutely bad . . . Second, a coherent, hierarchically ordered system of values is present. The leading value is social justice and other values are instrumental in relation to it . . . [it is suggested] that engagement in the fight to improve the situation of the oppressed classes is an indispensable attribute of all real values . . . without engagement in the fight for social justice every value turns into an antivalue. (Szpocinski, 1987: 47–8)

This was full thought control in action: everything possible was done to make sure that whatever information of any kind media audiences received would be 'system-supporting', ie directly and unambiguously supportive of the communist system and its values.

After each political crisis introducing the successive periods of the 'retreat' from communist totalitarianism the media became somewhat more open and honest in portraying reality, but without structural change, backsliding in this respect was always possible – and in fact became the norm.

### Communist Authoritarianism

The events of 1956 ended the Stalinist period in Poland and introduced a brief period of democratization, followed by transition to communist authoritarianism.

On the media scene, political controls were loosened, the tendency to maintain a centralized, monocentric system was weakened (at least for a time) and much greater freedom of speech and pluralism were allowed. As a result, the number of newspapers and periodicals grew almost twofold between 1958 and 1960; a great many regional and local newspapers appeared; the two non-communist parties began to publish dailies, the Roman Catholic Church stepped up its publishing activities (providing 'an alternate source of information': cf. Pisarek, 1988) and many ethnic minorities began to bring out weeklies and monthlies; the strident propagandistic tone of the news media disappeared. In 1956–7 especially, the print media provided a forum for open political debates, for exposing the atrocities and distortions of the Stalinist period and for highly critical coverage of the party and government policies. At the same time, propaganda and persuasion stopped being the only functions of the media which now performed the full gamut of functions vis-a-vis the receiver. Media content serving a directly political purpose now accounted for a much smaller proportion of overall media fare than before. The category of 'system-indifferent' content appeared, or rather grew considerably in importance. It was heavily censored and purged of anything that could be construed as politically undesirable, but it did not entirely serve the purpose of educating Homo Sovieticus.

By this time, then, the goal had been changed to one of cognitive control, on the principle that 'he who controls everything people *are allowed to know* is unquestionably the master. He has no need to fear that his power might be undermined by any organised movement or opposition' (Kolakowski, 1989: 65; emphasis added). All the content of the official media had to be either system-supporting or system-indifferent: no system-opposed content was allowed.

The mood of that period is well reflected in programmes on historical subjects broadcast in the years 1958–60:

> There are two changes. First, a departure from the antagonistic vision of the world typical of the previous period . . . The second change, which has greater consequences, is the departure from a coherent, hierarchically ordered system of values . . . social justice is no longer presented as a leading value to which all other values are instrumentally subordinated. Patriotism, development of culture, good politics, the fight for the freedom of others also become autotelic values. Their promotion to the rank of values is no longer dependent on their being linked with the fight for social justice. (Szpocinski, 1987: 48)

### Post-communist Authoritarianism

As far as the official media were concerned, the years 1971–89 can be divided into four periods, clearly reflecting events on the political scene:

(a) liberalization in the early 1970s and then a return to stagnation, centralization of control and concentration in the mid-to-late 1970s (cf. 'Komunikowanie masowe w Polsce . . .', 1981); (b) great opening up and liberalization in 1980–81 (cf. *Raport o stanie komunikacji spolecznej . . . ,* 1982); (c) strict censorship and obligation to follow the official line during and immediately after the period of martial law (cf. eg Passent, 1990); (d) gradual loosening of controls and a reorientation of propaganda policy in the mid-to-late 1980s (cf. Jakubowicz, 1990b).

Again Andrzej Szpocinski's study provides a telling illustration of trends in media content. In the years 1973–85,

> . . . there [was] a clear departure from the antagonistic vision of the world. In this respect they are a complete negation of the cycle of programmes from the beginning of the fifties . . . the problem of the choice of values and favouring such or other traditions lack the dramatism so typical of the Stalinist period. The historical heritage, the Polish heritage, at least, is presented as generally positive (antivalues in radio shows on Polish subjects disappeared). (Szpocinski, 1987: 48–9)

Then, in 1982–4,

> . . . there [was] a retreat from the non-antagonistic vision of the world so typical of the 1970s, and a reversion to the ethical principalism of the 1950s. For the broadcaster of the 1980s there is no doubt that good and evil exist in history. Unlike the 1950s, however, this belief does not lead to unequivocalness and absoluteness in judging past events . . . Historical knowledge – the programmes say – is always many-sided and contextual; therefore, every historical fact can be interpreted in many ways. (Szpocinski, 1987: 49)

Thus, even in the immediate aftermath of martial law, official propaganda lost the certainty resulting from the ability to apply unequivocal criteria in judging social reality. Indeed, the system of values promoted in the programmes in the 1970s and the 1980s was unordered, inconsistent and incoherent, says Szpocinski.

In general, despite all the ups and downs caused by the political situation, media content underwent considerable change. The ratio of 'system-supporting' to 'system-indifferent' content changed in favour of the latter. 'System-supporting' content lost much of its strength of conviction and certitude: the 'ideological code' of defining reality underlying it had spent all its persuasive force and was even seen as something of an embarrassment.[5]

Also, a new category of content appeared on television in the 1970s: western programming, shown in great profusion (cf. Jakubowicz, 1989). Though carefully screened to contain nothing directly or flagrantly pro-western, this programming is hard to classify as merely 'system-indifferent'. After all, it did introduce 'the cosmology of the West' (Mrozowski, 1987) into television programming. Also, it provided vivid images of life in societies governed by organizational principles different from those prevailing in Poland, contradicting the official version of the 'inferiority of the West', which in itself encouraged pressures for change.

Thus, this content was 'system-challenging' at best, if not downright 'system-opposed'.

This category of system-challenging content does not refer to western programming alone. For example, much of the effort of the 'Solidarity' press has been to reclaim and present to its readers banned areas of Polish history, passed over in silence in official publications as not in accordance with the official version or highly politically sensitive. Publications of this kind did not directly oppose the communist system, but did present a challenge to its project of thought or cognitive control.

Audiences were also exposed outside the official media to growing quantities of 'system-opposed' content. In the 1970s, the 'alternative public sphere', composed of the Catholic press, grew in importance. Also, an 'opposition public sphere', consisting of underground periodicals, appeared and became a major factor in providing a focus for the growing opposition to the system (cf. Jakubowicz, 1990b, 1990c). In 1980–81, the 'Solidarity' press was a major source of system-challenging and system-opposed content, dedicated as it was to 'undermining the foundation of the government's claims to legitimacy' (Labedz, 1988: 43) and 'socking it to the Commies' (Szarzynski, 1989: 1). After the imposition of martial law, the underground press continued to play its role (Jakubowicz, 1990c).

As a result, the official media began to reorient their propaganda policy in 1987–9 in order to steal the opposition's thunder. Bowing to the inevitable, including the existence of other, wholly autonomous public spheres with their own definitions of reality, the official media nevertheless continued to pursue the goal of limited cognitive control, based on 'the all-important insight that to be effective, hegemony in the public sphere need not be absolute, merely dominant' (Dahlgren, 1987: 31). If one were thus to sum up the evolution of thought and cognitive control strategies across the three stages of the evolution of the communist system in Poland (communist totalitarianism, communist authoritarianism and post-communist authoritarianism), one could arrive at the schematic representation of media content typical of those stages shown in Figure 5.1.

*Official Media: Need-fulfilment Denied*

The above brief overview of the evolution of the Polish media would suggest that there was a considerable degree of 'dynamic interaction' between an active audience and the media and that the media proved quite responsive to audience needs (cf. Palmgreen et al., 1985). In fact, however, that would be an erroneous impression. Despite the superficial changes sketched above, the media system throughout the whole period consistently denied the satisfaction of fundamental audience needs and operated in a psychologically destructive way.

Research into the Poles' social and political attitudes conducted in the 1970s and 1980s has shown that democratic values were placed at the top of their popularly accepted hierarchy of values. Among them such values as

Figure 5.1    *Varieties of media content at different stages of the evolution of the communist media system in Poland (schematic representation)*

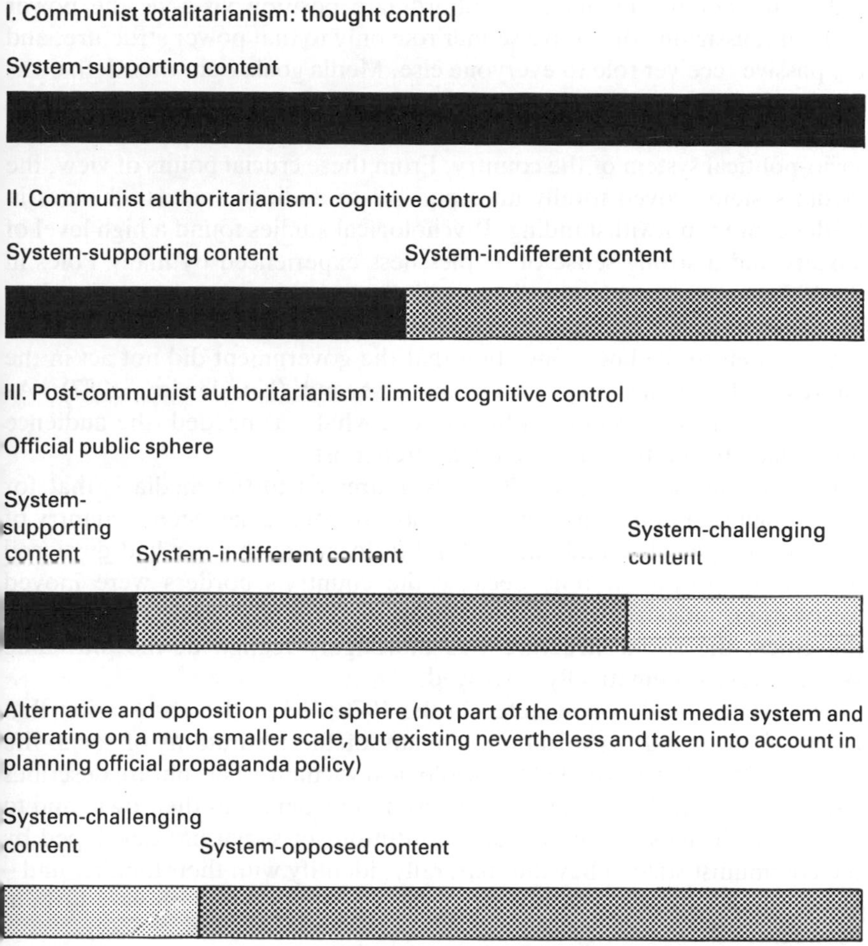

I. Communist totalitarianism: thought control

System-supporting content

II. Communist authoritarianism: cognitive control

System-supporting content          System-indifferent content

III. Post-communist authoritarianism: limited cognitive control

Official public sphere

System-
supporting                                                                    System-challenging
content          System-indifferent content                          content

Alternative and opposition public sphere (not part of the communist media system and operating on a much smaller scale, but existing nevertheless and taken into account in planning official propaganda policy)

System-challenging
content          System-opposed content

'freedom of speech' and 'ability of all citizens to influence the running of the state', took pride of place. This was accompanied by resentment of 'a centralized system of government which has the decisive say in all matters concerning society'. In other words, many Poles rejected what Stanislaw Ossowski (1967), a noted Polish sociologist, has called a 'monocentric social order'. The democratic option, including particularly its 'freedom of speech' dimension, is valued equally highly by skilled workers and college-educated members of the intelligentsia. Generally speaking, support for the democratic option grows with education which promotes both a greater interest in public affairs and competence for active and informed participation in them.[6]

Meanwhile, the fundamentally undemocratic socio-institutional model of the Polish media (Jakubowicz, 1990b), forming part of the organizational principle of communism, remained unchanged all through that period, denying freedom of speech and helping maintain the monocentric social order. It kept the media in a subordinate position vis-a-vis the power structure, assigning the active sender role only to that power structure, and the passive receiver role to everyone else. Media goals were thus defined as those of dominance, cultural and ideological homogenization of the population, and orienting media content to serving the perpetuation of the socio-political system of the country. From these crucial points of view, the media system proved totally unresponsive to audience needs, changes in media content notwithstanding. Psychological studies found a high level of anxiety and a strong sense of helplessness experienced by many Poles in the 1970s, most strongly associated with the fact that there was no freedom of speech and association in the country, with other causes (such as lack of equality before the law, conviction that the government did not act in the interests of the majority, etc) coming second (Koralewicz, 1987). As changes in media content fell far short of what was needed, the audience was denied the gratifications that mattered most.

One of the most deeply felt needs addressed to the media is that for self-recognition in media content.[7] Post-war Poland has been a country of great geographical, social and cultural dislocation: the war had displaced millions of people (if only because the country's borders were moved westwards), industrialization brought in its train large-scale migration to the cities; the social structure was thoroughly realigned; the old value systems were systematically destroyed.

Sociological studies conducted in the 1970s led to the observation that much of the social organization of many of the institutions of social life amounted to what was called 'a sociological vacuum'. This phrase describes a situation in which Polish people refused to recognize as their own, and to identify with, most structures and institutions of social life developed by the communist state. They did, naturally, identify with their families and – at the other extreme – with the nation as a whole, but with very little in between.

In consequence of the ensuing sense of disintegration and disorientation, displacement and rootlessness, the need for self-recognition, for affirmation of identity, for reinforcement of a sense of self addressed to the media was greatly intensified.[8]

The fulfilment of this need was specifically and deliberately denied to the Polish media audience in that the media were expected to inculcate new values, ideas and beliefs, rather than to reflect existing ones. The goals of dominance and cultural and ideological homogenization of the Polish population, of educating the 'new socialist man', of performing persuasive and propaganda functions – all militated against satisfying this deep-seated need and providing this crucial gratification. Accordingly, much media content was perceived as an imposition and rejected as such. As we will see below, this was not an unimportant factor as far as the media's role in Poland's crises was concerned.

However, the matter goes far beyond that. As has been said, totalitarianism is a system of power seeking to eliminate opposition by, among other things, destroying the whole fabric of society, all forms of social organization not subordinated to totalitarian control and – ultimately – individual identity. Thus totalitarianism involved a conscious, politically enforced systematic redefinition of human ontology, adopting as its primary targets the sphere of friends and family, education and religion. The following remarks by Kolakowski refer to the Soviet Union, but can be taken as applying to Poland during the Stalinist period just as well:

> The supreme goal of information control by a regime which aspires to total power is . . . to make [people] helpless and unable to resist – to deprive them of any identity other than that dictated and defined by the agencies of state power . . . [in the Soviet Union under Stalin's rule] individuals were supposed to be completely isolated in the face of the quasi-omnipotent state. The all-pervading secretiveness and embargos imposed on an enormous amount of quite trivial and innocent information were chiefly at the service of this goal: to make people helpless, frightened, isolated and eventually liable to admit that voluntary and internalised identification with the system was the only means of gaining a minimum of not merely physical but mental safety. (Kolakowski, 1989: 66)

Thus, the goal of totalitarianism in all communist countries was to use information control as part of a strategy of coercion and fear to make people active accomplices of the system, in as much as they were to be afraid not only of expressing wrong ideas, but of not expressing correct ones and not acting to manifest their support of the system they hated. This in turn produced self-denial and psychological semi-suicide: positive behaviour such as this tends to be partly internalized because people who have behaved under compulsion as if they loved their oppressive political environment end up half-loving it.

Even in the later, post-totalitarian stages of Poland's post-war history, up to the fairly relaxed 1970s, the destructive psychological effects of media operation were powerfully felt, giving rise to extreme tension and a sense of alienation and frustration among the people. However much system-indifferent and even system-challenging content there was in the media, they certainly failed accurately to reflect Polish social reality. The discrepancies between the ideologically motivated portrayal of reality in the media, reality itself and the social perception of it gave rise to an acute society-wide case of cognitive dissonance.

Cognitive dissonance leads to an impaired sense of personal dignity in that continuous reception of information known to be false is an insult to one's dignity, since it indicates that the sender does not take the receiver's cognitive abilities seriously. 'In the 1970s almost everyone in Poland experienced such a threat to their dignity' (Koralewicz, 1987: 9). Tension was intensified further because people were obliged to act on the basis of this false information: they felt their actions to be senseless, their sense of frustration rose and their self-esteem was diminished further.

All told, cognitive dissonance in Poland gave rise to acute psychological discomfort. Taken in conjunction with the frustration bred of the conviction that open rebellion was impossible, it led to a variety of responses among the people, from commitment to struggle against the system, through conformism, to withdrawal from the system, 'internal emigration' and actual emigration.

Even after the onset of *glasnost*, when the 'propaganda of success' turned into what some call 'propaganda of failure', the underlying message of truthful reporting could be interpreted as being part of a very subtle strategy in terms of social engineering, seeking to reinforce the system and discourage challenges to it (Curry, 1988).

However the message of *glasnost* is read, the fact remains that Poland has had upheavals aplenty which have altered needs, values and expectations addressed to the media. If media structures and functions remained practically unchanged throughout the communist period, this was not because gratifications obtained matched those sought, but because of an absence of alternatives acceptable to the power structure while the media system itself remained unresponsive to pressures for change. The impossibility of obtaining the gratifications sought by the audience was a major reason for popular discontent and an important contributing factor in all of Poland's post-war crises, as well as of the terminal crisis of communism in Poland in general.

## Media and Crisis in Poland

One way the media contributed to the terminal crisis of communism in Poland was by preventing the leadership itself from becoming fully informed about the situation. Once again, Kolakowski's comment about the Soviet situation is also quite apposite with reference to Poland:

> A closed system in which information is measured out according to one's place in the hierarchy of power is bound to prevent the rulers themselves from being properly informed, thus frustrating their efforts to acquire an undistorted image of events and resulting in wrong decisions . . . This self-disinformation is built into the power system, corroding it from within. (Kolakowski, 1989: 68)

That, however, is only a partial explanation of media's role in the terminal crisis of communism in Poland. The media make a direct and potentially very important contribution to the development of society's system of values, aspirations and expectations and of individuals' subjective feelings as to how far they have gone on the way to realizing their aspirations, and how achievable they are. And here the communist system was caught in a bind. Lack of success in fulfilling its promises led it to use the media to create a symbolic environment providing 'proof' that the system was working as well as definitions of reality in line with propaganda policy. The power structure's not infrequent feeling of helplessness in dealing with the intractable reality often led it to mount propaganda and other media campaigns as 'substitute action', giving it the feeling that at least it was doing something to control the situation. This in turn exacerbated the confrontation between aspirations and expectations and reality, as well as appraisal of chances for the attainment of those dreams and hopes. Thus, propaganda was self-defeating and counter-productive, all the more so that its crudeness and clear manipulatory intent further undermined its credibility and enraged the audience. It was thus a classic case of the boomerang effect.[9]

Cognitive dissonance gives rise to efforts to reduce it, in the form of both cognitive and practical motivation. Cognitive motivation leads the individual to seek information more in line with his/her own perception of reality and intensifies his/her interest in the actual state of affairs. Since the late 1970s, failure to obtain information of this sort often led individuals and groups to decide to launch underground newspapers or other forms of information distribution (cf. eg Raina, 1981, esp. Ch. 3). Practical motivation leads to action aimed at changing the existing state of affairs and its subordination to the norms and ideals espoused by the individual or group. Avenues for such action were blocked, however, leading to extreme frustration which would ultimately explode into a full-scale crisis.

After each crisis, media temporarily became more responsive to audience needs, only to revert to their old ways as ideology again triumphed over reality, partial and half-hearted social and economic reforms failed to produce results and a new economic downturn began. A new cycle would then begin.

## Epilogue

The 'Solidarity'-led government announced from the start that it would strive to create an open and pluralistic system of broadcasting, providing access to everyone and serving two-way communication between the authorities and the people. However, fear that its tough economic policy and austerity measures might provoke dissent and unrest, especially if they failed to produce an economic upturn in a relatively short period of time, and that the unchecked operation of scores of newly emergent parties might destabilize the political situation, has led it to approach the implementation of that policy with caution.

The new government was determined to maintain control over the main nationwide broadcasting organization, ie to preserve its status as that of a government agency for as long as possible and to use it as an instrument for promoting its own policies. Access by other parties to Polish radio and television has proved less easy than might have been expected. Abolition of the broadcasting monopoly has still not happened at the time of writing (October 1990), a year after the 'Solidarity'-led government came to power, although it was expected soon. All in all, the broadcast media and government policies in the field of broadcasting have caused a lot of frustration (mainly among political elites and competing parties and organizations) and come under widespread criticism – for many of the same reasons as they did under communist rule.

The portents are that policy may soon swing towards the other extreme – an unregulated free market in the field of broadcasting with very few safeguards against crass commercialism, concentration of capital and foreign domination.

Both policy orientations have very little to do with the original 'Solidarity' platform on mass communication (Jakubowicz, 1990c). Such, however, are the vagaries of politics and the contrasts between what a political force says when it is in opposition, and what it does after it has assumed power.

## Notes

1 This periodization of Poland's post-war history is widely accepted. Walery Pisarek (1988) uses it in his overview of the strategies of communication for development in People's Poland giving the four periods their more commonly used names: 1949–56 – the period of forced and total mobilization; 1957–70 – the period of 'ascetic stabilization'; 1971–80 – the period of 'modernization and dynamic development', with shifts from lofty ambitions towards frustration; 1980–88 – the period of emergency and 'national revival'.

2 See the special issue of the journal *Nowe Drogi* (1983). The 1980 crisis leading to the birth of 'Solidarity' has been studied with particular intensity (see eg Bialecki, 1987), but the findings can be said to refer to the causes of most of the other crises as well.

3 For accounts of the beginnings of this system in the Soviet Union, see Brooks (1986) and Johnson (1988).

4 Andrzej Szpocinski's (1987) content analysis of these programmes covers all the four periods of Poland's post-war history mentioned above and, as we will see, provides an eloquent illustration of the media's content and goals over that period. (Szpocinski, however, uses somewhat different period categories: he sees the years 1951–3 as a period of 'the revolutionary assumption of power'; the years 1958–60 and 1973–5 as 'the situation of relative stabilization', and the years 1982–4 (during and after martial law) as 'a situation of danger'. Despite the relative similarity of the late 1950s and early 1970s, the crisis of 1970 was a dramatic watershed event, assigning the second period to a different stage of post-war Polish history.)

Given the nature of the programmes and their didactic intent, considerable thought and care must have gone into determining the precise approach adopted at any given time. Thus, they can be taken as highly indicative of official propaganda policy.

5 This is true even of the main evening newscast of Polish television, used as a direct mouthpiece of the power structure. It gave up the use of the 'classical' arguments of the 'inferiority' of capitalism (class exploitation, structural contradictions, alienation, unemployment, military imperialism) and was reduced to portraying western countries as plagued by natural disasters and crime.

6 This is in keeping with general tendencies whereby modernization and socioeconomic development activate 'stimulators of communication democratization' (Oledzki, 1984; Jakubowicz, 1985) which naturally form part of a broader push for the democratization of society. In Eastern and Central European countries, they certainly promoted a demand for the democratization of mass communication (Jakubowicz, 1987).

7 Blumler (1985) points to the importance of the 'social identity' motivation for media use

as well as to the fact that social group membership and affiliations, formal and subjective, feed audience concerns to maintain and strengthen their social identities through what they see, hear and read in the media. Reinforcement of group affiliation, values and identity is an important – though so far neglected – dimension of gratifications sought in media content: possessors of certain social identities are likely to seek reflection and confirmation of their own roles as members of particular social groups. Meanwhile, consistent failure to find such reflection and confirmation and to obtain gratification of the self-recognition need in media content generates an overwhelming feeling of frustration and alienation in members of the audience.

8 Partly along similar lines, it may be argued that patterns of media use in media-saturated societies, which confound earlier visions of diversity and 'personal symbolic universes' constructed by individuals guided in their selection of media content by their own tastes, preferences and needs, result from the fact that amidst all the potentially fragmenting pressures of the contemporary world, the majority of the audience may be using the media to retain some sense of identity, to stay within a familiar (even if artificial) environment and to seek satisfaction of a variety of other psychological needs, previously satisfied in direct, interpersonal contacts. As pre-industrial society collapsed, the emerging mass culture was called upon to play a culturally integrating role to hold together society where the process of massification' resulted in the disappearance of community. Things may perhaps have come full circle. Audiences may be using the media to join into supra-national 'media communities' sharing a similar symbolic environment and hence a similar range of experience (cf. Jakubowicz, 1990a).

9 This was realized also by party authorities. In 1979, after nearly a decade of 'the propaganda of success' and just a year before the birth of 'Solidarity', the province committee of the party in Wroclaw had this to say in an internal document on the public mood prevailing at the time: 'In the light of the current situation, the propaganda activity carried out by the mass media is judged very critically. Among the many critical remarks, provoked primarily by television news, there stands out the comment that the press, radio and television do not help [the party], but quite the contrary – irritate and alienate people and cause growing frustration' (Adamus, 1985: 80).

# 6

# Violence and Terror in and by the Media

## George Gerbner

The purpose of this chapter is to examine the role of media violence and terror in provoking a siege mentality, and their more general functions in governance, research and policy.[1]

Much of the controversy over press coverage of violence and terrorism revolves around who should control the news – public authorities, private media corporations or information sources. Media are the cultural arms of any establishment. Private media relate to public authorities as church did to state in medieval times. It is a symbiotic relationship of mutual dependence and tension.

Western industrial societies relegate news control to private media as long as that poses no threat to established law and order. If, when or whether it does is a political and legal issue. News sources have few rights in the game. At best, they trade control over information for visibility or notoriety.

Struggles for participation, representation and power are shifting from military and political arenas to new cultural spheres. We have entered an era in which control by camera is gradually reducing the need for control by armed force.[2] 'Arms control' and reduction become more feasible as cultural controls (often more efficient and certainly more entertaining) gain in effectiveness.

Live coverage of terrorists, forced manifestos, extensive publicity of unrest and protest, in other words anything that lets insurgents speak for themselves, risks wrestling control of cameras and context, even if briefly, from the system. When that happens the state (army or police) threatens to crack down or actually steps in to restore control and settle political scores, often more than the provocation warrants.

The abduction of one government official and the murder of another in October 1970 gave the Front de Libération du Québec the leverage to communicate its manifesto to the public of Canada and the world. This challenge to control of mainstream media plunged Canada into its worst peacetime crisis. Prime Minister Pierre Trudeau invoked, and Parliament approved (with 190 in favour and only 16 New Democratic Party members opposed), the War Measures Act. Hundreds were arrested, liberties were suspended, and the press was muzzled for over five months (see chapter by Dagenais in this volume – ed.). The structural consequences of the

October Crisis' for Canadian broadcasting were described by Raboy (1990a: 204–8).

Highly publicized insurgent terrorism served to justify the imposition of military dictatorship, followed by even greater state terrorism in Argentina and Turkey. Onyegin's (1986) study of the Turkish case shows how killings were lumped together with legitimate strikes and protest demonstrations to criminalize and stigmatize political opposition and pave the way for the military. But the relatively crude and unpopular military rule may give way to cultural pressure. Anxious and insecure people lacking clear-cut political alternatives may accept, and appear to welcome, a crackdown even by 'democratic' authorities if it can be presented as relief from a terrorist or other criminal menace.

Comparative studies of labelling and coverage of terrorism reveal unreliable statistics and blatantly political uses. The authoritative chronology of transnational terrorism by Mickolus (1980) showed that the frequency of incidents peaked in 1972 with 480 that year, and subsequently declined. Nevertheless, US media and government policy put increasing emphasis on terrorism, justifying interventions in the strategic Middle East. Iraq was removed from the US list of nations sponsoring terrorism in 1982 and given extensive credits and arms to use against Iran, until it invaded Kuwait. Syria was similarly rewarded for taking a stand against Iraq in 1990. There was no comparable consideration or coverage of equally widespread state terrorism in many countries of Africa, Latin America or Asia.

Although international terrorism against states receives most attention, Bassiouni (1981, 1982) and others point out that terrorist acts by states and in a national context are far more numerous. 'Disappearances', bombings, kidnappings and state violence in many countries, often unreported, claim housands of times more victims than do well-publicized acts of anti-state and international terror.

While the physical casualties of highly publicized terrorist acts have been relatively few, the political and military uses have been far-reaching. Less than 1 per cent of all casualties of international terrorism in 1985 were American, but they prompted the forcing down of an Egyptian airliner and the bombing of Tripoli (probably based, as it turned out, on false intelligence).

Wurth-Hough (1983) documented the role of US network news coverage of terrorism in selecting events and defining issues according to political preference. Paletz et al. (1982) analysed *The New York Times'* coverage of the IRA, the Red Brigades and the Fuerzas Armadas de Liberacion Nacional (FALN) from 1 July 1977 to 30 June 1979 and found no basis for the charge that coverage legitimizes the cause of terrorist organizations. On the contrary, 70 per cent of the stories mentioned neither the cause nor the objectives of the terrorists; almost 75 per cent mentioned neither the organization nor its supporters; and the 7 per cent that did mention names placed them in a context of statements issued by authorities.

In another study of US network news, Milburn et al. (1987) noted the frequent omission of any causal explanation for terrorist acts, and the attribution of mental instability to terrorists and their leaders. (Similar acts directed against countries other than the United States were more frequently explained.) The implication, the researchers noted, was that 'you can't negotiate with crazy people'.

Knight and Dean (1982) provided a detailed account of how the Canadian press coverage of the siege and recapturing of the Iranian embassy in London from Arab nationalist 'gunmen' served to assert the efficiency and legitimacy of violence by the British Special Forces. In the process of transforming crime and punishment into a selectively choreographed newsworthy event, the media 'have to some extent assumed the functions of moral and political – in short, ideological – reproduction performed previously (and limitedly) by the visibility of the public event itself'. It is not accidental, the authors claimed, that highly publicized and 'morally coherent' scenarios of violence and terror have made public punishment unnecessary as demonstrations of state ideology and power.

Typically isolated from their historical and social context, denied legitimacy of conditions or cause, and portrayed as unpredictable and irrational, if not insane, those labelled terrorists symbolize a menace that rational and humane means cannot reach or control. Paletz and Dunn (1969) studied the effects of news coverage of urban riots in the United States and concluded that the attempt to present a view acceptable to most readers failed to illuminate the conditions in the black communities that led to the riots. News of civil disturbance shares with coverage of terrorist activity the tendency to cultivate a pervasive sense of fear and danger, and the consequent acceptability of harsh measures to combat it.

DeBoer (1979) summarized survey results in five countries and found that although terrorists claimed relatively few victims, the media coverage cultivated a sense of imminent danger that only unusual steps could overcome. Six or seven out of ten respondents in the United States, the United Kingdom and the Federal Republic of Germany favoured the introduction of the death penalty for terrorists. Similar majorities approved using a 'special force' that would hunt down and kill terrorists in any country; placing them 'under strict surveillance, even though our country might then somewhat resemble a police state'; using 'extra stern and harsh action' unlike against other criminals; and 'limitations on personal rights by such measures as surveillance and house searches' in order to 'combat terrorism'.

The symbolic functions and political uses of 'wars' on drugs and 'drug lords' have joined images of violence and terror as highly selective and ideologically shaped portrayals. They serve as projective devices that isolate acts and people from meaningful contexts and set them up to be stigmatized.

Stigma is a mark of disgrace that evokes disgraceful behaviour. Labelling some people barbarians makes it easier to treat them as barbarians would

Calling them aggressors justifies aggression against them, presumably to uphold the dictum that 'aggression must not pay'. Classifying some people as criminals permits dealing with them in ways otherwise considered criminal. Proclaiming them enemies makes it legitimate to attack and kill them. Naming some people crazy or insane makes it possible to suspend rules of rationality and decency towards them. Labelling a person or group terrorist seems to justify terrorizing them.

Stigmatization and demonization isolate their targets and set them up to be victimized. The cultural context in which that can precipitate social paranoia and political crisis is the historically unprecedented discharge of media violence into the mainstream of common consciousness. The ultimate victim is a community's ability to think rationally and creatively about conflict, injustice and tragedy.

Humankind may have had more bloodthirsty eras, but none as filled with images of violence as the present. We are awash in a tide of violent representations such as the world has never seen. There is no escape from the massive infusion of colourful mayhem into the homes and cultural life of ever-larger areas of the world.

Of course, there was blood in fairy tales, gore in mythology, murder in Shakespeare. It *is* a violent world. Systematic torture, 'death squads' and other forms of terror rule many states. Wholesale violations of human rights keep Amnesty International busy. Media spotlight, selective as it is,[3] makes massacres and genocides more difficult to hide. Such facts are often invoked to argue that violent story-telling is not new and that it still did not make us into monsters.

Well, that may be debatable. The US is the undisputed homicide capital of the world. It also leads all industrialized countries in jailing and executing people.[4] But if real-life and cultural violence and terror stem from common cultural roots, the mechanism cannot be simple imitation. If it were, we would all be reeling under the blows of our children and stalking the streets as muggers rather than potential victims. Our research of over 25 years suggests that the dynamics of violence and terror are much more complex, even if not much less repressive.

Violence is a legitimate and necessary cultural expression. It is a dramatic balancing of deadly conflicts and compulsions against tragic costs. Even catering to morbid and other pathological fascinations may have its poetic or commercial licence. Historically limited, individually crafted and selectively used symbolic misanthropy is not the issue. That has been swamped by television violence with happy endings produced on the dramatic assembly-line, saturating the mainstream of our common culture.

Audience appeal and broadcaster greed are said to play a part in the prevalence of violence on television. But neither these nor other historic rationalizations can fully explain, let alone justify, drenching nearly every home in the rapidly expanding 'free world' with graphic scenes of expertly choreographed brutality.

The incremental profits of manufacturing and exporting such a troubling

commodity as images of violence (as distinct from other dramatic qualities)
is hardly worth its human and institutional risks and costs. Most highly
rated programmes are non-violent. Using 'sex and violence' appeals in
programme promotion has little effect on ratings (Williams, 1989).
Economies of scale in cheaply produced violence formulas may have some
financial advantages to programme producers. But there is no general
correlation between violence and the ratings of comparable programmes
aired at the same time.

Why would mainstream media, the cultural arms of established society
undermine their own security for dubious and paltry benefits? Why would
they persist in inviting charges of inciting to crime? Why would they suffer
public and legislative criticism and face international condemnation?
Halloran (1977) suggested an answer when he wrote that the conventional
hand-wringing about the media overkill, focusing only on imitation and
incitation to crime, misses the point. His own research on protest
demonstrations showed that in featuring even trivial or irrelevant violence
the media achieve certain 'positive' symbolic values.

A 'positive' value equal to that of profits is, of course, power. A
marketplace is an arena of control by power. Left to itself it tends towards
monopoly, or total power. Violence is a demonstration of power. Images
of violence project hierarchies of power – gender, racial, sexual, class and
national power – that the mass-cultural marketplace cultivates through its
control of dramatic imagery rather than through consumer choice or
commercial need alone. A marketable taste for a nightly quota of violence
may be acquired more through assiduous cultivation from infancy rather
than free and broad choice. The need for it may be political as much as
commercial: to get, hold and wield (or cater to) power. Media violence is
its cheapest and clearest symbolic expression.

Violence in its most reliably observable form is a physical show of force.
It is making one do or submit to something against one's will on pain of
being hurt or killed. It demonstrates who has the power to impose what on
whom under what circumstances. It illuminates the ability to lash out,
provoke, intimidate and annihilate. It designates winners and losers,
victimizers and victims, champions and wimps.

In real life that demonstration is costly, risky and disruptive. In
story-telling it is usually clear, compelling and instructive. Violent stories
symbolize threats to human integrity and to the established order. They
demonstrate how these threats are combated, how order is restored (often
violently), and how its violators (though rarely its violent enforcers) are
themselves victimized. Far from only inciting subversion, they display
society's pecking order. In tragedy, rare in commercial entertainment, the
hero dies unjustly but the idea lives on to triumph perhaps another day.
The story-teller relinquishes control; s/he cannot help us any more; it's up
to all of us to fight injustice. In formula violence with happy endings
offenders die but the hero lives on to protect good people another day.
Who is who and what is what depends on who has the right looks and the

badge; the story-teller keeps our fate under control. Things will turn out all right if we are on the right side (or look and act as if we were). Crime may not pay in the world of dramatic fiction, but violence always does – for the winner. A tragic sense of life – energizing, empowering – does not deliver viewers in the mood to buy.

The power to define violence and project its lessons, including stigmatization, demonization and the selective labelling of terror and terrorists, is the chief cultural requirement for social control. The ability and protected right to mass-produce and discharge it into the common symbolic environment may be a decisive (if unacknowledged) concentration of culture-power in domestic and global policy making.

Media violence is a political scenario on several levels. As a symbolic exercise, it is a demonstration of power: of who has it, who uses it, and who loses it. As a subject of media research, it has been a source of funding and ammunition for various positions in a debate purportedly about violence but really about media control and reform. The media themselves shape and manipulate the terms of the debate. Legislators milk the political juice in it.

In the US, the assassinations of President John Kennedy, Senator Robert Kennedy and the Reverend Dr Martin Luther King, Jr led to the establishment in 1968 of the National Commission on the Causes and Prevention of Violence. Its Mass Media Task Force commissioned me to provide a reliable analysis of violence on television. That was the beginning of what has become the longest-running ongoing media research project, called Cultural Indicators. The project relates the analysis of television content to a variety of viewer conceptions and social consequences. It has provided research support for movements for media literacy, critical analysis and reform, and some protection to broadcasters against unjustified claims and scapegoating.

The Task Force Report by Baker and Ball (1969) presented our analysis. It established a standard format for tracking violence in network drama and revealed the high level of its frequency, a level that has not changed much over the years. Equally important was its systematic description of television violence not as a simple act but as a complex social scenario of power and victimization.

Media coverage of the report mentioned only the amount of violence, followed by charges and denials of violent imitation and incitation. The pattern of press reporting of media violence research, to which we shall return, focused on the potential threat individual acts of aggression and violence might pose to law and order. The social dynamics of violence and victimization, with its suggestion of power-play and intimidation, were of no media interest.

The Task Force called for remedial action by government and the media which, like many others that followed, went unheeded. But it moved Senator John Pastore to ask President Nixon for a larger investigation to safeguard public law and order. That investigation resulted in what are generally called the Surgeon General's Reports.

A Scientific Advisory Committee to the United States Surgeon General found indications of a causal relation between violence on television and 'aggressive behaviour" among some viewers (Comstock et al., 1972). In 1980, another Surgeon General's Advisory Committee was formed to review and summarize progress since the 1972 Report (Pearl et al., 1982). Both reported that television cultivates exaggerated beliefs about the prevalence of violence and heightens feelings of insecurity and mistrust among most groups of heavy viewers, and especially among women and minorities.

The Cultural Indicators research, the source of these conclusions (see Gerbner et al., 1986a, 1986b), also found that viewing cultivates a commonality of perspectives among otherwise different groups with respect to overarching themes and patterns found in many programmes. That tends to erode traditional differences among divergent social groups. The outlooks of heavy viewers are closer to each other than are the outlooks of comparable groups of light viewers.

Subsequent research refined and extended these findings into many areas of television 'cultivation' (see Signorielli and Morgan, 1990). These studies and their implications represent a new approach to media effects research, with special relevance to violence.

Research on the consequences of exposure to mass-mediated violence has a long and involved history. Most of it has focused on limited aspects of the complex scenario. It has been motivated (and dominated) by institutional interest in threats of individual imitation, incitation, brutalization and subversion. Much research has concentrated on observable and measurable psychological traits and states – such as aggressiveness – that were presumed to lead to violence and could be attributed to media exposure.

Research on aggression has been the most prominent 'media violence story'. Although ostensibly critical of media, it may have been the preferred story because it is the easiest to neutralize and the least damaging to basic institutional interests and policies.

Aggressiveness is an ambivalent concept with positive as well as negative connotations. It is a traditional part of male role socialization. Its link to most real violence and crime, which is socially organized and systemic rather than personal and private, is tenuous, to say the least. It can even be argued that too many people submit too meekly to exploitation, injustice indignity and intimidation.

Approaches that focus on aggression and lawlessness view violence from the law enforcement point of view. They distract attention from official violence and state terrorism, and from economic and social conditions most closely related to individual violence and crime.

Traditional effects research models are based on selectively used media messages and campaigns. They focus on selective exposures 'causing' attitude change, viewer preferences, etc. They miss the essential and unique feature of television culture: its universal, stable and pervasive cultivation of conceptions about life and social relationships in large communities over long periods of time.

Television is a relatively non-selectively used medium. Virtually inescapable exposure to televised images of violence goes on from cradle to grave. The television answer to the age-old media cause-and-effects question 'what comes first, the chicken or the egg?' is: the hatchery. Television is at the centre of the new cultural hatchery.

The recurrent notions of 'powerful' audiences 'resisting' cultivation, producing their own 'popular culture' and their own 'uses and gratifications' are irrelevant to the new approach to television cultivation. They focus on differences in perception and response but ignore or minimize the commonalities television cultivates, commonalities decisive for broader issues in matters of public policy.[5]

Seldom asked and rarely publicized are these broader questions of policy. They deal with victimization and control, as well as with aggression. The key question is not what 'causes' most violence and crime, as that goes far beyond media. It is: what contribution does constant exposure to certain scenarios of violence and terror make to different groups' conceptions of their own risks and vulnerabilities, to a society's approach to conflict, to the distribution of power, and to the likelihood of its abuse.

These questions do not fit the typical media violence story. They are more likely to challenge their assumptions and expose their social and political functions. It is not surprising, then, that they are seldom asked, rarely publicized and, as we shall see, sometimes strenuously resisted or distorted.

US children are born into a symbolic environment of six to eight violent acts per prime-time hour (where four-fifths of their viewing is concentrated), four times as many in presumably humorous children's programmes, and two entertaining murders a night. Contrary to the hype that promoted them, most actual uses of cable, video and other new technologies make the dominant patterns penetrate even more deeply (but not more cheaply) into everyday life.[6]

Television viewing is a time-bound activity. One must give credit to the creative artists and other professionals who seize opportunities – few and far between though they may be – to challenge and even counter the massive flow of formula programming. But most people watch television by the clock, not by the individual programme.

The overarching dramatic messages and images found in many programmes tend to cultivate common conceptions most relevant to public policy making. Violence is the most vivid and prominent of these inescapable presentations. Studies by Sun (1989) and Signorielli (1986) show that the average viewer has little opportunity to avoid frequently recurring patterns such as violence. Large audiences watch violent programmes scheduled in time periods when large audiences watch television.

The world of prime time is cast for its favourite dramatic plays – power plays. Men outnumber women at least three to one. Young people, old people and minorities have many times less than their share of representation. Compared to white American middle-class heterosexual males in the 'prime of life', all others have a more restricted and stereotyped range of roles, activities and opportunities, and less than their share of success and power. But they have more than their share of vulnerability and victimization.

The cultivation of conceptions of self and society implicit in these portrayals begins in infancy. For the first time in human history, major responsibility for the formative socializing process of story-telling has passed from parents and churches and schools to a small group of global conglomerates that have something to sell.[7]

The moderate viewer of prime time in the US sees every week an average of 21 criminals (domestic and foreign) arrayed against an army of 41 public and private law enforcers. There are also 14 doctors, six nurses, six lawyers and two judges to handle them. An average of 150 acts of violence and about 15 murders entertain us and our children every week, and that does not count cartoons and the news. Those who watch over three hours a day (more than half the people) absorb much more. Graze the channels any night for just 15 minutes. Chances are that you can linger over bodies (on or off screen) who had been threatened, terrorized, beaten, raped, killed and perhaps mutilated. And they will not be just any bodies. Most likely they will be bodies of women, violated often just as curtain-raisers to the real 'he-man action'.

The violence we see on television bears little or no relationship to its actual occurrence. Neither frequency nor type resemble trends in crime statistics. They follow marketing strategies that inject relatively cheap dramatic formulas into otherwise often dull 'action programs'. But, as we have suggested, the action goes far beyond markets and profits.

Our ongoing research (Gerbner, 1988, etc) has found that exposure to violence-laden television cultivates an exaggerated sense of insecurity, mistrust and anxiety. Heavy viewers buy more guns, locks and watchdogs for protection than comparable groups of light viewers. A sense of vulnerability and dependence imposes its heaviest burdens on women and some minorities. For every 10 white males who commit violence in network television drama, 12 are victimized. For every 10 white women violents, 16 suffer victimization. For every 10 foreign or minority women, 22 become victims, doubling the ratio of vulnerability (Signorielli, 1990). The pattern of violence and victimization presents a mean world in which everyone is at risk (but some more than others). Happy endings assure the viewer that although evil and deadly menace lurks around every corner, strong, swift and violent solutions are always available and efficient. Contrary to charges of liberal bias, our research shows that a political correlate of television viewing is the virtual collapse of a liberal orientation (Gerbner et al., 1982).

These are highly exploitable sentiments. They contribute to the irresistibility of punitive and vindictive demands and slogans ranging from 'lenient judges' to capital punishment. They make the politics of a Willie Horton and a Willie Bennett hard to resist.[8] They lend themselves to the political appeal of 'wars' on crime, and drugs and terrorists that heighten repression but fail to address root causes.

Riding the wave of citizen activism and reformist zeal of the late 1960s, Senator John Pastore espoused television violence as his 'issue' and held a series of legislative committee hearings on it. In a climactic session in 1974, I reported our findings on both the incidence of violence and an indication of what the most pervasive consequences of exposure might be. But the cultivation of insecurity and dependence seemed too complex and 'academic' for Pastore. He kept pressing for an answer to the law-and-order question: 'Does it lead to violent behavior?' Pastore's support was needed for the renewal of our research grant. I finally gave him the answer he wanted which, while true, was not the most significant new research finding.

A decade of commissions, research reports and committee hearings had produced no lasting policy change. A short-lived 'family hour' (which only its originator, CBS, ever observed) resulted in an anti-trust legal challenge and quick retreat even from existing network programme codes.

Upon Pastore's retirement, a House subcommittee headed by Lionel Van Deerlin took up the television violence cudgels. A group of newly elected and more independent-minded and militant members and staff than previous committees, armed with critical research, decided to cut through the ritual. Dragging their reluctant chairman along, the 'Young Turks' produced a well-documented draft report in 1977. It was the first time that a committee had attempted to draft a report, let alone legislation. Furthermore, the draft called for an investigation of the structure of the television industry as the only way to get to the roots of the 'violence problem'.

When the draft mentioning industry structure was leaked to the networks, all hell broke loose. Big political contributors in Van Deerlin's district were contacted. The National Association of Broadcasters (NAB) threatened reprisals on other bills dear to Van Deerlin's heart, including a rewrite of the Communications Act of 1934, the basic law of American broadcasting. Members of the subcommittee told me that they had never before been subjected to such relentless lobbying and pressure.

The report was delayed for months. Van Deerlin caved in and tried to downplay the recommendation. The staffer who wrote the final draft was summarily fired. The day before the decisive vote, a new version drafted by the NAB lobbyist was substituted. It ignored the evidence of the hearings and gutted the report, shifting the source of the problem from network structure to the parents of America. The press featured the watered-down version as the long-awaited 'anti-violence report'.

The surrender was in vain. The rewrite bill was scuttled anyway. Van Deerlin was defeated in the next election. The broadcast reform movement collapsed. Foundation support for citizen action dried up. The coming era of market rule and private power, misnamed 'deregulation', saw the dismantling of most public protections built up through many years.

The Young Turks of 1977, smarting from their defeat and dismayed at the collapse of the public constituency for broadcast reform, made another attempt in 1981. Under the leadership of then Congressman Timothy Wirth, a series of hearings attempted to revive the media violence issue. Many of the actors of 1977 were trotted out on the same stage. Our Cultural Indicators Violence Profile was introduced showing record levels and continued cultivation of insecurity and mistrust, the 'mean world syndrome'.

But this was the 1980s and the 'public trust' concept of the Communications Act was in full retreat. Instead of all major networks, as at previous hearings, only CNN covered the hearing and only because its president, Ted Turner, was the lead-off witness. The hearing was billed 'a forum for dialogue among interested parties', and went nowhere. There was no general press coverage, no report and of course no bill.

Only one reference was made to our most telling basic findings. Representative Cardiss Collins, the only woman on the subcommittee, noted that our 'research shows that when women and minority types encounter violence on television they are more likely to end up as victims than the majority types'. Then she said: 'You stated, "The real questions that must be asked are not just how much violence there is, but also how fair, how just, how necessary, how effective, and at what price".' And she wondered aloud: 'Are you saying that the price to the well-being of our society is much too high?' (United States Congress, 1982: 230–31). No one on the subcommittee followed up her question, or my answer.

The last substantive remark of the hearing was made by Representative Al Swift, who, recalling the fiasco of 1977, concluded that 'We ought to be careful in our frustration of what television is doing to us that we do not take an axe to the tail of the tiger and think we have accomplished something. We may have accomplished a little bit, but it is the other end of the tiger that is ultimately going to get us'. (United States Congress, 1982: 235).

The tiger is riding high. The cultivation of mistrust and paranoia in everyday life robs civilization of its civility. Hospitality and kindness to strangers seem quaint if not irresponsible anachronisms. Children learn early to beware of adults and, when they grow up, to stop for no one on the highway. When a 6-year-old Italian girl whose father fell unconscious at the wheel ran bleeding and crying on the highway for 30 minutes while cars zipped by, the shock prompted a searching of souls, and of media. 'We have begun to show the cold glacial face for which only recently we used to rebuke other countries that once were richer than ours', said an article in *Corriere della Sera*. *L'Unita* lamented that in the age of television, 'A sheet of glass has been interposed between us and the world that once and for all eliminates real, tangible, and sensitive awareness of others' (reported in

*The New York Times*, 19/7/90: A1).

A never-to-be-declared state of symbolic emergency is pitting white male heterosexual 'prime-of-life' middle-class power against the majorities of humankind living in the ghettos of America and what used to be called the Third World before the Second collapsed into the First. The Cold War may be winding down; the war on poverty has turned into a war on the poor. The cultural props for imperial policy are shifting from their anti-communist rationalizations to a sharp and selective offensive against real and concocted terrorists, narco-terrorists, petro-terrorists and other dark demons. An overkill of violent imagery helps to mobilize support for taking charge of the unruly at home and abroad.[9]

Movies of the decade follow or lead and, in any case, cash in on the trend. With theatrical distribution dominated by a few chains, local cinema-goers have less and less to choose from. Escalation of the body count seems to be one way to get attention from a public punch-drunk on global mayhem. *Robocop*'s first rampage for law and order in 1987 killed 32 people. The 1990 *Robocop 2*, targeting a 12-year-old 'drug lord', among others, slaughters 81. The sick movie *Death Wish* claimed 9 victims in 1974. In the 1988 version the 'bleeding heart liberal' turned vigilante disposes of 52. *Rambo: First Blood*, released in 1985, rambled through Southeast Asia leaving 62 corpses. In the 1988 release, *Rambo III* visits Afghanistan, killing 106. The daredevil cop in the original *Die Hard* in 1988 saved the day with a modest 18 dead. Two years later, *Die Hard 2* thwarts a plot to rescue 'the biggest drug dealer in the world', coincidentally a Central American dictator to be tried in a US court, achieving a phenomenal body count of 264.[10] But the decade's record goes to the 1990 summer children's movie and tie-in marketing sensation and glorification of the culture of martial-arts violence, *Teenage Mutant Ninja Turtles*. With its 133 acts of mayhem *per hour*, it was 'the most violent film that has ever been marketed to children and given a "PG" rating', reported the National Coalition on Television Violence.

As the Cold War turns into a new Holy Alliance, the superpowers can concentrate on securing their ever more precarious hold on the remaining privileges and shrinking resources of a world liberated from some bankrupt forms of domination but increasingly free and open to symbolic invasion. The floodgates are opening for unrestrained penetration of media violence 'Made in the USA' in the name of democracy. Few countries are willing or able to invest in a cultural policy that does not surrender the socialization of their children and the future of their language, culture and society to 'market forces'. That is more likely to contribute to the resurgence of chauvinism, clericalism and neo-fascism than to open, diverse and humane democratic cultures around the world.

The mass production of images and messages of violence plays a perhaps small but pivotal part in the new imperial network. The questions we must ask are those of Congresswoman Collins: how just and how necessary, not just how much? And how long can the 'benefits' outweigh the costs and the risks? Isn't the price much too high already?

Bombarding viewers with violent images of a mean and dangerous world remains, in the last analysis, an instrument of intimidation and terror. This is not an isolated problem that can be addressed by focusing on media violence alone. It is an integral part of a market-dominated system of global cultural commercialism that permeates the mainstream of the common symbolic environment. Only a new international environmental movement, a cultural environmental movement dedicated to democratic media reform, can do justice to the challenge of violence and terror in and by media.

## Notes

1 For an extended summary and analysis of research on media violence and terror see Gerbner (1988). Parts of this chapter have appeared in an earlier version (Gerbner, 1991).

2 The 'dominoes' of Eastern Europe fell ever more rapidly as television cameras, not guns, were turned the 'wrong' way. Even in Romania where armed resistance was attempted, showing the execution of the Ceausescus on national and world television put an end to it.

3 Political priorities and media attention make reporting of loss of life around the world not only selective but also unequal. The CIA-assisted bloodbath of 'communists' in Indonesia in 1965, 'one of the worst mass murders of the twentieth century', received scant notice at the time (see eg *Columbia Journalism Review* 12/90: 8–14). The 'whole world witnessed' the 'Tiananmen Square massacre' – or did it? (see Munro (1990) and Black (1990)). In any case, the similar crackdowns in Kwangju, South Korea, in 1980 (under US tutelage), and in Burma in 1988, had no worldwide witness. Studies of disaster news conclude that in terms of media space and time allocated to it, the death of one Western European equals three Eastern Europeans, nine Latin Americans and twelve Asians (Adams, 1986).

4 One of every 133 Americans will become a murder victim (US Bureau of Justice Statistics Technical Report, 3/87: NCJ–104274). The US rate of killings is 21.9 per 100,000 men aged from 15 to 24. The rate, for example, for Austria is 0.3, for England 1.2, and for Scotland (highest after the US) 5.0 (National Center for Health Statistics study published in the *Journal of the American Medical Association* and reported in *The New York Times*, 27/6/90: A10). Between 1985 and 1989 the number of homicides in the US nationwide increased 22 per cent (Congressional hearings reported in the *Philadelphia Inquirer*, 1/8/90). The US rate of incarceration is 407 per 1,000,000 citizens. This compares to 36 in the Netherlands, 86 in West Germany, and 100 in England. While the prison population in the US doubled in the 1980s, the crime rate rose 1.8 per cent, suggesting that the 'need to incarcerate' is out of proportion with the actual crime rate but is a political response to culturally generated insecurity and demand for repression (see, for example, a study by criminologist Nils Christie reported in *The Philadelphia Inquirer*, 5/7/90). There is no evidence that capital punishment is a greater deterrent than a life sentence (Phillips and Hensley, 1984: 109), or that it relates to lower crime rates (Gartner, 1990). Cross-cultural comparative studies suggest that killing – both legal and illegal – and 'the need to incarcerate' stem from common cultural roots. 'Acts of violence', concluded criminologist Gartner (1990: 102) 'may be a part of a common cultural desensitization'.

5 Todd Gitlin (1990: 191) writes: 'Some of yesterday's outriders of youth culture have become theorists scavenging the clubs, the back alleys and video channels for a "resistance" they are convinced, a priori, must exist. Failing to find radical potential in the politics of parties or mass movements, they exalt "resistance" in subcultures, or, one step on, in popular styles, or even – to take it one step further – in the observation that viewers watch TV with any attitude other than devoted rapture. "Resistance" – meaning all sorts of grumbling, multiple interpretation, semiological inversion, pleasure, rage, friction, numbness, what have

you – "resistance" is accorded dignity, even glory, by stamping these not-so-great refusals with a vocabulary derived from life-threatening work against fascism – as if the same concept should serve for the Chinese student uprising and cable TV grazing.'

6 Two-thirds of home video recording is of network programmes. Video rentals bring movies rarely permitted on television and usually restricted (R-rated) in cinemas into the home for unrestricted viewing. Yang and Linz (1990) found that in a representative sample of 30 such videos only one did not portray violence, and six out of ten included sexual violence.

7 Just as many intellectuals find it difficult to recognize the severe limitations media impose on concepts of pluralism and choice, many writers who see television as just another artistic outlet find it difficult to accept the responsibility of the creator for what is a native environment rather than a freely chosen artistic product. The biographer of Stephen J. Cannell, writer of some of the most violent television programmes, complained that 'It is difficult to imagine any other medium in which the artist is burdened with as much guilt and social responsibility by as many people as on television' (R.J. Thompson, 1990: 42).

8 Willie Horton was of course the 'furloughed criminal' in the contrived Bush 1988 campaign commercial. Willie Bennett was a real near-victim of the 'Stuart case' in Boston in 1989. When white suburban businessman Charles Stuart described a black man as the murderer of his wife, the police quickly accepted and publicized his story. A small army of police invaded and terrorized black neighbourhoods and picked up Bennett as a likely suspect, while demands for more jails and the death penalty echoed in the hysterical media coverage. Stuart identified Bennett in a police line-up as the killer. Later the killer turned out to be Stuart himself.

9 How selective the menace can be is suggested by the fact that the US invades, bombs (the poor districts), takes control and delivers to the old oligarchy an over-independent Panama (coincidentally, soon to take possession of the Canal), ostensibly to capture a head of state and former CIA-client charged with narcotics traffic, but releases an Orlando Bosch who blew up a Cuban airliner killing 73 civilian passengers aboard (*The New York Times*, 18/7/90: 1).

10 Count by Vincent Canby (*The New York Times*, 16/7/90: C11). Canby observed that William Wellman's 1931 *Public Enemy* shocked viewers and critics (*The Times* reviewer noted its 'general slaughter') despite the fact that each of its eight deaths takes place offscreen. But, Canby observes, 'death and mortal injury were treated with discretion then, at least in part because the then-new Production Code took a dim view of mayhem for its own sake'.

# 7

# Crisis as Spectacle: Tabloid News and the Politics of Outrage

*Peter A. Bruck*

## The Crisis-in-the-story

Crises do not exist in the world. They exist in discourse. Crises are not real events, but are evaluations of the significance of what is happening. Crises are special knowledges based on perceptions of disruptions of existing states of affairs which construct the changes as sudden, unforeseen and difficult to cope with. Crises cannot be seen, but are constructions of value orders. They are events connected to regimes of imperatives of actions which are conceived of as resolving the troubling consequences of events.

In other words, we can say that crises are specific forms of discourse which build on specific codes of significance. These codes combine knowledges of past events with specific anticipations of immanent or future consequences, thus distinguishing crises from catastrophes and making them more complex sociological problems than mere disasters. These codes of significance include normative dimensions related to the regime of imperatives directed towards actions of resolution, thus allowing the exercise of authority, the establishment of failures and the attribution of guilt and responsibility with the ensuing sanctions.

News media can therefore be said discursively to produce crises. They tell stories which are routinely and ritualistically structured in such a way that their reports can be read as standing in for 'reality'. The discourse of crises requires the devices of realism even more than everyday media discourses. In this way, specific efforts are invested so that happenings are read by the media-consuming public as crises.

Crises are always related to specific points of view. These points of view are determined by one's degree of emotional involvement in events, one's place in the power and class structure of society, ethnic–cultural background, faith commitments and others. Crises as constructed by the media generalize a specific point of view to create a sense of shared affectedness and general interest.

At the same time, crises are discourses which have privileged positions of speakers and sources such as victims and eyewitnesses, experts and observers, responsibles and managers.

Crises can be easily classified into those which deal with larger social collectives, political and economic structure and those which deal with small groups and individuals, matters of their life and death, physical or mental well-being.

This chapter deals specifically with the way tabloid news media treat and develop crises. I will outline some of the features which crisis reporting takes in a tabloid newspaper. The empirical case which I will be using for this examination is the story of a series of murders in a hospital in Vienna, Austria, which was constructed by the tabloid paper into a crisis of an entire health care system and its political control by government. In addition, I will discuss the relationship between the news format of this paper and the specific form of crisis understanding which it is able to produce for its readership. Finally, I will discuss some aspects of the adequacy of this understanding for the public's ability to deal democratically with the circumstances which gave rise to the events.

## Murder Crisis

On 7 April 1989, the office of the Austrian state attorney in Vienna issued a warrant against a nurse who worked in the department of internal medicine at the city's second largest hospital. Waltraud Wagner was under suspicion of having murdered eight or nine elderly, chronic care patients. The nurse had confessed to the killing of numerous patients, the *Neue Kronen Zeitung* reported in a banner headline (8/4/89:1).

Ms Wagner apparently had quite a short temper. The next day, Sunday, the *Neue Kronen Zeitung* printed a front page picture of a pudgy woman with oval glasses, to illustrate the headline 'Everyone who angered me got a free bed with dear God' (colloquially: those who made trouble for me got a free ride to the next world) (9/4/89: 1). The paper also knew the details of the 'horrifying' confession of the 'murder nurse'. Using injections and medications, the nurse 'controlled life and death' in the hospital (9/4/89: 2–3).

The nurse was not alone in her crime. New warrants were issued and four more arrests were made. The *Neue Kronen Zeitung* covered them on the front page plus seven pages of 'picture reports'. Five nurses, the paper said and added exclamation marks, had cooked up the murder plans over glasses of new wine (10/4/89: 1). The famous Viennese locale of the 'Heurigen', the vineyard inn where the new wine was served fresh from the barrel, had been used not to socialize but to develop murderous schemes. The schemes were effective and not all too elaborate: 'Nurses jumped two at a time at defenceless sick!', headlined the paper (10/4/89: 2–3).

Their horrible deeds had not gone unnoticed. One year after the fact, a man stepped forward. He was a *Krone* reader and 'had his eyes opened' by the paper. His testimony covered the top half of the front page: 'I was witness to a murder in the bed beside me' (11/4/89: 1). Inside, over a large

photograph of endless crosses at a mass grave site, the reader could see
testimony that: 'Nurse Waltraud killed a patient next to me' (11/4/89: 2–3).

Nurse Wagner was a ringleader. She had started to dispose of
cantankerous patients and developed the supposedly foolproof method of
a 'mouth-rinse'. Largely immobile and weak patients were drowned in
their beds when given excessive amounts of water to drink, the *Neue
Kronen Zeitung* found out. It also knew of another nurse that had helped
put the police on the track: 'When she's on duty, the witch, one goes out!'
(12/4/89).

Nurse Waltraud also had a good memory. Using the files of the ward,
she was able to put together a list of nearly 50 men and women and indicate
the method of murder. The *Neue Kronen Zeitung* printed a facsimile of the
list. It sat down at a table the two investigating police officers from the
murder squad to tell the paper's readers their impressions of the 'witch of
Lainz' (Lainz being the district and name of the hospital). Fresh from the
cross-examination of the suspect, the police offers reported that Waltraud
Wagner was smart and cold-blooded. Initially she stuck to ice-cold denials,
but finally succumbed (12/4/89: 2–3).

The crimes of Waltraud Wagner and the other nurses were multifold.
The *Neue Kronen Zeitung* told of stolen bank books, tortured and starved
patients, and the disappearance of poisonous medications from the ward
(16/4/89: 1; 8/4/89: 1; 20/4/89: 1).

The most significant aspect, however, was yet to be revealed. Nurse
Dora, who had worked with Waltraud Wagner and the others, 'let it out':
'Terror and sex reigned in the death-ward of Lainz' (22/4/89: 1). Having
obtained a snapshot from a ward party, the *Neue Kronen Zeitung* showed
Ms Wagner sitting on the lap of a man in a white doctor's coat whom she
laughingly tries to prevent from reaching into her décolleté. Inside, on a
double page spread, the paper printed the inside story of the death ward:
'Sex and wine, death and terror, wild feasts, commando-actions. And
Christ on the cross was the – Jimmy' (22/4/89: 14–15).

And this was not all. Not having got enough sexual satisfaction from the
doctors at work, the *Neue Kronen Zeitung* wrote, the nurse worked in
secret as a prostitute (23/4/89: 1). A headshot without glasses and with
short hair was captioned: 'In a sexbar in Vienna murder-nurse Waltraud
was known as "the piglet who would do everything" (see page 7)' (23/4/89:
1). Page seven repeated the term piglet four times, showed pictures of the
exterior of the strip bar, and gave details as to prices and service (23/4/89:
7).

**Tabloid Formats**

The success of tabloid formats cuts across different media and national
systems. American TV is notorious for the day-time talk shows of Geraldo
Rivera, Sally Jesse Raphael, Phil Donahue and Oprah Winfrey. North

American news broadcasts were fundamentally altered by the development of 'eyewitness' formats, and the UK daily press is world famous for its notorious Fleet Street papers. Tabloid formats have also been more and more successful in Canada with the Toronto based *Sun* group being the main promoter. After the fall of the Berlin Wall in 1989, the West German tabloid *Bild Zeitung* started selling in the GDR and reached within weeks a circulation of over one million. The two hottest projects in the media business of continental Europe in 1991 are the expected start-ups of two new tabloids in Berlin and Vienna with more than half a billion US dollars at stake in advance investments.

Unique among existing tabloid media, however, is the *Neue Kronen Zeitung*, published in Vienna. At present, the *Neue Kronen Zeitung* is a world leader in terms of market dominance by any newspaper, tabloids included. Only 30 years old, it has a hold on 63 per cent of circulation in the Austrian capital, and the commercial success of this newspaper has reshaped Austrian journalism and politics, the *Kronen Zeitung* being the mass medium most fervently supporting Kurt Waldheim as president of the republic.

Media scholarship has been generally scarce on the success of tabloid formats, and has rarely exceeded the stating of the obvious and documenting their commercial success (Audley, 1983: Goldblatt, 1988). Recent analyses by Knight have focused on a textual reading of the tabloid format of evening TV newscasts (Knight, 1989).

## Notions of 'tabloid'

The term tabloid has been used frequently to refer to smaller size newspapers, printed on newsprint, with regular publication schedules, professional distribution and single copy sales. The size of newspapers is, however, only in the rarest of cases a useful criterion for distinction between different media products and their cultural form. The German *Bild Zeitung* is, for instance, produced as a broadsheet of sometimes only 16 pages, but has to be counted at the same time as among the highest circulation tabloid papers in the world. On the other hand, more and more upper market newspapers including financial ones like the Canadian *Financial Post* choose the smaller size.

A narrower use of the term tabloid refers to smaller size papers sold at supermarket checkout counters across North America, including *News of the World, National Enquirer, The Star,* and *The Globe.* The reporting of the supermarket tabloids focuses on the sensational and bold, on quick cures and miraculous events. They fill their pages with the latest celebrity gossip, tales of instant fortune and freakish disaster. These papers deal to a considerable extent with situations which could be seen as crises if the stories were more believable and directly connected to the empirical evidence of the world readers live in. Their journalism, however, covers the realm of the fantastic and sometimes the crazily invented, and most of their consumers know and accommodate this in their reading strategies.

Supermarket tabloids differ from newspapers in that they offer no news coverage or reporting of general events under deadline pressure. Rather, they offer a cyclical processing of a limited number of themes and plots whereby the situational details and individual characters in the stories are changed.

Among the tabloid papers one can also subsume the increasingly successful special interest papers, including student papers and freesheets, many of which have no general circulation, but reach only restricted geographic-sectoral or institutional readership. A good number are giveaways financed entirely by advertisements and commercial inserts.

For the purposes of this chapter I am concentrating on dailies in the tabloid format. These papers are of particular interest because they regularly and routinely construct crises. Unlike the supermarket tabloids they enjoy a relatively high credibility with their reading public in terms of telling stories which provide a definite sense of reality. They are integrated into the natural attitudes of everyday life (Schuetz, 1967; Garfinkel, 1967) to the extent that they lead most readers to believe that what sense they make of the world will naturally be shared by all others. Their increasing market success includes the displacement of 'objective journalism' by 'tab-journalism', ie a change in the reality effect creating strategies routinely employed by the newsworkers. These papers participate in the construction of a general public sphere as they cover politics and economics as well as crime and sport. They are among the key media agents in the democratic processes of their respective body politic, and many an 'affair' has been the result of their efforts.

For analytical purposes, a number of journalistic elements can be identified to make up the tabloid format of the written daily press. The newspapers appear daily, have only one section and are addressed to a general readership. Their street sales exceed subscription, and they are distributed largely through kiosks or vending machines and not through home delivery. Their front page is taken up almost entirely by bold headlines and/or a large picture, and few lines of reporting text. The headlines throughout the paper are large and glibly formulated. Little or no attribution is used in the reporting, but an extensive space is given to the columns of individual and highly opinionated commentators. Many tabloid papers carry a poster picture of a semi-nude girl on page 3 or 5, and crime and sex stories occupy most of the general news pages. Politics and economics are reported in highly personalized ways focusing on the deeds and fates of individual people rather than structural relations or analytical insights. Much use is made of what Barthes (1972) has called statement of fact.

These tabloid dailies routinely use crises as key material for their content, particularly on the front page. The breach of the 'normal' order is foregrounded. The normalcy of order and its breaches covers a wide range from trivial to moral questions, from individual killings to international politics.

### The Textual Exploitation of Crises

In tabloid dailies, crises are not just reported. They provide the material for a description of the world in turmoil. The use of strongly evaluative and richly connotative characterizations is a key technique employed to increase the sense of disruption, the severity of the crisis, and the overall significance of the event. In the case of the *Neue Kronen Zeitung* reporting of the murder crisis in Vienna, the killings on one ward by three nurses turned the entire hospital into a 'death-clinic'. The tabloid's well-established strategy of routinely adding 'colour' to the events strengthens this impression, and the descriptions of emotional details are used in the effort to produce the events as objects of emotion for the readership.

The main suspect in the Vienna case was also the central figure described by the *Neue Kronen Zeitung*, and her emotional and psychological make-up was focused on by the use of allegedly verbatim quotes from her daily dealings with patients. In addition, the entire reporting effort around her sex life has also to be understood as part of this strategy.

Contrast structures are skilfully employed in the descriptions in order to heighten the emotions and the impression of disruption whose suddenness is often specifically emphasized. The *Neue Kronen Zeitung*'s murder crisis is an excellent example. The stereotypical image of the nurse as a helping angel was repeatedly alluded to and set against the constructed reality of the cold and cynical murderesses who thirsted for power. Charity and caring were not on their minds, but rather comfort and pleasure. They had no compassion for others. Instead, they were filled with selfish desires.

Using the most classical and sexist of contrast structures, the *Neue Kronen Zeitung* named the lead suspect a 'witch' and constructed her in the image of a prostitute who did her work not only in order to get money but also because she couldn't get enough sex. The images of the voracious whore and devious witch were the key elements in the contrast structures to render plausible and understood the events in the Viennese hospital. This main contrast structure was then combined with a number of other elements like the quotations of blasphemy (calling Jesus Christ 'Jimmy') in order to create a heightened sense of outrage. Most contrast structures use age-old dichotomies to render the new and confusing intelligible and understood (see Smith, 1978). The portrayal of women in the media is a case in point. As Stephens describes for the news ballad 'Murder upon Murder' from the year 1635, the female transgressor in the story was described as a 'filthy whore' who 'sotted up' her accomplice's mind and who lived with him 'a vile and loose life' with 'their hearts . . . bent on cruelty' (Stephens, 1985). The *Neue Kronen Zeitung* used similar lexical items to interest its readers in the problems of the Lainz hospital and to provide them with a sense of knowing.

In the course of the reporting in the *Neue Kronen Zeitung*, the events were portrayed as outrageous, the main characters in the story were made to look outrageous, and, finally, the reactions of the responsible officials and politicians were made to appear outrageous. This all led strategically to the situation that the *Neue Kronen Zeitung* had to name itself as the agent to resolve the crisis and to find with the solicited help of its readers the proper solutions. The paper headlined among others: 'Suffering and death of the aged concerns everyone – *Krone* readers discuss Lainz: POLITICIANS, YOU LOOK AT THE HOSPITALS FROM THE INSIDE!' (18/4/89: 1); 'Secret city hall report confirms accusations from *Krone* readers: LAINZ PAVILLION WAS THE BLACKSPOT OF VIENNA'S HOSPITALS!' (3/5/89: 1).

Thus, the *Neue Kronen Zeitung*'s strategy of creating outrage is in this case of the murder crisis – as in others – carefully complemented with a staging of placating efforts to present solutions, however spurious or cosmetic they might be. Moreover, it is part of the specific hallmark of this tabloid and arguably also part of its enormous journalistic reach that it combines the reportorial construction of crises consistently with a self-presentation as agent of solution in combination with its readers.

## Sensationalism as Crisis Resolution

The crisis codes of significance of tabloid papers include a set of elements which create the events as something special, something sensational. The use of exclamation marks can be said to index this strategy. Of the 14 page-one headlines concerned with the Lainz murders in the *Neue Kronen Zeitung* in April 1989, 12 ended with a big, bold exclamation mark.

Media sensationalism is by no means a new phenomenon or one restricted to or invented by tabloid papers. And when connected to moralizing it is considered to be doubly effective in attracting a numerous, and properly outraged, readership. Already in the 1600s, sensationalism and moralizing was the staple of English newssheets, and the underground newsbooks of eighteenth-century France were no less fierce in their attack on 'the wickedness of morals' and the manifest evil around them. Today and then, sensationalism is or was rarely used by the papers without being accompanied by a strong and stern moral message (Stephens, 1985).

Media sensationalism requires profound disruptions of normal life as its preferred material, and life's end, particularly if it comes suddenly, violently and unexpectedly, is one of the sure sellers. For all those who continue to live it is an exercise of looking at the threshold to the forever unknowable Other, the kingdom of death, and tabloid papers negotiate the blinded gaze from the realm of the living continuously when they report crimes, fear of crimes and accidents.

Provided that there is an institutional context to the events of such reports, ie the actions can be reported as not just private outbursts of individual maliciousness or insanity, they become material for the sensationalistic construction of crises. Three sets of roles are available and necessary to the reportorial staging in order to achieve a crisis. The human community needs to be split into perpetrators or transgressors, objects or victims, and authorities and responsibles.

When the *Neue Kronen Zeitung* reported the killing of over 50 patients on a geriatric ward of a Viennese hospital, the paper constructed the three transgressors almost exclusively as murder nurses, and the main suspect was 'discovered' to be the insatiable sex-maniac who devoured male doctors on the ward during the day, and not having been satisifed by such activity, also worked as a secret prostitute in a strip bar at night, aggressively hailing in customers from the street when idle. At the bar, the paper reportedly found her known as the 'piglet who does everything', while on the ward she was seen to be the 'witch'. An enormous reportorial and textual investment in the perpetrators and transgressors leads to the sensationalistic effects. For a number of weeks the *Neue Kronen Zeitung* ran up to eight pages daily on the story, detailing the personalities of the nurses as well as the horror of the patients and the victimization of powerless and defenceless terminally ill people.

With this reporting the paper succeeded in constructing an even wider sense of crisis for the entire nursing profession and the hospital and general medical delivery system in the city of Vienna. Journalists worked night-shifts as nurses' helpers to be able to report the answer to the question of 'how patients can still trust nurses' since an 'entire murder brigade of nurses, and who knows how many accomplices, were able to commit an unprecedented series of cruelties'. Under the headline of 'Are you also a murderess, nurse?', the paper incites the outrage of nurses by reporting in pious factualness that nurses' helpers were spat at in supermarkets, staff nurses had their tyres slashed, and neighbours greeted a trainee nurse in her apartment building with 'Haven't you been arrested yet?' After first creating a scapegoat out of the entire nursing profession in Viennese hospitals, the *Neue Kronen Zeitung* used reports of their outrage to turn against politicians and their insensitive ineptness.

Sixteenth- and seventeenth-century news ballads often used direct admonitions and some undisguised preaching. In a news ballad from 1562, the writer ensured that the readers got his point by using the following words: 'What might these monsters to us teach/which now are sent so rife/but that we have Goddes word well preach/and will not mend our life?' (Stephens, 1985). The twentieth-century tabloid *Neue Kronen Zeitung* uses a strategy more adequate to the secularized circumstances of contemporary Austrian life, and draws lessons by searching out culprits in the administrative and political elites which control and run the hospital system. Secret reports are uncovered and published and accusations are made. A unity of action is textually constructed to bring the paper and reader together and admonish the power bloc ruling the Viennese health care system.

Sixteenth- and seventeenth-century news books and news ballads were often able to narratively resolve the disruption and undo the crisis by having transgressors express remorse and offer advice to those whom they are now made to see endangered. Like the twentieth-century drug abuser turned counsellor, a 1577 murderess confessed all and went on to preach to the young: 'They should always have the fear of God in front of their eyes, render obedience to their parents and friends' (Stephens, 1985: 94).

Through the treatment of the topics of its coverage, the modern tabloid daily *Neue Kronen Zeitung* presents its readers with a conception of what constitutes a crisis. Crises are seen to occur less in the workings of government and virtually not at all in complex relations of business or trade, unless they are able to be presented in terms of everyday life as matters of life and death, personal corruption or vice. In this sense, sensationalization is associated with a shift in reportorial focus from the conduct of collective affairs to individual fate, from systemic flaws or structural injustices to murder and rape, individual injury or enrichment. Notions of crises are connected with the personal and the private, rather than the institutional and public. The coverage emphasizes details of personal tragedy rather than analysing events within their institutional or socio-political context (see also Knight, 1989; Weiss, 1989).

The problems of an entire high-tech health care delivery system are journalistically captured in the murder story (see also Bruck, 1989b; Doyal, 1979). The adequacy and inadequacy of modern medicine is made visible solely through the 'bloodied hands' of nurses who were unable to cope with the stresses of working on an understaffed ward for the aged terminally ill. Their work routines and the ward's staff organization are not made visible by a reporting which focuses on the construction of dramatic personalities. Positively characterized as evil, the nurses are shown as holding their life and actions and with them the entire functioning of the hospital system in their hands, while the patients and their relatives are made out to be entirely powerless victims. The powers of the 'murder nurses' are only rivalled by those of the incompetent politicians, showing finally only the tabloid paper to be on the side of the readers and vicariously on the side of all those who are powerless.

### Sensationalism and Spectacularization

Sensationalism is a form of telling a story which uses strongly evaluative characterizations, admonishments and detailed descriptions. Tabloid formats use additional strategies to deepen the impression of their stories and of crises. They try to create a visual sense of happenings by a variety of means. Tabloids show a proliferation of large (often colour) photographs at the expense of print throughout their pages and mimic increasingly the image-oriented presentation style of TV news reporting, which – as Knight (1989) has argued – gives audiences an impression of authenticity and immediacy. The tabloid daily *Miami News* defines itself as 'the newspaper for people who watch television' (Bordewich, 1977).

The sensationalistic effect of tabloid news is based on the selection of specific contents like violent crime and disasters with accompanying photos selected for shock and titillation value. At the same time, tabloid newspapers employ a number of means to personalize coverage. They focus in their news stories on 'ordinary people', devote much space to quotes by individuals about subjective emotional experiences, and close-ups or portrait shots dominate their photo-journalism.

The murder crisis in the Vienna hospital was reported by the *Neue Kronen Zeitung* most definitely in sensationalistic and personalizing terms. But it was more than that. In the step-by-step revelations of the 'murder nurse' as a 'killing witch' a special staging came to be used in order to make visible and demonstrable to the readers the heinous techniques of murder. The 'mouth-rinse', where a special feeding cup was used to drown already weakened patients, occupied many days of coverage as it was an allegedly undetectable method of killing. The powers of the nurse assumed magic qualities which then gained an occult aspect when her night-time voraciousness as a prostitute was discovered.

This step-by-step uncovering and the use of different angles on the story by reaching further and deeper to present evidence of violence and sin are not mere textual techniques directed towards the specific representational qualities of the story which is being told. Rather, they are major techniques used to put the readers in a relationship with the events in the story, to construct them as spectators. I would refer to this technique as the spectacularization of the murder crisis.

As Debord (1983) has argued, a spectacle is not a collection of images, but a social relation among people, mediated by images. Spectaculariza-tion in this sense is not merely a means to inflate the importance or alter the texture of events, but it is also a means to position the readers and to excite them into passivity.

In order to be effective, spectacularization requires a specific type of development. On the level of the story there needs to be the progression – however quick or drawn out – from the state of complete ignorance and darkness to the all illuminating and profoundly clear. Specific dramatic and narrative attention is paid by tabloid news to this dimension, and the *Neue Kronen Zeitung* deployed all means in the telling of the story of Lainz.

The strategies of reader address used by the *Neue Kronen Zeitung* differ in degree and kind from those used by other tabloids like the *Sun* papers in Canada or the *Bild Zeitung* in Germany. Generally, readership participa-tion is stressed, with 'You said it' columns containing photos and responses by members of the public to current issues. Headlines are kept informal using idiomatic language and frequently making use of word games and puns. The reporters are characterized as compassionate, caring, involved and even partisan rather than detached and objective, suggesting an additional closeness to the readers.

The readers of the *Neue Kronen Zeitung* in the Lainz story were addressed by multiple strategies, representative of how the paper generally constructs its readers into subject positions. These strategies include the direct hailing of the paper's readers, and their regular calling up as witnesses with name and/or picture identification in news stories. The paper then claims to be the voice of the readers by directly quoting them and generalizing from those quotes to what should be done to resolve problems and crises. It pursues causes in the name of the readers and outrightly claims to represent them and their generalized interests. In these instances the paper shows itself as acting as political, social and economic counsel on behalf of readers. The paper attempts to create a sense of unity among its readers and includes itself within this group. It then narrates this social entity as the active agent in the solving of social problems, most often criminal cases (Bruck, forthcoming). In the case of the Lainz murder story these strategies were connected to generating specific forms of reader sentiment. These sentiments were carefully constructed in the news text providing the stylistic resources for a politics of outrage.

The spectacularization used by the *Neue Kronen Zeitung* can be additionally read as a special technique to cope with a crisis. As a rational-functional means, spectacularization permits focusing on crisis events, and as an emotive-adaptive means, it allows feelings and experiences to be channelled. Discursively, it achieves the distancing between the spectators and the seen, between the readers of the tabloid paper and the happenings which might be cause for anxiety and concern. This distancing is not achieved on the level preferred by intellectuals and reformist administrators, that is on the cognitive and rational level. The events are only marginally contextualized and linkages to systemic factors or institutional dynamics are made only incidentally. Rather, the distancing is made on the structural level of the story-telling.

Spectacularization builds on the natural attitude of everyday life (Schuetz, 1967) and the common-sense knowledge that one cannot be the observer and the observed at the same time (Garfinkel, 1967). That which is observed is distanced by the act of viewing. At the same time as the spectator is assured of being removed, he/she is also 'visually' kept sufficiently close to be excited. The spectacularization of tabloid news media dramatically creates this distance between the world, its hostile and often deadly forces, and the readers, looking for safety and assurance, while offering them a chance to participate vicariously.

This generates a special quality. Even if one is among the affected, the hurt or the grieving, one is also audience, viewer and spectator. No matter the loss, the angst and the personal turmoil, one can also partake in the 'pleasure' of watching. The spectacle pays off every one of its spectators; no one is excluded from profiting from the loss.

Spectacularization is not only a special treatment in the media production of crises, but it needs crises, big crises, material which can be turned into crises. At the same time, spectacularization is a strategy of coping with crises. However illusionary this might be in material and substantive terms, it is most pleasurable in discursive terms.

This analysis of the murder-crisis story and particularly of the strategies of reader address is based on the assumption that media formats are key factors in determining the discursive treatment of media contents (Bruck, 1989a). Further, tabloid formats and spectacularization strategies (see Knight, 1989; Bruck and Raboy, 1989) are considered to be on one pole of a discursive treatment continuum of formulaic presentational forms.

Content specific format variation and contextualization strategies could be said to make up the other pole. Changes in media formats and discursive strategies are important factors in the market-driven development of popular culture. Tabloid formats are cultural forms of news production which disempower members of society, yet in a pleasurable way. Their spread and increasing market success suggests that the complexities of modern life and survival in a systemic world create special pressures on individual members, leading them to consume discursive solutions. Further research would be needed to clarify how this is related to democratic involvement and participation.

# 8

# Media in Crises: Observers, Actors or Scapegoats?

*Bernard Dagenais*
*translated by Anna Fudakowska*

In all societies, media are called upon to play multiple roles. From monitoring the surroundings to the creation of the collective imagination, from social control to the function of play (Voyenne, 1982: 49), scholars have discerned innumerable facets to the place occupied or which should be occupied by the media in our societies. It is, however, in moments of crisis that the dimension of these roles takes on its full meaning.

Although in normal times everyone perceives the media as being integrated into the social setting, in times of crisis they tend to come into their own and acquire an autonomy which had not previously been attributed to them.

In fact, a crisis allows a new side of the media to show through. Media then experience, in their own way, an identity crisis and start to question themselves. In fact, a society in crisis also creates a media crisis. And the excitement provoked by a crisis in different sectors of society also reaches the media.

In western democracies, every important crisis places the media in a nearly inescapable cycle which develops in the following manner. In the first place, at the start of the crisis, the media assert their role as essential elements of democratic equilibrium by circulating information in order to allow the developing crisis to be followed and the real stakes to be understood. At this stage, all restrictions to the free circulation of information become the object of strong contestation. The examples of the Falkland Islands, Panama, Grenada and even the Persian Gulf War confirm this stage.

Later, as soon as the action begins to diminish in scope and the players' activities can no longer be considered hard news, the media begin to question their own role in the crisis. At this point the question is raised of whether this or that media was the object of manipulation, and whether, in its quest for images, the electronic media in particular did not warp reality.

In a third stage, socio-political circles will bring judgement to bear on the media's behaviour in its coverage of the crisis. And the media will respond to them by affirming that, yes, they may have made a few mistakes, but democracy emerged strengthened thanks to the widespread distribution of information.

The cycle ends with a parallel double dialogue: that of political and scholarly analysts who cast their wise gaze on the place occupied by the media during the crisis; and that of the journalistic spokespeople who vigorously defend their attitude during the crisis.

We want to study this question through the October 1970 crisis in Quebec. Let us recall that in October 1970, two cells of the Front de Libération du Québec kidnapped, in the space of one week, the British Trade Commissioner in Montreal, James Richard Cross, and Quebec's Labour Minister, Pierre Laporte. The federal government declared a state of 'apprehended insurrection' and invoked the War Measures Act, suspending civil liberties and providing the police with emergency powers. A day later, the Minister was found dead in the boot of the car used for his kidnapping, while the Trade Commissioner was released about 60 days after that.

These events gave way to an unprecedented crisis in Quebec which disrupted the whole population, prompted a sudden awareness of the precariousness of democracy and, according to some people, went so far as to imperil this same democracy.

The media played a major role in this crisis. On its own, the Montreal daily, *La Presse*, published 585 different articles about the crisis during the month of October 1970 alone. Because of the obvious interest sparked by the events, the crisis then developed with lightning speed. In two weeks, all of Quebec society suddenly found itself disrupted, ceased to live at its regular pace and, at certain moments, felt paralysed in its usual activities. The Premier of Quebec installed his headquarters in a Montreal hotel. Business conventions and social events were cancelled. Because of the pervasive presence of the military and of the police, even the underworld had to slow down its activities.

Inspired by the strategy of Brazilian revolutionaries (revealed by the media), the members of the FLQ planned the first kidnapping with the aim of attracting the world's attention to the conditions of life imposed on francophone Québécois and to gain the release of their imprisoned associates. In their communiqués, the FLQ always insisted that broad press coverage accompany the latest development in events (Fournier, 1982).

From the start, then, the media were associated with the crisis, in various different ways.

## The Circulation of Information

### First, Observers

At the beginning of the October Crisis of 1970, the media played a completely traditional role by relating the development of activities as they unfolded. Because it involved the kidnapping of a public figure, the media broadcast the news. First of all, they faithfully reproduced, without critical distance, all facts, rumours, hypotheses, declarations and contradictions in circulation.

In the heat of the action, they allowed all of the elements composing reality to circulate, without restriction or discrimination. In this sense, they were at first neutral observers of a reality that they transmitted unquestioningly.

For the revolutionaries, the kidnapping of Cross was a means of liberating Quebec from under its yoke. For the police, it was the biggest manhunt ever organized. For the business community, it was a threat to economic stability and the occasion for a new flight of capital from the province. For the clergy, it was evidence of the decline in moral values. For politicians, it was democracy under direct attack and incitement to a crazy adventure in anarchy. For the public at large, it was an overblown news story (Dagenais, 1990).

The media would allow each of these groups to express itself and to distribute the perception of reality which it had developed. At this point, all the events, all the reactions, every aspect of the crisis was reported through the prism of each social actor who spoke up (Dagenais, 1989). The media provided a platform for these intervening parties but no more than that.

In addition, the journalists became front line observers. 'The journalists note' that the number of police 'appears' to be greater than usual at government headquarters, newspapers reported (Trait, 1970: 37). With the passing of the deadline fixed by the FLQ, 'newspaper observers feared the worst for Mr Cross' (Trait, 1970: 42).

Quebec Premier Robert Bourassa stated that the first kidnapping was a ridiculous and useless act which could only discredit all those who advocate Quebec independence, and the media amplified this declaration.

The FLQ published its manifesto in which it condemned the world of finance and its vassals, and the media took up these accusations. The government accused the media of playing into the hands of terrorists. And the media reproduced the accusation blaming them. Someone announced that the British Trade Commissioner had been killed and the media transmitted this information.

The media translated the present moment with such intensity that the action unfolding before their eyes became their sole horizon. And, during this time, the population followed the reading of the communiqués, the government's replies, the ultimata, the concessions.

The Monday following the Cross kidnapping was a statutory holiday in Quebec. However, eight (of 14) dailies published special editions devoting their front pages to the kidnapping of Laporte. The news editor of *La Presse* recalled that for his special edition, 'reporters and photographers covered the metropolitan region for hours and hours, verifying all rumours, questioning witnesses, gathering comments; neither the fatigue, the long hours, nor the tension gripping the city reduced their unflagging

wish to present a complete picture to the reader' (12/10/70).
The funeral of Pierre Laporte was broadcast live on state television.

## A Mirror

The media were therefore a mirror of reality. A sometimes faithful, sometimes distorting, mirror. They conveyed the positions of all those who availed themselves of speech. They took stock of the same facts, broadcast the sometimes diametrically opposed conclusions of the various actors and juxtaposed contradictory opinions. Thus, one could learn from the same media that the head of the Parti Québécois, René Lévesque, advocated negotiation, that a London editor recommended a subtle approach and that firmness was demanded from New York. The media therefore rendered available a vast range of possibilities for interpretation.

By acting as a mirror in this way, the media simultaneously amplified the reality that they were describing while reflecting back to infinity the image they were receiving of reality.

## A Witness

They were witnesses to reality as well. The role of the witness renders truthful that which it sees. Media were thus more than neutral observers taking note of events as they developed. They bore witness and because of this, gave a character of existence and credibility to the events and the discourses they conveyed, as they conveyed them.

This role of witness was played in very active fashion. The media wanted to see and to hear. They demanded to be present at all stages of negotiation in order to ensure that the public's right to information was well served, as the only possible way of ensuring a true democracy.

## A Transmitter

The media made themselves the spokespeople of all the groups which expressed themselves, colouring with their point of view the relation of events themselves.

It was through the media that the FLQ made its conditions known to the government. It was through them that the government replied. And it was through the media that the whole population followed the development of the events and made known its own reactions.

The Quebec Justice Minister spoke to the kidnappers via the media. Canada's Minister of External Affairs addressed the kidnappers during a special Canadian Broadcasting Corporation television programme. Five days after the kidnapping of Cross, a Quebec Ministry of Justice representative proposed to all the radio stations that they broadcast a message asking the kidnappers to prove that Cross was still alive.

Upon Laporte's death, Canada's Prime Minister, Pierre Trudeau addressed the nation on television. 'For the first time, every citizen in his home, workplace, car was witness to a decisive political action: radio became a public telephone between two powers and we were all plugged into the same line', affirmed the president of Radio-Québec at the time (*Le Soleil*, 24/10/70).

## But Manipulated Observers

From its first communiqué, the FLQ specified that it wanted the media to be associated with its action. 'The political manifesto which the FLQ will forward to the authorities must appear in its entirety on the front page of all major Quebec newspapers . . . Moreover, this manifesto must be read in its entirety and commented on by the political prisoners, before their departure, during the course of a broadcast of at least thirty (30) minutes . . .' (Trait, 1970: 30).

Further on, the FLQ specified that 'the political prisoners can be accompanied . . . by at least two political columnists from two of Quebec's French-language dailies' (Trait, 1970: 31). There is no doubt that the kidnappers wanted to make this kidnapping a media event, especially as they affirmed the goal of attracting world attention to the plight of the Québécois.

The idea that information was being manipulated returned frequently during the crisis. In the first place, the media were accused of having been skilfully manoeuvred by the FLQ which used them to speak directly to the population and in order to create the crisis.

Then the journalists were accused of manipulating information to further a cause of which they approved. The journalists, in turn, accused the proprietors of the press of manipulating information in order to serve the authorities.

Finally, the journalists accused the state of manipulating information through the power of censorship that it acquired under the War Measures Act.

Politicians, journalists and opinion leaders, each insisted on demonstrating that the information that was circulating was not the reflection of reality but rather the propaganda of their adversaries.

Were the media then the accomplices or the victims of this manipulation? Several days after Cross was freed and his kidnappers had departed for Cuba, the newspaper *Québec-Presse* (13/12/70) published the transcript of an audio tape recorded by the kidnappers prior to their capture.

On this tape, the kidnappers confirmed having 'deliberately pitted two private radio stations against each other so as to have more coverage by counting on the vice of this type of enterprise: competition and profit . . . We used the great capitalist press, we used radio stations to make our ideas known in order to reveal, to show, that we are in agreement with the demands of the Québécois'.

In fact, information was, and remained, uncontrolled until the imposition of the War Measures Act which set up an official state of censorship that was never applied, but was sustained by a real self-censorship, and by the death of the minister Laporte, which made any support for 'the band of cold-blooded assassins' impossible (Trudeau, 1970).

## Next Actors, but Neutral Ones at First

The media played an important role as mediator of the crisis. By acting as a channel of communication between the kidnappers and the government, while allowing the population to follow hourly the events as they developed, the media became an active component of the crisis. For it was not so much the events themselves that participated the tensions but rather the knowledge of these events. In more ways than one, the media became an integral part of the crisis. Information, normally the business of the press, became an event in itself. Every discovery, every media hypothesis became the business of the public.

From the very first week, journalists' homes and offices were searched, and some reporters were arrested by police. At the other extreme, some newspaper editors moralized about the role of the journalists in the electronic press.

The names of certain prominent journalists were mentioned as possible observers during the expected exchange of political prisoners.

The Montreal radio station, CKAC, by broadcasting the FLQ manifesto, and the daily newspaper, *Montréal-Matin*, by deciding to publish the text, forced the hand of the government which then felt obliged to authorize the circulation of a document which had become public anyway.

If the crisis had international repercussions, it was because of the media. If the crisis succeeded in implicating all sectors of society, it was because of the media. If the crisis had the impact that we say it did, it was also because of the media. The kidnappers who abducted Laporte did so only after the media had signalled to them the kidnapping of Cross.

## But Soon, Involved Actors

Like every other social group in the collectivity, the journalists became partners to the socio-political crisis. They sought, through their positions and decisions, to orient the development of events. In this process, journalists abandoned their positions as observers and became actors in the developing drama.

They did not hesitate to let the government know their point of view. Editorialists lavished advice on the state, indicating the best way of administering the crisis, counselling the government not to give in at any price (Jean-Paul Desbiens – *La Presse*), or to consider the weight of even one human life (Claude Ryan – *Le Devoir*).

Soon they were no longer the neutral support or the mirror of events. They spoke when they could have chosen to remain silent. They broadcast information which they could have placed on the back burner. They became the victims of threats, of bitter criticisms and condemnations and some of them even lost their jobs because of their attitude during the crisis. Thus, journalists with the Quebec City daily *Le Soleil* and news reporters for radio station CJMS publicly dissociated themselves from their employers' editorial policy.

The editor-in-chief and publisher of *Le Devoir*, Claude Ryan, organized and led a movement in support of a negotiated settlement. For this, he would be directly connected to an alleged conspiracy aimed at the setting up of a provisional government.

One columnist wrote in early November that despite the military presence in Ottawa and the fear of an insurrection, the only battle in sight was taking place between the politicians and the media (*Chronicle Telegraph*, 3/11/70).

### And then, Censored

Soon after the beginning of the crisis, some editorial writers had incited journalists to exercise restraint. The President of the Canadian Broadcasting Corporation, George Davidson, instructed the English and French networks of the crown corporation to make less commentary regarding the kidnappings. After the introduction of the War Measures Act, which included the suspension of fundamental liberties such as freedom of the press, freedom of information and freedom of expression, journalists were pushed into exercising harsh self-censorship.

The Quebec Justice Minister, Jérôme Choquette, threatened the media directly with legal proceedings if they went too far. The control of information by the state posed the problem of free circulation of information in times of crisis.

At the very beginning of the crisis, journalists had been arrested by the police and their materials seized. The Professional Federation of Quebec Journalists (FPJQ) complained to the Quebec Justice Minister that part of the copy destined for the October issue of the magazine *Le Quartier Latin* was seized during a search.

With the imposition of censorship, the voice of the government was no longer blurred by opponents. A full-scale attack on the behaviour of the media during the crisis then developed. In fact, everything developed as if the crisis was simultaneously unfolding on three fronts. First of all the facts. Something happened and the media recounted its development blow-by-blow, sparing no detail of the affair.

After the description of the event, different social bodies pronounced themselves on the event. The facts now served only as background to a setting before which diverse currents of opinion confronted each other. Expression and opinion were the order of the day.

Thirdly, when each social group had exhausted all possible discourse on the developing event, the role of the media was evaluated. One does not ask what had been the media's role. They are accused of lacking social responsibility and of having circulated unacceptable statements in an improper way.[1]

## Multiple Criticism

From the perspective of someone observing the media, their role does not appear too positive. The simple fact that media broadcast ideas opposed to one's own makes them into an enemy. In fact, in a crisis, every social body that perceives an attack on its room to manoeuvre unremittingly condemns the attitude of the media.

And so the media were accused of having created the reigning climate of tension, by not having controlled information. They were held responsible for the degradation of social consensus and were considered accessories of the FLQ – whereas, later, scholars would accuse them of having failed to situate the developing event in its true context.

In fact, once the details of the drama had played themselves out, attention refocused on the media. They were attacked from all sides. The issue was the quality of information in times of crisis. From this point on, the media no longer followed the events. They became themselves a source of events.

Criticism emanated from all sectors. And so not only did journalists blame their colleagues, but politicians, police, different social bodies and ordinary citizens directed their anger against the media. Most certainly, mistakes in the media's behaviour could always be found to justify the violent critiques which were levelled against them. But first and foremost it was their general behaviour which was blamed.

Prime Minister Trudeau himself set the tone of the critiques: 'It would be desirable that the media exercise moderation concerning these problems. To accord them all of this publicity is a mistake, as it is what the perpetrators of the kidnappings desire the most. I think that it is also a mistake to encourage the use of the expression "political prisoners" in describing the bandits' (*La Presse*, 13/10/70).

### The Police Forces

The police deplored the attitude of the press in this affair. 'By publishing all sorts of rumours without verifying their authenticity, and harassing headquarters with questions, the journalists are doing considerable harm to the work of the police, declared a representative of the Montreal police. While doing its best to understand journalists' responsibility to inform the population, the Montreal police wants them to show a greater concern for accuracy in the accomplishment of their work' (*Le Devoir*, 14/10/70).

*Le Journal de Montréal* reported that several highly placed federal functionaries were accusing the media of having no sense of proportion in their coverage of the events: 'Besides harming the work of the police by broadcasting the messages before the police are even aware of them and by meddling with the *felquistes'* communiqués to the point of blurring all significant fingerprints, the reporters were accused of putting on the air often unverified news which only led to confusion and sensational competition' (14/10/70).

## The Governments

Prime Minister Trudeau asked for more reserve and discretion from the media. He thought they were giving too much publicity to the FLQ. In Quebec, several members of the national assembly (legislature) and government ministers criticized the media sharply.

The Liberal Party whip, Louis-Philippe Lacroix, accused the journalists of being responsible for the death of Pierre Laporte. He charged that they were collaborating with people who were against authority and reproached them for not supporting the legitimate elected government. He labelled them the grave-diggers of democracy. Legislature member Henri Coiteux accused the journalists of being 'a gang of parasites, failures, pseudo-intellectuals'. The Minister of Tourism, Fish and Game, Claire Kirkland-Casgrain, reproached the media for distorting facts and for their lack of competence.

Cultural Affairs Minister François Cloutier stated that there had clearly been abuse of freedom of the press. 'It is inevitable that in a situation of crisis, there be restrictions on information', he said. For him, 'the use by the FLQ of some radio stations exceeded the normal rules of liberty in a democracy' (*Le Droit*, 5/11/70). Premier Bourassa himself affirmed that it 'is normal, following the events which we have experienced, that we proceed to examine the limitless freedom of expression which Quebec enjoys' (*Le Droit*, 13/11/70).

## The Media

Several days after the first kidnapping, the editor of the daily *La Presse* criticized *Le Journal de Montréal* for having dared to publish the FLQ's manifesto. But *Le Journal* had only published the text of a communiqué found during an earlier kidnapping attempt the previous summer.

In his editorial of 14 October 1970, Roger Bruneau of *L'Action* wrote these words about some of his colleagues: 'In our opinion, many news items were communicated a little too rapidly on the weekend by radio and television throughout the province. Several of these news items, some more sensational than others, were later proven to be either false, incomplete, or premature. The rapidity with which they were communicated, the context in which they were communicated . . . created quite a troubling atmosphere under the circumstances and contributed to increasing the state of excitement into which the population felt it was plunged.'

'The real struggle', wrote *La Presse* editorialist Jean-Paul Desbiens several days after the first kidnapping, 'was played out between the governments, the media and the FLQ. The FLQ comes out the winner, because the governments have given up. And they gave up because of the intervention of the media' (10/10/70). He added in a later editorial that 'there would be a lot to say about the lack of intellectual rigour on the part of the written and spoken press' (24/10/70).

*Québec Presse* noted that some monumental errors were committed by the electronic media during the crisis and that they could have had tragic consequences. Information could no longer be entrusted to amateurs incapable of facing up to every eventuality (25/10/70). And the editor of the weekly *Le Petit Journal* wrote: 'I believe that the unrestrained freedom of the press led little by little to the death of a Quebec minister' (25/10/70).

Even James Cross did not have kind words for the media upon his liberation: 'The news media were either thoughtless, ruthless, or stupid . . . It should have been obvious that the speculation that (my) letters possibly carried a coded message, could create a dangerous situation for (me), or prevent (me) from sending any further messages' (*Globe and Mail*, 15/12/70).

The role suddenly played by radio in Quebec society surprised everyone, with its immense power and the absence of clear ground rules concerning the use of the airwaves.

## In Defence of the Media

Faced with these attacks, the journalists defended themselves. Left to fend for themselves against the charge of responsibility for having created the crisis and provoked a man's death, they countered. For the Ottawa region's Professional Association of Journalists, the fear to which it is essential not to succumb springs from ignorance of the facts.

For Claude Lemelin, editorialist at *Le Devoir*, 'in times of crisis, the press should play a systematic opposition role. The news media have the duty to act as a counterweight when, on the occasion of events which shake up a society, the large majority of opinions converge' (*Le Soleil*, 9/11/70).

*The Montreal Star* political columnist, W.A. Wilson, noted that 'The reigning secrecy seems dangerous to me. A well-informed public is much better protected against panic and rumours. Rumours are born from the muteness of the authorities'. According to Rod Blaker, of CJAD, 'the public has an absolute right to know the events and to be aware of the context in which the authorities are making their decisions.'

When the journalists are accused of having betrayed reality through their way of covering news, when they are accused of having missed out on their strictest duty to social responsibility by broadcasting the most hare-brained rumours, the media do not try to justify themselves regarding the details with which they are reproached. They counter instead with a dialogue of principle based on the nobility and the necessity of their task, on the defence of the public's right to know, on the premise that one who knows can behave more wisely than one who does not. The tendency is to defend an institution under threat, and not a journalist who may have done his or her work badly.

'Informers, commentators, analysts, journalists were not any less shaken up than others', wrote *Le Devoir* assistant editor Michel Roy, in the magazine *L'Actualité*. 'This would seem to be evident and yet it must constantly be recalled insofar as the public, demanding of the press, has the tendency sometimes to consider the journalist as an imperturbable recorder of the news, a cold and disembodied witness to a situation in which he would never be involved' (Roy, 1970).

Journalist Gilles Constantineau summarized the phenomenon in this way:

> It must be coldly acknowledged that that is what is amazing. During almost an entire weekend (that of the Laporte kidnapping), in one of the most dramatic affairs of the time, everything is brought to public attention by means of electronic information before the official – and helpless – representatives of authority are even informed. All of the norms are scoffed at: administrative, police, even diplomatic . . .
>
> The effects of this new phenomenon of communication and participation, can be questioned. There is no evidence of any panic on the part of the population, and the opposite would have been astonishing: in a climate of public tension, terror is born from ignorance of the facts and from uncertainty, not from the total awareness of everything that is going on. Errors, excesses? If they happened, radio stations must be recognized as having gone to extreme lengths at verification and filtering, and the television stations, particularly those of Radio-Canada, manifested a heightened sense of proportion and level-headedness. (*Le Soleil*, 14/10/70)

As the attacks continued, the Professional Federation of Quebec Journalists decided to defend itself against the accusations brought against the media:

> Journalists (and in particular those of the two Montreal radio stations) have effectively served as intermediaries between the FLQ and the authorities. Who apart from them could assume this new and serious task, which befell them and which they took on without soliciting it?
>
> In the climate of extreme tension, there were, effectively, errors – the broadcasting for example of rumours which were found to be false and which, as soon as possible, were refuted by the journalists themselves. Here must be understood the enormous difficulty sometimes presented to journalists by the differences between real information (emanating from a *felquiste* cell) and a rumour thrown out by practical jokers, given that, in both types of cases, it is about anonymously and clandestinely transmitted information. Here also must be understood the difficulty presented to journalists by the near total secrecy with which police activity is surrounded and the near total inaccessibility of government officials . . .
>
> It is infinitely preferable for everyone that the widest possible range of information be broadcast simultaneously and proportionately with the events, at the risk of conducting some mistaken facts or misinterpretations. Otherwise, all of society will be served up to the game of false rumours. Ignorance is often born from panic. To a large degree, the survival of democratic attitudes depends on the free transmission of information, as much for those who govern as for the citizens. (*Montréal-Matin*, 15/10/70)

The Federation's President, Gilles Gariépy, considered that journalists had done their work well. He reproached Prime Minister Trudeau for not accepting that the media can be something other than a loudspeaker for established authority.

## Partner to Social Equilibrium

As a social partner, the media were victims of the same critiques as the police or the governments. Some people congratulated them on their conduct, others blamed them severely and finally several supported them throughout the crisis. In fact, the media served the crisis. In this sense, different groups used them to their advantage. And the media served social equilibrium. By precipitating the crisis, the media in effect helped explode the profound discontent that then reigned in Quebec. They allowed Quebec to live the end of terrorism.

By providing everyone with information pertinent and useful to their decision making, as emphasized by the journalists' federation, the media on the one hand played a beneficial role; on the other hand, according to the criticism levelled against them, they abused their freedom by indiscreetly broadcasting everything which fell into their laps.

We realize that by freeing speech, the media helped bring into the open the profound discontent which brewed in Quebec. They served as relatively harmless outlets for an entire category of people. They allowed the channelling, through free expression, of a mass of energy which otherwise could not manifest itself. In fact, they were the pacifiers of physical violence.

Furthermore, in this essentially political crisis, by plunging the population into 'instantaneousness', the media unburdened the Québécois collectivity of the historic weight which it carried in its collective memory, that is to say, 'the tragic sense of fatalism that many people experience when thinking about the destiny of Quebec' (Ryan, 1971: 163).

By criticizing the media for its incidental errors, one is really attacking the periphery of this social institution, a little as though one looked from close-up at a fruit's peel and saw nothing but the flaws, while forgetting the nutritious values that it contained.

The media served the October crisis. The crisis used the media. The collectivity experienced the crisis through the media. And the media suffered the crisis. The role of the media, then, is understandable only in the system and through the social system in its entirety.

In that sense, the media invented neither political violence, nor political discourse. They certainly influenced the use of violence by the publicity they provided to some of its forms, but they did not create it. The media did not imagine the event, they described it.

### Conclusion: Observers, Actors or Scapegoats of the Event?

Throughout the crisis, the media were severely criticized for their irresponsible role. How did the media pass from being observers of the political scene to being meddlesome actors and finally scapegoats?

Every socio-political crisis necessarily draws the media into the mechanism of the event. While in normal times, in democratic societies, the work of the media is exercised in a normal way, with neither constraint nor censorship, in times of crisis, the media are subjected to multiple pressures and must adjust their behaviour according to the demands of the principal players.

What conclusions can we draw from the words of some and the thoughts of others? Are media responsible for crises by amplifying the events? Or are they irresponsible for throwing oil on to the fire? Or are they one and the other or neither one nor the other? The answer is not to be found in what the journalist says or does, but in the way of looking at what is done or said.

In fact, there are always two levels of analysis when one looks at the media: (a) journalism as a social function and (b) the journalist as an individual. Between these two levels of analysis, a particular kind of dialectic is drawn.

In order to exonerate the errors which they make along the way, the journalists always speak of the social function which they fulfil and which is essential to healthy democratic development.

In order to contest the social function of the media, politicians add up the errors made along the way by journalists and then conclude that the social function which they fulfil is deplorable.

To tell the truth, in order to understand the social role of the media, one must stop focusing on the traps into which they fall. The blunders of politicians could be added up to infinity. This does not detract from the democratic context in which they operate.

The media are then social actors but journalists remain observers of social reality. They are at the same time accessories of the forces which use them and victims of those who condemn them.

### Notes

1 These three phases correspond to the three distinct types of argumentation developed by Sproule (1980): description, interpretation and evaluation.

# 9

# Media and the Invisible Crisis of Everyday Life

*Marc Raboy*

On 6 December 1989, late in the afternoon, a young man armed with a semi-automatic rifle burst into a classroom at the École Polytechnique de Montréal (the engineering faculty of the University of Montreal). He separated the people present into two groups, men and women. Then, according to witnesses, he cried: 'You're all a bunch of feminists. I hate feminists', and opened fire. In a rampage through the building lasting barely 15 minutes, he murdered 14 women. Then, he killed himself.

The Canadian media reacted to this spectacular 'event' in a thoroughly predictable manner. The detailed description of the carnage, reaction of the authorities and representatives of various elite groups, portraits of the killer and his victims, the survivors in mourning, and theories of the experts occupied newspaper headlines, television specials and radio hotlines in the days to come.

But the aftermath of the drama was most notably marked by what we would call a *discursive struggle* – a rush to name things in a certain way, in the wake of this occurrence (see Pêcheux, 1988). In fact, the interpretation of what had happened was the object of unprecedented conflict for such a case, and the media were there every step of the way, both taking positions and acting as a platform for the different interests involved.

In spite of themselves, and through the classical coverage that they accorded to the event, the media bore witness to the profound social unease revealed by this 'act of a madman' as it was called by the press. The force with which different ideological tendencies imbued their efforts to interpret the meaning of the event indicated just to what extent the changing relations between men and women constituted a real social crisis,[1] and the behaviour of the media demonstrated, once again, to what extent these important institutions are themselves in a situation of crisis.

An abundant literature attests to the mass media's limitations in contextualizing and explaining the meaning of social information (eg Tuchman, 1978; Carey, 1986; Miège et al., 1986). The phenomenon of spectacularization, and the reasons for its emergence as the dominant mode of presenting the news, have been equally well documented (eg Debord, 1983; Knight, 1989). The tendency of mediated information to support the various institutionalized forms of power has also been the object of numerous important studies (Glasgow University Media Group, 1976, 1980, 1982, 1985).

Media have reported on sensational 'news stories' since the early days of the mass circulation press. During the past 25 years, many political groups, as well as individuals, have had recourse to spectacular deeds precisely with the main goal of attracting the attention of the media – in full understanding, whether conscious or unconscious, of the ground rules that govern their operations (see eg Gitlin, 1980; Schmid and de Graaf, 1982; Raboy, 1984).

The anti-feminist multiple murder in Montreal was not this type of event, however. While carried out by a single individual acting alone, it was clearly directed at an identifiable social group: women on the way to achieving a certain degree of professional success.

In general, the media did everything possible to obscure this fact. Of course, the 'facts' were diligently reported, according to standard journalistic norms. But that was precisely the problem, because the routines of journalistic reporting, and the rules governing the separation of fact and opinion, ended up muddling a situation that was rather remarkably transparent. In this case, to paraphrase Stuart Hall, the media's ideological role was in sustaining a set of representations of reality which was 'not so much false, as a *false inflection* of the "real relations" on which, in fact, they depend' (Hall, 1977: 324).

In their 'news' formats, the media basically stuck to the narrative of the drama, each one telling the story in its own habitual manner. The representation of reality varied from one medium to the next according to each one's perception of its audience as a potential market.

Where the media normally take an institutional position on the important issues of the day – newspaper editorials, for example – they were remarkably, even uncharacteristically, prudent. Even more so than usual, editorial commentators behaved like transmission agents for the representatives of social power.

Yet, in the spaces designated for the expression of various points of view – columns, opinion/editorial pages, and to a lesser degree, certain radio and television public affairs programmes – the potential role of media as a forum for symbolic sharing and exchange through communication was partially realized. There, at least, the social issues were underscored and discussed.

On the whole, the media contributed little to structuring and orienting the public debate prompted by the Polytechnique murders. Their efforts were, rather, directed primarily at making the event fit the reading of society that they present to their publics in normal circumstances.

But a public debate ensued nonetheless – and in the weeks and months that followed, even a year after the event, the debate over the significance of the event became the story.

# Highlights of the Narrative[2]

*Thursday 7 December*  As the event had occured late in the day, the following morning's newspapers had a few hours – a very few – in which to react. The front page of *La Presse* stuck to a straightforward description, headlined: 'Insane marksman kills fourteen women'. The text described the act as one of 'unusual violence against women', while a second article on page 2 quoted the murderer's cry: 'You're all a bunch of feminists. I hate feminists.'

The Gazette devoted three front-page articles to the event, including one by its city columnist, Jack Todd, whose column usually appears on page 3. The most outstanding feature of *The Gazette*'s coverage, however, was a photograph of the inert body of a dead woman in a cafeteria seat while a man in the background removed Christmas decorations from the cafeteria wall. The photograph was sold by *The Gazette* to an international distribution agency, and was eventually published around the world.

*Friday 8 December*  Coverage now moved into high gear. *La Presse* announced, in a tabloid-style reverse band across the top of its front page, 'Ten pages of articles and photographs on the Polytechnique killings'. The lead story focused on the murderer ('The killer had three obsessions: Women, war and electronics'). The sub-title indicated the meaning of the act: 'The antifeminist murderer carried with him a "hit list" of 15 well-known women'. Readers were told various biographical details about the individual, Marc Lépine, and it was revealed that a letter found on his body blamed feminists for having ruined his life. The article named some of the public figures appearing on Lépine's hit list.

Among the articles and photographs about the victims and police procedures, there was a reaction story about Quebec's political leaders. The premier declared that society could not accept that violence should become an outlet for irrationality and despair. The minister of education worried about the quality of services available for social deviants. The minister of public security called for looking into better forms of gun control. The leader of the opposition appealed for silence as the only appropriate public response to such a horrific event. These official reactions set the tone for the perspectives that would be repeated in the media, notably by editorialists, in the days to come.

Elsewhere in *La Presse*, a clergyman called it 'an occasion to reflect on the meaning of life'; a female student said, 'So much violence everywhere has me scared'; a male student said, 'What upsets me the most is my feeling of powerlessness and sadness'. The random reactions mingled with those of elite figures ('Cardinal deeply shaken'), experts ('Multiple murder an individual phenomenon') and survivors ('Mother feels pity for crazed killer'). On page 2, the paper's star columnist, Pierre Foglia, described an interview with the killer's neighbour.

Among these, one report stood out. By bizarre coincidence, the mayor of Montreal was personally close to one of the victims, the daughter of a city councillor and occasional babysitter of his own children. 'For the mayor of Montreal', reported *La Presse*, 'the apparent motive of the mad killer shows that many men have not yet accepted an equal role for women in society.' It was the first cited reaction that interpreted the event in this way.

Further inside the paper, the city columnist 'wonders' whether the killer had not chosen this 'male bastion' deliberately in order to make these future women engineers pay for his inability to share power with women. (16 per cent of Polytechnique students and 3 per cent of faculty were women, according to a separate article in the paper.) 'Women's' reactions were grouped together and presented in a scattering of articles deeper inside.

In the editorial space, *La Presse*'s publisher (who rarely appears in print) reproduced the theme introduced by the leader of the opposition: 'This is not a time for analysis or opinion. It is a time for silence. It is a time for personal reflection . . . Out of respect, in collective mourning, we shall remain silent.'

However, on the following page-and-a-half, the newspaper reprinted the viewpoints of various official representatives, from the Prime Minister of Canada to an association of centres for battered women. The premier of Quebec described the act as 'an incomprehensible crime', while for two (male) researchers it was 'the tip of the iceberg of masculine rage against women'. Could they be talking about the same thing?

An interesting variance was found in *The Gazette*'s coverage, which paid less attention to official reactions (except for the mayor of Montreal – who was, however, framed as someone close to one of the victims, rather than as a politician). In columns and news stories, *The Gazette* picked up the theme of gun control. Its editorial, while recognizing the targeting of women as a central element, was nonetheless entitled 'Beyond Understanding' – reiterating the motif of powerlessness and incomprehensibility expressed by the premier of the province as well as ordinary citizens. Rather than citing institutional spokespeople, *The Gazette* opened its pages to readers – whose views ranged from a call for the return of the death penalty to denunciation of the front-page photograph of a bullet-riddled victim. The paper's political columnist was critical of the politicians' responses so far: 'All women were the target of the executioner at the École Polytechnique . . . Madmen invent nothing. They act out the furtive fantasies of the sane.'

Television columnists, meanwhile, found that TV was 'shockingly inadequate', unable to break its routines and interrupt regular programming to deal with the event.

*Saturday 9 December*   A wounded survivor held a press conference at which she described how she had tried to reason with the killer in the ill-fated classroom: 'He told us he was struggling against feminism. I told him we were only women studying engineering, not necesssarily feminists . . . That's when he started to shoot.'

*La Presse* published a truncated version of Marc Lépine's hit list, with photographs of five of the high-profile targeted women, including one of its own columnists. (Montreal police released only some of the names, and a summary of the content of Lépine's letter.) This later sparked some debate among journalists' organizations about the news judgement and notion of public interest that could justify publication of such information.

*La Presse* columnist Foglia deplored the fact that media and the public had painted Marc Lépine as 'a monster'. There are no monsters, only ordinary people 'like you or me'. Any of us can fall into a demented state at any time, he wrote. That's just the way it is: 'When it happens, it's awful. But it has nothing to do with anything. *It's death, man.* [English in original] . . . There's nothing to be done about it.' Postmodern chronicler par excellence, Foglia lashed out at the legions of psychologists, feminists and journalists who saw a 'macho neuropath' behind the act.

The weekend sections began to present some critically distanced analysis, suggesting a need to examine the social meaning of the event. A former woman president of the Quebec Order of Engineers was quoted stating 'The Polytechnique is the strongest symbol of women's penetration of a non-traditional sector. The killer was sending a very strong message'. For columnist Francine Pelletier (who *La Presse* had revealed to be on Lépine's list), the message was 'the price for the emancipation of women is death'. One journalist noted that 'it is impossible to react to this drama without thinking about the relations between men and women' – but then hastened to add that one should not build a theory based on a barbaric incident that only lasted five minutes. He concluded, however, that the act was the expression of 'a malaise that really exists: the difficult adjustment of numerous men to the changing role of women and relations between the sexes'. A colleague of his wallowed in self-pity meanwhile, complaining that 'feminists of both sexes have not lost any time interpreting the event through their own ideological grid'.

*The Gazette* followed in a similar vein, but with an absence of anti-feminist sympathy and with a certain break in journalistic routine – for example, on the front page, a woman news reporter described her personal feelings about the event as a woman, about its effect on her daily life. Columnist Todd re-examined the theme of everyday violence against women. *The Gazette*'s ombudsman responded to written and telephoned protests from several hundred readers outraged by the front-page photograph of the murdered woman. The paper defended its publication of the photograph, but announced that proceeds from the sale of international rights would be donated to charity.

*Gazette* columnists and feature writers were more explicit and homogeneous in characterizing the act as one of violence against women and specifically directed at feminism, 'the logical consequence of the rape, wife-beating, sexual harassment, incest, prostitution, pornography and the glorification of violence and male aggressivity in our popular culture' (Bauch, 1989). A political columnist noted the refusal of politicians to recognize this fact, taking solace in the more comforting view that it was the isolated act of a madman.

The leitmotiv of the first days carried over into the following week. As 10,000 people attended the civic funeral, columns, editorials and news reports reiterated the well-established positions of the first few days. The ineffable Foglia, for example, related his desire to howl in the face of the moralists, 'those frocked and unfrocked clergymen, the clergymen of nonviolence and the clergymen of feminism'. Social violence, he declared, is an aesthetic question: 'He didn't like women, this much is clear . . . But perhaps women didn't like him either'. *The Gazette* and *La Presse* called for gun control; Quebec City's *Le Soleil* saw no indication of deeper social unrest, while for Montreal's *Le Devoir* this display of anti-feminist terrorism saw women's success as the cause and the symbol of its own failures.

### Analysis

During the weeks that followed the Polytechnique killings, one had the impression the media were paying more attention than before to certain types of 'news' concerning relations between the sexes. One journalist at *The Gazette* dug into the dry statistics of criminality and family violence showing that one Canadian woman in ten suffers violent aggression in her own home, and that conjugal murder was on the rise (Bagnall, 1989). But the report showed that this information had been available for some time: 'They could have seen it before if they had wanted to'. A therapist was quoted saying 'Society will not reflect unless there's an act that projects it into a crisis. The killings at the University of Montreal have provoked a crisis' (Bagnall, 1989).

As the *real* story – violence and aggression against women – returned to the back pages, episodic flurries brought it back to life. On 6 February 1990, the Canadian Broadcasting Corporation's national radio news led off with a story about an attempted rape in a downtown Calgary street, in front of passive bystanders. A few weeks later, a federal cabinet minister's sexist remarks about an opposition politician got him into hot water.

Did this represent a real change as a result of the Polytechnique event, or was it illusory? In other words, did the event actually *provoke* a crisis, reflected in increased media coverage, or had it *signalled* an existing crisis that the media had been dealing with in a 'non-crisis' (ie *uncritical*) way? The evidence points to the latter.

Research conducted in the summer of 1990 showed that, with certain exceptions, attention to the problematic aspects of relations between men and women remained essentially unchanged in Quebec and Canadian newspapers as a result of 6 December 1989.[3]

In the francophone press, articles dealing with sexual aggression, conjugal violence, pay equity and feminism as a political movement were more numerous before the event than after. The only exception to this was gun control, which had generated virtually no press reports between January and December 1989, and more than 50 times as many during the following six months.

In the anglophone press, articles on battered women, sexual aggression and women in the workplace were more numerous before than after the event. Articles on family violence, sexual harassment and women's rights were roughly in the same proportion. Articles on sexual discrimination, sexual stereotypes, feminism and gun control were slightly more numerous after 6 December 1989.

One can note quickly that with the single exception of gun control in the francophone press, there was no appreciable modification in the importance afforded the various subjects raised in the public debate that followed 6 December 1989. Indeed, in several areas we found considerably *less* attention paid to these subjects in the months that followed the Polytechnique murders (francophone press: sexual aggression, feminism, pay equity; anglophone press: battered women, sexual aggression, women in the workplace).

In April 1990, when a mass circulation Quebec magazine published an article attributing anti-Semitic remarks to a well-known businessman, protests rained from all quarters. The text in question was even more injurious towards women and their place in society than it was towards Jews, however, but critics were painfully slow to point this out (Raboy, 1990b).

Seven months later, a marginal local journalist published a book-length pamphlet entitled *Manifeste d'un Salaud* (A Swine's Manifesto), purporting to be a critique of the rhetorical excesses of radical feminism. Characteristically, the book was the focus of a brief but significant flurry of diversionary and divisive polemic in the press, coinciding with the anniversary of the killings (Côté, 1990).

In a situation like the one we have just described, media are quickly overwhelmed by the crisis. Thus, by applying the usual norms of journalistic coverage and definition of what constitutes news – in short, by accentuating the spectacular and the unusual instead of the everyday and the mundane – the media embark on a course that they can not easily control afterwards.

Under these circumstances, it was unthinkable for media to treat the Polytechnique event any differently in their news formats. This resulted in certain aberrant situations that angered parts of the audience and that managers eventually came to deplore (publication of a sensational photograph; publication of the hit list targeting prominent women). In their editorial formats, they were careful to remain within respectable limits, using the reactions of political authorities and other elite representatives as indicators. Nonetheless, the elements of a public debate were brought out by certain columnists and others with access to media platforms.[4]

We can postulate that the overall impact of this coverage was something similar to the one described by Schmid and de Graaf in their study of terrorism: that media coverage of violent acts intimidates members of victim groups (Schmid and de Graaf, 1982). It focuses on the act of aggression rather than the social consequences, by accentuating events rather than processes. The coverage of 6 December 1989 followed this pattern.

According to Quebec journalists themselves, the media obscured the real nature of the event, taking an unduly long time to recognize its sexist character. They failed to report properly 'the great distress felt by all women in Quebec at that moment'. It was 'an unprecedented social phenomenon', according to the journalists (*Le Devoir*, 1990).

According to Gaye Tuchman, 'news imparts to occurrences their *public character* as it transforms mere happenings into publicly discussable events' (Tuchman, 1978: 3, emphasis in original). Media activity is situated principally in the symbolic sphere: it consists of making sense. This is to say, Marc Lépine killed 14 women, but for an entire population that was not *directly* touched by the event (ie all those who experienced it in a public, rather than a private, way), it acquired its meaning through the media. Media thus 'constructed reality'. By emphasizing the 'inexplicable' nature of the event, for example, the media left the entire female half of the population naked before its own vulnerability, denying not only the notions of resistance or positive preventive action, but even the possibility of a clear understanding of what had happened. In some cases, this went so far as to attempt to submerge reality altogether.

This singular aspect of media coverage was noted and denounced by feminist analysts (Malette and Chalouh, 1991). Some political authorities, seconded by their acolytes in the media, spared no efforts to camouflage the social character of the killer's act – its sexism, its misogyny, its anti-feminism. This must be seen in a framework of discursive struggle – of the struggle to name things for what they are. In our news system, the description of events is often followed by conflicting attempts to interpret their meaning. These struggles generally emanate from the centre of the media system – news pages of major dailies, radio hot-line shows, television public affairs programmes – and eventually wind up on the margins, in specialized, small-circulation journals, books, alternative video, documentary films. Social analysis, on the other hand, follows an opposite course: it usually begins in so-called marginal media, which are driven by other forces than 'events'. Analyses, especially radical ones, eventually find their way into the mainstream when the mainstream media are no longer able to ignore them (Raboy, 1984).

It is always problematic to call something by its real name. In the case we are considering here, the appeals for 'silence', the insistence on classifying the event as something 'incomprehensible' – as if it were a kind of social unidentified flying object! – were simply attempts to repress and to camouflage the obvious, motivated by a fear of confronting reality and taking the consequences.

Prejudicial signification, of which sexism is an example, is a form of domination. So is the ideological position that denies that our society is sexist. When one factors in the effects of media spectacularization, social experience and its principal means of representation, language, are deprived of their expressive force, and become objects of consumption. This is disempowerment (see Bruck and Raboy, 1989).

The use of feminist discourse is exactly the obvious: a form of empowerment. Here, for example, is an alternative way of describing what happened at l'École Polytechnique, taken from a student newspaper of the following day. With one or two arguably excessive choices of terminology, it corresponds perfectly to the journalistic canons of objectivity and balance, yet we never see this language used in this way in reporting in the mainstream press:

> Fourteen women were executed at the Polytechnique, several others wounded. Their crime: that they were women? That they were students in a discipline traditionally reserved for men? I think (I WANT TO BELIEVE IT, I want desperately to believe) that it was an isolated act, that the killer belongs to no particular group, that his act represents no general way of thinking. But one thing we know for sure: a man has killed some women. It appears that he set up the following equation: woman student in Engineering = non-traditional vocation = potential feminist = danger . . . (Bérard, 1991: 76)

Women have brought into public view some of the hidden aspects of their oppression, but the affirmation of feminist values and the feminist critique of society has been intercepted by the media, writes *québécoise* journalist Colette Beauchamp in her ground-breaking study, *Le silence des médias*:

> If you are a coherent feminist, you lose all credibility – not in the eyes of the public, but within your own profession. You pass for a fanatic, an object of frustration, a maniac. You run the risk of not only slowing down your career but of being shown the door altogether. If you provide a platform for feminists . . . you will be accused of using the media to serve a cause . . . as though not taking women into consideration and giving the floor to the representatives of power more often than is their due had nothing to do with ideology and activism. (Beauchamp, 1987: 245)

Except for a few isolated interventions, the feminist point of view about the Polytechnique had to await the publication, several months after the fact, of a book of articles assembled by a small publishing house. Much of the discussion dealt precisely with the problems posed by the media (Malette and Chalouh, 1991).

Ericson and his colleagues (1987) have shown that, in spite of the vast range of potential sources available to journalists, they tend to limit themselves to spokespeople for important institutions. Individuals without institutional affiliation do not figure in news reports, unless they have been involved in tragic events. The coverage of the Polytechnique confirmed this finding.

According to one study, more than half the newspaper articles appearing during the week following the event featured people speaking about it. Aside from individuals directly involved, commentators fell into two broad categories: authorities and women. But articles relating women's viewpoints grouped several speakers together, while in most cases, authorities were allowed to speak on their own. On the whole, three times more importance was accorded to the views of a person in authority than to those of a woman (Legault, 1990). There was thus a manifest imbalance in the news by virtue of the fact that certain actors were deemed more deserving of speech due to their social status and their subscribing to dominant ideological precepts.

More than anything else, journalism is about the relationship of order to conflict (Ericson et al., 1989). Through the media, the representatives of social power make claims to knowledge. The most important news is that which represents authority as power legitimated by knowledge. The essence of media and crisis reporting is that authorities will always claim to find order in situations of conflict, and conflict where none exists.

At the same time, the media relegate all non-authority, non-powerful actors to second-rate status (when they are not excluded altogether). News thus becomes a means of communication at the summit of the 'knowledge structure of society', while those at the bottom of the structure remain spectators.

The notion of knowledge as spectacle is also denounced by James Carey, for whom 'The purpose of news is not to represent and inform but to signal, tell a story, and activate inquiry . . . [but] the press, by seeing its role as that of informing the public, abandons its role as an agency for carrying on the conversation of our culture. We lack not only an effective press but certain vital habits: the ability to follow an argument, grasp the point of view of another, expand the boundaries of understanding, debate the alternative purposes that might be pursued' (Carey, 1989b: 82).

Carey's theoretical contribution to communication studies is fundamental. According to him, there are two ways to think about mediated communication, as 'transmission' or as 'ritual'. In the first case, communication is comparable to an electric circuit linking sender and receiver; in the second, it is an intersubjective process of sharing and exchange (see Carey, 1989a).

Press reports can be separated into those that manifest a transmission approach, simply relating the details of an event, and those that, in more of a ritual mode, try to contextualize the event and analyse its repercussions for society.

Another study of the Polytechnique coverage compared press reports on this basis. Ninety per cent of articles in a tabloid daily and two-thirds in a general mass circulation paper were of the transmission type. All of these were 'news' articles. On the other hand, while much fewer, articles of a ritual type were found across various categories – news, editorials, columns, opinion pieces (Reuillard, 1990).

The case of Montreal's École Polytechnique demonstrates that we need the media to structure and sustain public debate, not only in *times* of crisis, but in *situations* of crisis in 'normal' times. But the news emanates from newsrooms which operate according to their own institutional rules and imperatives, and these have nothing to do with this social need.

With respect to what ought to be their primary function, then, the media also find themselves in a state of perpetual crisis – if we can describe crisis in the terms used by Antonio Gramsci more than 60 years ago (Gramsci, 1930: 276): 'The crisis consists precisely in the fact that the old is dying and the new cannot be born; in this interregnum a great variety of morbid symptoms appear.'

## Notes

I would like to thank the students in my Laval University seminar on 'Public communication, society and democracy' (winter 1990) who shared their thoughts on this subject with me, as well as journalist Francine Pelletier and psychologist Sheilagh Hodgins for their generous and constructive advice.

1 In the dictionary sense, where 'crisis' is defined as a 'critical point in the course of events . . . a vitally important or decisive stage . . . a turning-point . . . a state of affairs in which a decisive change for better or worse is imminent' (*Oxford English Dictionary*, 1971: 605).

2 The following section is based on a more detailed summary presented in full in Raboy (1990c). That paper analysed coverage of the event in two mass circulation, general-interest Montreal dailies, *La Presse* (French) and *The Gazette* (English). The other three dailies published in Montreal at the time were the popular tabloid *Journal de Montréal* (French), the elite *Le Devoir* (French), and the tabloid *Montreal Daily News* (English) which ceased publication on 16 December 1989.

3 See Raboy (1990c: 14–15). The research consisted simply of a comparison of the occurrence of certain themes in Canadian newspapers before and after 6 December 1989, using the standard industry sources that index these newspapers.

4 One aspect that has sparked some discussion among critical francophone commentators concerns the relative openness and lack of hostility to feminist perspectives of English- as opposed to French-language media (see eg Saint-Jean, 1991; Émond, 1990). This was indicated by the results of our own inquiry as well. While a proper cross-cultural investigation of this question is far beyond the scope of the present chapter, we would suggest that a partial explanation for this can be found in recently adopted affirmative action hiring practices by certain media. An exceptional 44 per cent of journalists employed by *The Gazette* are women, for example (Beauchamp, 1987: 224), and while most of the newspaper's 'stars' are still men, it should not be surprising if this situation had an impact on the culture of the newsroom which was eventually reflected in the pages of the paper.

# 10

# Media and the Commodification of Crisis

## Lorna Roth

Media labelled it the 'Mohawk crisis' – constructed, broadcast, lived: the present end of hundreds of years of failed communications, lack of understanding, incommensurable value systems. Masked Indian Warriors wearing camouflage, uttering perfect 'sound bytes' in a confrontational manner, feeling free behind disguises to construct brand-new personae along the flat lines of the television cartoon caricature: 'the animated Warrior in confrontation with the public-relations face of a militaryman reminding us, ironically, of the old cigarstore Indian'. The Indian/cowboy face-off, right out of American movie vernacular, riveted the attention of Canadian publics, whose eagle eyes peered at every moment of every day of the action.

And after it was seemingly over, the 'lands' saved for Mohawk grandchildren and after the disengagement process had camouflaged everything 'back to normal', another battle started on public turf – this time over who would have rights to use the crisis for the purposes of profit. Opposing sides once again took their places: non-native entrepreneurs with visions of board games, video games, lunch boxes, dolls, characters in simulated crisis-drama for children only, who had strategically foreseen the opportunity for becoming millionaires, right from the beginning of the summer, *versus* the Mohawk Nation Office, whose defence fund could be expanded by the sale of crisis memorabilia – T-shirts, hats, paintings, Indian art and artefacts wrapped in the forms of commercial appeal. Is this what cultural politics is all about? – a spectacle of image-events produced and then reproduced as commodity forms to be sold, to be consumed nostalgically, or 'to make history forgotten within culture' (Debord, 1983: 192).

North American culture: a culture of commodities; the commodification of culture; the transformation of politics into marketable packages – packages of political fragments, extracted from their contexts and re-presented in fashionable formats. The show goes on without exception. The conflict and drama of crises, narrowly defined by media gatekeepers, ups the ratings, increases potential profits and closes down alternative meanings. She/he who owns the media controls the frameworks. Media construct crises to appear to have no histories in their objectified versions: crises as commodities.

11 July 1990: a hot summer day in Kanehsatake, a small Mohawk Indian community approximately 40 kilometres west of Montreal, Québec, Canada: a force of 100 Sûreté du Québec police officers attack a golf course road blockade of armed Mohawk protesters. One police officer dies; a confrontation over land rights, which should have been resolved hundreds of years ago through a negotiations process, escalates. Canada's 'Indian summer' of 1990 begins. It is a summer no Canadian will ever forget. It is a summer many international television viewers will never forget either. It is the summer that 'multicultural' Canada's public relations strategy and image of cross-cultural tolerance became visibly and audiovisually tarnished.

## Indian Summer 1990: A Reconstruction

In 1989–90, Canadian media resources and attention were concentrated on the Meech Lake Accord debates about Canada's constitutional future (designed to make Québec a partner in Canada's constitution). Over the years, the Meech Lake Accord, which finally failed to pass in June of 1990, had been the subject of vicious critiques by many Canadian anglophones, members of ethnocultural and visible minority communities, women, as well as Aboriginal peoples, for their having been left out of the constitutional agreement. Historically, however, the final defeat of the Accord was orchestrated by a Manitoba Cree Indian legislator, Elijah Harper, and resulted in a growing sense of cultural and political empowerment for native peoples across the country.

With attention focusing exclusively on this defeat and its implications, the confrontation that began to escalate at Kanehsatake and the neighbouring town of Oka in July 1990 took the media by surprise. Not well acquainted with the specificities of native issues, such as land claims/sovereignty/native-non-native relational history, mainstream journalists scurried about in order to adequately research and clarify the context for the conflict. As a result, the quality of media coverage at the beginning of July, when Québec provincial police attacked the Mohawk barricades, was sketchy at best.

The 'crisis' revolved around a land conflict between the Mohawks of Kanehsatake and the governments of Oka, Québec and Canada. From early March until the end of September, the Kanehsatake Mohawks stood firm in their opposition to the expansion of a golf course on to a piece of contested land that is claimed by both them and the municipality of Oka, Québec, a neighbouring community. What appeared initially to be a struggle over a stretch of proposed golf course land eventually became redefined as a battle over a larger terrain: the Mohawks' and other Aboriginal nations' rights, places, perspectives, representation and participation in social, political, economic, cultural and media institutions in Canadian society.

The conflict between the Mohawks and non-native claimants for the land actually began hundreds of years ago when King Louis XIV of France granted 240 square miles of land to the Seminary of St Sulpice in Oka,Québec, for the Indians' use and benefit. Between the years 1800 and 1940, the seminary sold almost all of the land for its own profits. Neither the granting of the land nor its sale invalidated Aboriginal title, 'which can be extinguished only by treaty or by an explicit act of the government. But the Mohawk Nation never ceded its sovereignty; nor was it ever conquered. The Mohawk land claim at Oka has never been judged on its merits by any court of law' (Raphals, 1990: 413).[1]

In 1961, these very lands became the site of a nine-hole golf course in Oka, despite opposition by the Kanehsatake people. In 1989, the municipality of Oka unilaterally decided to permit the golf club the right to expand its playground over an additional 55 acres. The proposed expansion included an area called 'the pines', which has been used by the Mohawks of Kanehsatake as common lands and a sacred burial ground.

Negotiations to stop the project failed and in March 1990, the Mohawks decided to use 'other' means to oppose the extension of the golf course. On 11 March 1990, a small group of Mohawk people set up a road blockade preventing access to the golf course. It was (wo)manned 24 hours a day by residents of Kanehsatake and by members of the Warrior Society, an organization whose objective is the defence and protection of Mohawk rights. During the protest, members of the Warrior Society wore camouflage clothing and put handkerchiefs over their faces for anonymity even throughout the hottest of summer days. They also each took on a pseudonym for the same purpose, and over time became well known for their unique and crafty public personae.

On 10 July the Mayor of Oka, Jean Ouellette (who, along with several of his city councillors, has personal investments in the golf course development), requested that the Québec provincial police (Sûreté du Québec, hereafter referred to as SQ) enforce a Québec Superior Court injunction to tear down the blockade and make the land accessible to the general public. The Mohawks responded by further fortifying their barricades. Reinforcements (Warriors and plain-clothed civilian supporters) volunteered and were brought in from Mohawk and other native nations.

On 11 July, 100 SQ officers attacked the Mohawk blockade with assault rifles, concussion grenades and tear gas. Corporal Marcel Lemay of the Québec police force was shot and died a few hours later in hospital. The confrontation escalated after the announcement of Lemay's death. SQ officers responded fearfully and aggressively by surrounding Kanehsatake and blocking off all food and medical supplies from entry to the community. Within two hours, the Mohawks of the Kahnawake Indian Reserve, a community on the south shore of Montreal (about 40km from Kanehsatake), reacted with a show of solidarity by blocking the Mercier Bridge that links several south shore communities to Montreal. The bridge would remain closed until 5 September. During this time, deprivation of easy access to Montreal would cause high levels of frustration and, in some cases, racist demonstrations by non-native commuters who were to be inconvenienced with an additional four to six hours of commuting each day.

Upfront, publicly acknowledged negotiations between the Québec government's Native Affairs Minister, John Ciaccia, and the Mohawks began on 12 July and continued privately throughout the summer. At the Québec government's request, the federal authorities refused to participate in these officially, claiming that they did not want to jeopardize Mohawk/provincial government progress. In fact, they consistently refused the Mohawks' offer of 'nation to nation' discussions, on the grounds that it implied a political status with which federal officials were not comfortable. Furthermore, they argued that they would not talk with 'masked terrorists' and 'armed criminals'. Federal bureaucrats did, however, work behind the scenes to purchase some of the disputed land for the Mohawks who, in turn, disapproved because it bypassed the very principle underlying their protest: that land which already belonged to Mohawk peoples cannot be bought or sold by non-Mohawk peoples or governments.

Key Mohawk and government players in the conflict (federal, provincial and Six Nations Iroquois Confederacy officials[2]) struggled all summer to clarify the terms and preconditions for negotiations to take place in good faith. Some progress was made. By early August, Mohawks and a Québec Justice of the Superior Court, appointed by Prime Minister Brian Mulroney, agreed to allow 'the free movement of food and supplies in and out of the two communities, the free movement of Mohawk advisors, and the creation of an international team of observers to monitor events while negotiations take place' (*Globe and Mail*, 3/9/90).

Three nights of violent, racist outbreaks near the Mercier Bridge contributed to the decision on the part of the federal government to call for army assistance on 14 August. The army deployed 2500 troops to four locations near Oka and Chateauguay – the two communities adjacent to the Mohawk barricades. (As a point of comparison, it is interesting to note that the Canadian government deployed less than 1000 military troops to Kuwait during this same period.)

On 16 August, international observers took up posts at the barricades to monitor the conflict on behalf of international human rights organizations. On 17 August, the Canadian army replaced the SQ at the two community sites and on 27 August, Québec Premier Robert Bourassa requested that the army dismantle the Kahnawake barricades according to their own strategic schedule. Kahnawake Mohawks cooperated with the army.

On 1 September troops moved into Kanehsatake and for the duration of the month, negotiations started and stopped, anti-Mohawk activities continued in surrounding territory, and meetings/protests of native groups across the country continued. During September, troops squeezed the Kanehsatake Mohawk Warriors on to a very small piece of land on which was located a drug rehabilitation centre, otherwise known as the

Treatment Centre. Mohawk Warriors refused to back down from a potentially violent confrontation.

The army then began to isolate the Warriors from all outside communications sources, except the army itself. They cut cellular phone lines into the Treatment Centre, thus not only isolating the Warriors but also making it impossible for journalists still inside to file their stories. A wide array of organizations, including the Canadian Association of Journalists, the Fédération professionnelle des journalistes du Québec, Southam Press, the Canadian Civil Liberties Association and the European Parliament, protested about this breach of freedom of the press. The army, meanwhile, characterized those journalists who had chosen to remain inside the Treatment Centre as being afflicted with the 'Stockholm Syndrome' (the psychological identification of a hostage with the hostage-taker), thus delegitimating their reports.

In a practical sense, the isolation meant that *everyone* behind the barricades lost access to their outside information networks and sources. Not only were journalists unable to receive and send out information, but the Mohawks no longer had access to information about the level of public support they were getting from across the country. The conflict had reached a climax for the Mohawks.

The army strategy worked.[3] Failed negotiations with two levels of government and the army pressured the isolated, remaining Mohawk Warriors (32 men, 19 women and several children) to leave the Treatment Centre on 26 September, 78 days after the crisis erupted. They came out, one day ahead of an announced 'disengagement' date, taking the army, the SQ and the media by surprise and throwing them into temporary chaos. Violence was used by the armed forces and the SQ as the Mohawks were herded on to buses to be brought to Farnham, Québec, for 'processing'. Cameras filmed the whole disengagement event.

The Warriors were indicted for 'obstruction of justice', bearing firearms, using firearms in a threatening manner, wearing a disguise, death threats, participating in a riot, and other charges. Most were freed on bail to await court hearings and spent the autumn and winter of 1990–91 raising funds to pay their defence costs.

Some of the land surrounding 'the pines' was purchased by the federal government, though the status of the specific piece of contested land is still publicly unclear. It is believed that the deeds for the purchased land will be passed over to the Mohawks in time, as federal authorities develop a clear sense of who can fairly represent the interests of the majority of the Kanehsatake residents.

The army left both communities at the end of September, and the SQ/RCMP (Royal Canadian Mounted Police, Canada's federal police service) continued patrolling the areas, while discussions about long-term security needs were addressed. Both governments initially refused to establish Commissions of Inquiry into native/non-native relations in Canada, although the Parliamentary Standing Committee on Aboriginal

Issues conducted a hearing about the conflict.

Since the autumn of 1990, the federal government and the Mohawks have attempted to restart a widely supported negotiation process with Kanehsatake on land grievances and self-government. Progress has been slow due to disagreement on the terms of reference for these talks. Native peoples of Canada have called the 'end of the Mohawk crisis' the beginning of a new era in native/non-native relations. In April 1991, the federal government announced the establishment of a Royal Commission on Aboriginal Issues.

## Media Coverage of the Amerindian Summer

The Mohawk confrontation with the Canadian federal, Québec provincial and Oka municipal governments and their respective security services contested the myths and discourses about media objectivity and balance in Canadian society. Thousands of hours of broadcast coverage and hundreds of thousands of inches of print were generated by English, French, Mohawk and other Aboriginal media in an effort to cover the confrontation effectively. This attests to the importance that the media gave to the issues during the period of the so-called crisis.[4] But if we compare this huge quantity of space with the minimal amount of coverage that native issues are routinely allocated, the difference is appalling.[5]

Distinctions between English, French and Mohawk media coverage of the confrontations, the emergent issues, and the key players involved were fairly predictable from the various political and linguistic points of view. The essential differences were based on the historically specific perspectives and cultural attitudes brought to bear on the media analyses by journalists and their representative institutions.

Tending to fall back upon their 'pre-crisis' perspectives vis-a-vis language and cultural politics of the province, all media used the crisis situation as an opportunity to collect evidence for ongoing editorial positions regarding federal/provincial politics, ie constitutional arrangements, state/nation legitimation crises, native/non-native relations, racism, and other economic and identity issues.

The point that most strongly stands out after reading/viewing/listening to much of the English and French media output is a sense that the notion of balance had been interpreted quite differently. There are at least two ways of constructing balance in media products. On the one hand, balance might be implicit within each and every article or story. If this is the preferred method of approximating balance, then readers, listeners and viewers might be able to excerpt one story from a newspaper and/or a broadcast and expect that *at least* two sides will be represented within that one narrative.

The other means of achieving balance is by assuming that each medium is one whole product made up of various programme elements or articles, clustered around multiple points of view. In the latter model, it is assumed that the 'active' reader/viewer/listener of mainstream media will spend the necessary time consuming the medium's entire output and will eventually conclude that all aspects *taken together* provide a balanced overview of the issues. The inherent risk of this model is that media users will not invest appropriate amounts of time and will often choose to read/listen to/watch exclusively whatever aspects will reinforce their own initial attitudes.

Media coverage of the crisis, in general, opted for the latter form of balancing a range of views instead of attempting to balance out each story assignment. The French media, however, consistently covered a wider range of opinions about the crisis than did the English media, that is, it included more material, some of which might even be considered of a racist nature. For example, whereas the English media were faster to name anti-Mohawk effigy-burning and throwing of glass bottles at Mohawks as 'racist' behaviour, the French media provided a venue through which anti-Mohawk protesters could speak for themselves, and it let them do so without much analytical or critical commentary from journalists. Their tendency to frame issues in a linguistic manner pointed to English/French media differences in philosophical approaches to issues of freedom of expression and the responsible limits within which these freedoms are to be constructed.

Several practical factors may have contributed to this difference in viewpoint. Perhaps because many more of the players, such as the non-native residents of the communities involved, are French-speaking, the French media had easier access to spokespeople who could elaborate their positions articulately in French but not do so well in English. Another critical point is that very few Mohawks speak French because of a historical trust/alliance with the English, thereby making it difficult to do on-site interviews and provide easy access to information in French. This resulted in the recycling of the few Mohawks and other native people who could intervene comfortably in the media in French. It also gave a distinct advantage to the English media in terms of access to information disseminated by the various Mohawk groups. The third aspect which might account for the absence of the Mohawk voice on French media, particularly at the end of the summer, is that no francophone journalist remained at the Treatment Centre after the army narrowed the perimeters of the Warrior-controlled territory. This meant that the point of view of the Warriors could not be broadcast or printed by the French media. Of course, after the cellular phones were cut, the English media lost this right too, but they had access to the Warriors' perspective for a lot longer than did the French.

**Patterns within the 'Mohawk Crisis' Media Coverage**

In general, the media played three strategic roles in regard to the crisis. As *information conduits*, they each documented a range of aspects of the events and background, some critically, some in a rather distorted manner. As *constituency builders*, they contributed to the positioning of audiences around certain actions or in building up support for particular interpretive frameworks. As *mediators*, they enabled the public to participate in debates about the significance of the conflict to native/Québec/Canadian society and publicly share how it impacted on them personally.

The radio phone-in show was the most popular format on each of the English, French and Mohawk channels, although each cultural community handled the debates quite differently and in accordance with the frameworks within which each station editorially operates.

French radio was somewhat controversial at times and illustrates the use of radio as constituency builder. The most popular radio show host on a well-known station was alleged to have used his programme as an information base around which non-native protesters could organize. In other words, he was suspected of having used some of his radio access time to build popular support for anti-Mohawk vigilante groups involved in the confrontation. The position of the corporation which owns and operates this radio station has been that its objective throughout the summer was to provide a wide range of opportunities for people of all political persuasions to speak out about the issues and to express their attitudes. The owner argues that his station thus reflects diversity of opinion as required within the Canadian Broadcasting Act.

One of the most innovative uses of radio for diffusing tension was demonstrated by Radio Kahnawake, the Mohawk Broadcasting Service. 'Nat', the phone-in show host, used her English-language programme uniquely by inviting callers to explain their feelings throughout the crisis. She even encouraged some of the perpetrators of racism to call and evacuate their hostilities in her direction. This, she hoped, would substitute for physical brutality, reasoning that if, as Martin Luther King suggested, violence is the language of the inarticulate, the opportunity to speak might diminish the need to act physically. Nat received hundreds of calls over the summer. At the end of the callers' usually hostile comments, she would say 'Thank you' and hang up. She rarely lost patience and maintained a consistent level of diplomacy. What she did essentially was use radio as a means of catharsis – for diffusing hostile energy – in a mediating role.

Newspapers were the most consistent medium for provision of background about the issues of land claims, sovereignty, native culture and native politics. Ironically, at a time in Canadian history when an independent native press would have been invaluable as a tool for bridging the information gaps between native and non-native peoples in the country, federal funding for native-produced newspapers had been cut 100 per cent as of March 1990. So there was and still is a missing Canadian native voice in print – one which would have importantly complemented and informed the non-native population of the background to the critical issues which led to the confrontation.

Print media covered the issues from a fairly wide range of perspectives, although the English ones did not seem to give as much space to commentaries constructing the Warriors as 'criminals' or 'terrorists' as did the French press. Again, this seems to be a question of the degree of latitude within their notion of balance.

Montreal's *The Gazette* dedicated a lot of its resources to coverage of the crisis and had staff reporters at the Treatment Centre towards the end, so that English readers could get limited amounts of information from the 'inside' until the cellular phones were cut. *Gazette* editorials took into account the unique role of the media in constructing the character of the crisis and did not deny the subjectivity of various reports from behind the barricades. While giving ample coverage to native voices, *The Gazette* still managed to report on concerns of non-native citizens (commuters, business owners, etc). It did not often omit or ignore the broader contexts of the issue, nor did it fail to respond to criticisms of its coverage.

An outstanding example of problematic coverage was when *The Gazette* and *La Presse*, as well as a local television station (CFCF), naively announced the name of a beach to which Kahnawake women, children and elders were being evacuated for security reasons on 13 August. The information fed right into the planning strategy of anti-Mohawk vigilante gangs. During the evacuation, anti-Mohawk protesters arrived, baseball bats in hand, to prevent the Mohawks from landing at the publicly named beach. The evacuation site had to be abandoned for fear of potential confrontations, demonstrating the problem of the unrestrained application of the philosophy that 'more information is better'.

The media outlets responded to criticism at first with freedom of expression arguments, but later agreed that they would consider the potential impact of such information in the future. This is yet another example of the direct relationship between media and constituency organization.

### The Four 'Crises' of the Summer of 1990

'Crises' are named and evaluated in discourse as sudden disruptions in the everyday, routine state of affairs. By discourse, I simply mean the way in which people speak about a particular subject or object. When the media describe 'crises', journalists and the institutions which they represent are both 'coming from' and 'taking up' positions about a particular event or issue, while simultaneously trying to respect the journalistic principles of 'objectivity' and 'balance' underpinning North American media work. In other words, journalists don't just name crises, they contribute to the public construction of disruptive events as 'crises'. They give crises public attention and value.

Most media referred to the government/Indian confrontation of 1990 as simply the 'Mohawk crisis'. This is too monolithic a category. On the basis of media evidence. there are at least four ways of framing the crisis which occurred in Canada during the summer of 1990 within a larger context of cross-cultural communications and political problems.

First, there was the conflict and subsequent crisis between the Kanehsatake Mohawks and the various levels of governments over golf course ownership and land claims process. This conflict had major consequences on the quality of native/non-native relations across Canada and inspired widespread regional 'support' reactions. These took the form of Indian protests about local issues, and were anchored within larger questions of Aboriginal self-government. Roadblocks in protest at logging Indian-claimed lands in British Columbia, James Bay Cree Indians threatening to blow up the initial infrastructure of a proposed Hydro-Québec hydroelectric project on their territory, Innu protests over low-flying NATO planes in Labrador, Newfoundland, and many other political actions escalated in response to the Mohawks' land claims/human rights arguments.

These regional confrontations between First Nations' peoples and their neighbours became the basis for a second crisis related to more general environmental, political, social, economic and cultural developmental issues.

Thirdly, there was the crisis in certain politicized strata in Québec society regarding the place and significance of a 'sovereign Mohawk nation' in the context of their own political positions and discourses of nationalism and separation. This raised significant questions about the Québécois' affirmation that peoples of French ancestry are the key and sole victims of English colonization processes. In having to deal with native land claims and natives' usage of terms like 'sovereignty' and 'nationhood', Québécois have had to acknowledge that they, too, may be labelled in a parallel colonialistic manner by the Aboriginal peoples living in the province. This, understandably, did not sit well within the framework of their own claims.[6] Furthermore, the English media, having just come out of the failed Meech Lake debates and always searching for arguments to contest Québécois separatist policies, used the native discourses of sovereignty to contextualize and back up their own criticisms and political positions against Québec sovereignty.[7]

Fourthly, there was the crisis within the actual media institutions, particularly those within the geographical region of the Mohawk confrontation. This crisis consisted of a schism in the way journalists, assignment editors and management thought about native issues and the forms in which they are represented in the media. Questions about the absence of native people from routine media, other than in the odd news clip, abounded. So, the fourth crisis was that of the media having publicly to face their own poor representations of cultural and racial diversity within Québécois and Canadian media institutions on all levels of employment, portrayal practices and management. Starting fairly early in the crisis, journalists became preoccupied with self-reflexive questions.

What the Mohawk/government crisis showed us in this regard was that there were very few journalists in Québec who had enough background about native issues to take on the challenge of covering the complexities of the stories without several weeks of orientation and background research. Even more clearly, it made public the little-known and appalling fact that less than a handful of native journalists are employed by mainstream media institutions. In addition, it showed the Canadian public how poorly represented native nations are within mainstream broadcasting imagery and narratives, except when under dire circumstances, at which point coverage becomes a profitable commodity on the broadcasting market. English and French media documented the issue as an ethno-exhibitionist confrontation between two cultures engaged in disagreement over land rights. The drama, the objects, the costumes, the deep-rooted significance of the contested lands, and the constant threat of violence exposed by media throughout the summer made aspects of the confrontation very easy to extract symbolically and materially from their historical contexts and transform into marketable products.

## Commodification of the Mohawk Crisis

'Warriormania! Lasagna look the hottest ticket for Halloween' (*The Gazette*, 24/10/90: A3).[8]

'PR Role at Oka Won Army Over: Public Relations Goes to the Front' (*Globe and Mail*, 25/10/90: A5).

'Bridge Blockade a Boon for Sales of Binoculars' (*The Gazette*, 20/7/90: A3).

**[Excerpt from CBC Radio National News:
Friday 2 November 1990 – 7:00 a.m.]**

Announcer: Two men from Québec are hoping to strike it rich from the Oka crisis. They're building a merchandising empire based on the events of last summer. They've registered just about every name and symbol from the crisis, including the golf course, the Warriors, the army barricades, and even the nicknames of one of the Warriors, Lasagna. Carol Off prepared this report.

Lagarde: The idea came from my kids.

Off: André Lagarde is a self-employed Oka resident always looking for a good idea. So when he saw his children setting up barricades during the summer and forcing their playmates to negotiate, the entrepreneurial lightbulb went on. Lagarde and his partner went to the copyright office and registered everything they could dealing with the Oka crisis. Now they're ready to put out as many as 75 different products – from Warrior dolls to lunch boxes, all under the trademark Okanatake SuperWarriors Fan Club. The first item will be a game called Barricades and Negotiations – selling for $9.95.

Lagarde: In the package, there will be those barricade ribbons, that negotiation plan, and there will also be a club in the game.

Off: Children will be able to cordon off their room, the basement, or the street with colored ribbons. Children can also buy accessories to the game, like sandbags, or large slinky-type toys that can be used like the army's famous razor wire.

Lagarde: So if the negotiations is very bad and there is nothing to do, well you are going to put your slinky.

Off: The big money maker, though, is the SuperLasagna Junior video game. A warrior has to negotiate difficult terrain like a golf course, a lake, and of course barricades in order to find food and supplies. The only characters not included in the merchandising will be the people from Chateauguay and Lasalle – best known for throwing rocks at Mohawks on the Mercier Bridge. The entrepreneurs say they don't want to get into those kinds of negotiations. Carol Off, CBC News, Montreal.

And how did the clerk at the Canadian copyright office react to the entrepreneurs' request to sneak-register the very essence of Mohawk peoples' lived experiences and the symbols of their identity which they had created to represent the limits of their political patience – in the names of two Oka businessmen? Where is the justice when struggle over use of the pseudonym of Ronald Cross – 'Lasagna' – and his protest costume takes place in Lasagna's absence? Community and solidarity lose when history objectifies through media imagery and holds up forms and simulations for contemplation and purchase.

Media headlines begin and end the transformation process – the crisis used, not a wasted moment. Media post-mortems – editors determined to learn from the experience, to do it better next time – governments, the army, public relations consultants, the Warriors all fixated on the details, the breakdown in routines, the patterns left, the strategies, the responses: 'What worked best?' 'Where did *we* go wrong?' 'No, no, don't give us a general analysis. Be specific. Tell us how *we* did.'

Who will benefit from this knowledge? Can social change be conceived in terms other than crisis?

In a short time, the media's archive of staple images will become 'bodies of texts' and eager scholars over the next decades will research papers, dissertations, books, will capture historical essences and 'structures of feeling' (Williams, 1977: 128–41), will insert the images into new academic discourses on 'media and crisis'. Hopefully, some will use this as a basis for teaching media literacy skills and for deconstructing the media procedures which were so transparent during the periods of dramatic tension.

The 'Amerindian' summer provided Canadians and international audiences with first-hand data about some of the fragilities, inadequacies and scars within the media system. It showed how important it is to recognize that in moments of crisis, we begin to see very clearly how media systems operate, where protestors/state/media alliances/allegiances and conflicts develop.

Canadian mainstream media audiences are not generally accustomed to observing breakdowns in news routines, or seeing their own information sources disorganized. Where are the laws of media? Who gives the order? What to do with ill-prepared journalists, invisible assumptions blinding audiences with blatant inaccuracies, poorly researched analyses – improving only incrementally as time places history into its context.

Where is the cultural and racial diversity in the Canadian press? And where are the unemployed native journalists whose budgets and critical words were cut by federal government bureaucrats? Where are *their* voices in media institutions? And why is the colour of 1990 media in Canada, a 'multicultural' nation, still white?

The media are in trouble – taken off guard. The arbitrariness and biases of story/news construction are too transparent for comfort. Too many senior reporters on summer holidays, reporters who want to become stars by jumping from one media fence to another, and where, again, are all the native journalists? To where have their discourses on native sovereignty, equality and the cultural meaning of 'land' evaporated? And will *they* be paid for *their* commentaries, too? How many times can one 'native expert' or one native person be recycled through the mediasphere?

Viewers can see 'media crises' as rich fields. Here is access to and deeper understanding of media production processes and limits. The documentary power of the camera as witness and evidence – never closing down: 'unedited, raw footage' broadcast live, from the rough and unpredictable terrain, out there, near the contested 'pines'. Questions open opportunities to participate in discussions about freedom of expression and censorship: 'Can a journalist indeed be objective?' 'How is it that some of the most informative parts of the footage are left out of final edited products?' 'Is journalistic self-censorship a common practice?' 'Where is the native bias?' 'Where has the notion of balance disappeared in all this?' and 'Are media becoming participants in this crisis?': questions formulated by viewers in watching media producers grope for the best analyses that could be done, given the crude circumstances.

Relationships (alignments and ruptures) between state, Mohawk and media institutions become a central subject of discussion. Debates focus on media coverage, bias, conflicting views of journalistic norms, the question of whether an orthodoxy of interpretation could or should be imposed on cultural attitudes of journalists by Mohawk Warriors, by army dictates, by state request, by self-censorship. Also popular are deliberations about the social role of intellectuals, media–Mohawk–state manipulations, and the national history of political violence in regard to other native issues: positions articulated almost exclusively in the discourses of 'terrorism'.

Discourses of terrorism commonly frame media views of crises. *Official* discourses often attempt to deny the political character of challenge to the state. Media are expected to support the legitimate order of things. *Reactionary populist* discourses argue that all legal restraints should be bypassed in order to eliminate the enemy. *Alternative* discourses view terrorism as something which must be explained and not reacted to excessively by the state. *Oppositional* discourses are the voices of the perpetrators of anti-state violence. Denying space to this discourse is the goal of the official discourse-keepers. Oppositional voices are important.

They engage public attention and enable clearer understanding of the motivation of political actors/actresses. A typology of voices – four classes; unlimited examples in media texts of the Indian/government conflict.[9]

But missing elements stand out: private discourses of silent majorities – print, sound and video clips left out of news items by choice, the whispering voices of other Aboriginal peoples, afraid for their own land claims. The critical voices of journalists and commentators silenced in the mainstream, but not on the margins.

Radio Kahnawake – CKRK, Mohawk Broadcasting Service, an oppositional discourse: radio for the local community, with eavesdroppers (sometimes welcome) from neighbouring suburbia; CKHQ – Radio Kanehsatake, sister radio, close to the action. Possessing no official ID, no accreditation, results in no access to press conferences on the 'other' side of the issues. 'But it's *us* that this is all about!' they claim. 'No matter! Get that press card first. Learn the codes, play the music, sing the songs, do the dances, gotta follow the army's rules. Access to the privileged only, the obedient only, if you please.'

In Kanehsatake, two Mohawk women, fresh out of training school, eat, breathe, sleep and wake to the experience of a state of siege while living at the community's radio station between 11 July and 29 September – the duration of *their* 'crisis'. Voices connected to international venues – 'What is happening?' 'Please report what you see *now*, what the moves are.' Telephone as link to local, regional, national, international support networks.

The backfire begins soon *after* all is presumed to be calm. Neighbouring communities call CKRK for more and more talk about the 'crisis'. Can the Mohawks save *their* golf course too? Take down the shingles – 'We Mohawks do not rescue withering golf courses on non-native lands!' 'But you did so well with yours, why not *ours* too? We need you. Aren't you OUR radio too? You *were* during the crisis. What happened?' Do they actually think that Mohawks have become specialists in rescuing golf courses in one summer's duration?

Nat moves about the day schedule to get away from the neighbouring night monitors, nostalgically focused on the past. Nat wants peace of mind. The listeners take chase, jump about the day, find Nat, call Nat. Radio Tag. Psychological dependency is a difficult habit to break – the unanticipated byproduct of innovative radio.

The line blurs, yet another struggle begins. Community radio itself becoming a contested space, encroached upon by outside listeners, non-natives attempting to appropriate the last resource of all: Mohawk community airwaves – the roots of cultural expression, the route to social identity. Innovations at the media margins.

Where will it all end? This is no time for speculation. From land claimed throughout the country to water rights in James Bay to airspace in Kahnawake, a common pattern is discerned. Native nations have felt and lived it, some media have named it. It is not a crisis, it is not a disruption –

it is a mere continuation of a pattern of interaction established between natives and non-natives from times of early contact: cultural intrusions, national evasions, incommensurable values. Fresh codes – extended margins – are required to break the impasses, the bypasses, the overpasses and the underpasses.

Other margins are needed – symbols of political will and pioneering spirits. Margins are like edges of adventurous places and spaces, where pioneers explore for new perspectives, where novel frameworks originate. Here, they are the limits of one's imagination to be tested in the next cross-cultural challenge of Canadian society: how to rebuild native and non-native communities without the symbol of differences, the barricade, in between to block off the social possibilities of reconciliation.

### Conclusion

Art and artefacts of Amerindian cultures have always been traditionally collected, sold and purchased in recognition that 'folk art' is highly valued for its authentic difference from mainstream or dominant North American culture. In the late twentieth century, therefore, it would be expected that some aspects of the spectacular government/Indian stand-off would become subject to entrepreneurial opportunism. Warrior camouflage, army razor wire, television images, outstanding moments in the conflict – torn from their historic places – have indeed been re-emerging as items within the Canadian nostalgia market. Lived cultural and political processes, objectified and spectacularized in media texts, have been pulled from media vehicles and ethnically marked as objects, tokens of a radical transformation in Canadian history, which must not be forgotten: objects of historical memory, native kitsch.

The production of associative links through object ownership is nothing new to North American society. However, it is worth noting that Canada does not have as extensive a history of commodifying material or symbolic events as does the United States. Ever since the release of the *Star Wars* film in the 1970s, mass marketing of object-symbols from films and television have become common practice in the US. But the proliferation of memorabilia about the Mohawk/government confrontation represents a somewhat new phenomenon within Canadian society. For example, in 1970, after the FLQ (Front de Libération du Québec) crisis which challenged the constitutional relationship between Canada and Québec, nothing comparable was produced in terms of commodity nostalgia. There are no historical Canadian precedents for the entrepreneurial response to the Mohawk crisis. So what might account for its occurrence at this particular historical juncture?

Clearly, the media constructed and commodified the crisis in a sensationalistic manner, leaving out as much as it reflected. The vulgar appeal of the Mohawk crisis as a complex exhibition of objects and events to be displayed or manipulated derives from its potential to distract the consumer superficially from critical questions that might challenge the unworkable assumptions presently clouding discourses on serious political problems and relationships among Canadian/Québec/Aboriginal societies.

The confrontations of the 'Amerindian Summer' struck at the vulnerable centre of the complex relationships between Canada's three basic constituencies: the pre-Canadian, Aboriginal peoples or 'First Nations', the 'founding' nationals, the French and the English, and the new Canadians, recent immigrants. Political crisis in the Canadian state has been escalating since the 1960s. The failure of the Meech Lake Accord, the popular support for Québec separatism inside and outside the province, and ethnic/visible minority and Aboriginal challenges to the status quo attest to the recent discord within Canadian society. The events of summer 1990 dramatically problematized and publicized Canada's ongoing legitimacy crisis. Media projected Canadian society as a less-than-tolerant pluralistic nation, struggling somewhere between a public discourse on multiculturalism and a practice of responding to conflict with military strategy rather than with negotiations. Yet little media analysis has focused on these broader questions, with which Canadians are still grappling.

Everything that happened during the summer of 1990 is of considerable consequence to the future of a stable Canadian society and is a prototype of what might take place in other nations should communication between cultural constituency groups break down as severely as it did in this case. With Fourth World Aboriginal peoples being linked through satellite communictions and international networks, it is evident that the 'Mohawk summer' of 1990 was closely and strategically monitored by them, as well as by the broad international community.

On a superficial level, the Mohawks and other Aboriginal nations in Canada learned that violence gets media and government attention; the military learned that censorship works quickly to defeat the disenfranchised; journalists learned that they have a lot of homework to do in preparation for another possible cultural/racial confrontation; the public learned that Canada is not the ideal 'multicultural' nation it discursively claims to be; governments learned that strategies to deal with conflicts within non-native constituencies might not be culturally appropriate for Aboriginal peoples.

The negotiation process chosen by government and military officials was not particularly effective due to cross-cultural differences that seemed irreconcilable. Government representatives failed to understand the Mohawk belief in group consensus; Mohawks refused to name only *one* or *two* people to carry on negotiations on their behalf. Media people failed to research the cultural incommensurabilities well enough to convey to the public the point that the breakdown in the negotiation process was *not* due to a lack of good will on the part of the Mohawks, but rather to a set of cultural and political values to which they wished to remain loyal. The dreadful failure to communicate effectively during the hostilities should help to shift the material and the media grounds upon which native/non-native relationships in Canada are to be negotiated in the future.

The necessity to recognize and cope with the distinctions among native/non-native value systems (evident in the difficulties surrounding the choice of a 'representative' Mohawk negotiator) was shown to be integral to a clear and reasoned understanding of political, social, cultural, economic and media crises. Certainly, if Canadian and other peoples are going to use this experience as a basis for rethinking and revising interaction patterns with First Nations groups, the development of effective cross-cultural strategies to facilitate relationships between natives and non-natives, and *initiated* by both groups, will be of the utmost importance.

If Canadians have learned anything from the Mohawk/government confrontation, it is that no cultural community is monolithic and that *all* peoples must work respectfully to build new bridges to mediate intra- and intercultural differences. Furthermore, every conceivable peaceful means to facilitate this (re)construction process must be used. And when these bridges are built with the support of more enlightened Canadian journalists, the passageways across them must be left as free and undistorted as possible.

This is an opportune time to open the doors and windows of (inter)nationally controlled media, as well as political, social, cultural and economic institutions, to equal participation of First Nations peoples. The continued spectacularization and commodification of the Mohawk crisis will be an easy way to shift public attention from this arduous, energetic and democratic project.

## Notes

I would like to thank Gail Valaskakis, David Tomas, Loreen Pindera, Diana Bronson, Jack Cunningham, Marc Raboy, Bev Nelson, Conway Jocks and the David family of Kanehsatake for their invaluable comments on an earlier draft of this chapter.

1 This chapter represents the generally accepted public view that the land claim by the Mohawks, due to ancestral occupancy, is a valid perspective. It should be noted, however, that the Algonquins of Northern Québec believe that the contested land is, in fact, theirs, and point to their own ancestral occupancy as a basis for their position. The jury is still out on both claims.

2 In the seventeenth century, the Mohawks formed the Six Nations or Iroquois Confederacy along with five other Indian nations. The first Europeans signed peace and friendship treaties with this Confederacy, one of which was called 'Two Row Wampum', which specified that both the European and Iroquois communities would live side by side – each following their own laws, customs and lifestyles. These treaties are the basis for Mohawks' assertion of their sovereignty and why they continue to insist on nation-to-nation negotiations with the Canadian government.

In the 1800s, the federal government instituted a system of government on native lands modelled after that of Europe, and Band Councils became the only legitimate representative of the Indian communities according to the perception of the federal authorities. The Long House traditionalists then and now refuse to vote in Council elections as they do not recognize this form of 'imposed' government. As a result, to this day, there are many political and ideological divisions within the Mohawk communities. In the context of the 1990 Mohawk/government conflict, the Confederacy, as the Mohawk traditional governmental organization, represented the Mohawk position within the negotiation process.

3 Joe Scanlon, a consultant to legal and military authorities on communication strategies in crisis situations, suggests the following official responses to violent confrontations perceived to threaten the legitimacy of the state: (a) isolate those involved physically, controlling their movements, stopping them from making contact with others, stopping them from leaving the scene; (b) isolate those involved in communication terms, restricting contact to the authorities, ideally to those trained to deal with such incidents; (c) open up discussions with those involved, discussions carried on by skilled communicators, people often called negotiators; (d) develop the capacity to respond with significant force should the incident deteriorate; (e) stall for time (Scanlon, 1990: 5).

Clearly, this type of advice was not ignored by the Canadian authorities in the case of the Mohawk confrontation.

4 Video and audiotapes also became a valuable commodity for the police, who wanted them as a basis for reconstructing events and for identification of parties involved. Some were seized under protest. The issue of police seizure of tapes to be used as evidence is problematic to media institutions and compromises freedom of expression. Some cases have gone to court.

5 Ross Perigoe (1990) has pointed out that native concerns have largely been ignored in the Canadian media, except when there is a conflict to dramatize. As an example of this, he tells about a CBC *Newsworld* programme which ran in April 1990 about the portrayal of visible minorities in Canadian media. On the programme two Kanehsatake residents spoke from the audience about the golf course situation and criticized the two large English broadcasting networks, CTV and CBC, for not having paid attention to their polite requests for background media coverage, starting in March 1990: 'According to the speakers, whenever they called the local television news rooms to tell them about a planned protest, the question always came back, "Will there be any guns?" The media, in other words, were saying, "We'll only cover you if there is the possibility of violence." In some ways one might even conclude that the media were, by inference, counselling the Mohawks that violence or the threat of violence gets attention.

'It was a poignant moment, watching these people wrestle with insensitive media that understood conflict only in terms of barricades and rifles' (Perigoe, 1990: 12).

Several weeks later, the barricades were up, and the situation had escalated to an armed confrontation.

6 In December 1990, the pro-sovereignty Parti Québécois announced a new Aboriginal policy which would give native peoples some self-government powers and more of a partnership role in a proposed Québec sovereign society. This is probably a response to the Liberal government/Mohawk conflict and the Parti Québécois' recognition of the priority of native cooperation in the smooth governance of Québec.

7 Robin Philpot (1991) argues that English Canada was the only beneficiary of the hostilities in that it discursively and materially used the Oka crisis as an 'alibi' to challenge Québec's claim as a distinct society and to frame Québec as a racist and intolerant state.

8 'Lasagna' was the pseudonym adopted by a high-media-profile Mohawk Warrior.

9 The four categories of discourses were derived from the work of Schlesinger and Lumley (1985).

# 11

# On New Uses of Media in Time of Crisis

*Armand Mattelart and Michèle Mattelart*
*translated by Anna Fudakowska and Marc Raboy*

A certain idea of crisis is in crisis. What profound changes have undergone our ways of imagining and thinking about – not to mention resolving – crisis situations! We propose to address this question by attempting to measure the shifts or upheavals at work in the identification of these situations. This will allow us to pick up the thread of a reflection begun during the 1970s and which, at the time, resulted in a book we published together entitled *De l'usage des médias en temps de crise* (On Uses of Media in Time of Crisis) (Mattelart and Mattelart, 1979).

This retrospective way of thinking about crisis or crises, those of today in relation to those of yesterday, seems appropriate in order to outline the lines of rupture and of continuity between two periods when the media acquired a strategic status in the redefinition of public space and of the ground rules of democracy.

## The End of the Hero

### From Strategy to Tactics

Thursday, 27 November 1986, an immense student demonstration invaded the streets of Paris to protest against the university reform project drawn up by the government of Mr Chirac, prime minister in the 'cohabitation' period of the Mitterrand regime. The evening of what could have appeared to be a remake of May 1968, one-time student movement leader Dany Cohn-Bendit, drew a lesson in comparison between the two events: 'The unorganized have no political experience today while in '68 even the most viscerally anti-organization had a political project at the back of their minds, a vision of socialism or a utopia for which they had a whole strategy. In 1986, the absence of this political experience transforms all of the debates about ideas into demonstrations of affectivity. The motor is emotion' (*Actuel*, 1986: 57).

''68, is old hat. '86, is better than that', sang one of the slogans among many others in this demonstration overflowing with sly winks at the come-on lines of advertising language, rich in deliberate linguistic misappropriations, in humorous parody, all the while deeply immersed in the glare of the media. The spirit of 1968 had been splashed in red, 1986 was a gaudy green: and so, two moments of student crisis found themselves naturally confronted, separated by the interval of a generation; two explosive moments that were not only indicative of the atmosphere of their times but of the differential status of two crisis events and the particular experience each represented.

The first noticeable difference concerned the place occupied by the media. In 1986, the movement is resolved to be telegenic. At the scene of the student strike, media committees are among the first to be established. Right from the evening of the first demonstration, a major multi-screen debate takes place on TF1, 'the Voice of France' (which will be privatized soon afterwards). Also on TF1, Michel Polac's show, *Droit de réponse* (Right of Reply) features a live debate. The videotext network, Minitel, integrates itself rapidly into the movement's communication apparatus. *Le Monde* fields 2000 calls a day under the codename 'Students' (in 1968, France did not have enough phone lines; 18 years later, these have quadrupled while the number of videotext users is the highest of the major technological powers). Local radio stations in each city cover the demonstrations and broadcast demonstrators' speeches. From the outset music is a feature of faculty occupations and street marches. Rock and African music groups contribute to the festive air. For the actors of 1968, journalists had been suspect as they were seen to be tools of a system that manipulated and distorted information. In 1986, many of the former critics had moved into the system's professional command posts.

May 1968 had cried: 'Bourgeois press, rotten TV'. The street warfare of the time was one of tracts, banners and graffiti against the media and advertising, against a television and radio system padlocked by the Gaullist state, against the rise of mass culture then beginning to mark the emergence of France's consumer society: 'Change life, people and the media'; 'Say no to the transistor culture'; 'Newspapers are toxic. Read leaflets, posters, wall papers'; 'Free the books from the National Library'; 'The darkroom has enlightened the bosses. Counter-offensive, the strike continues. Kodak'; 'ORTF (French radio and television organization): break the chains'. (a pun on 'chaînes', which also means 'networks' – trans.)

The more the radicalism of May 1968 expressed itself by refusing to accept the institutionalized media and by creating its own supports which renewed (and went beyond) the revolutionary tradition of 'agitprop', the more the youth of 1986 appropriated the media scene, both in collusion with its codes and images, and distanced from them. In its playful way, with its tendency to dress up sharply the discoveries of the daily media environment, 1986 sounded the death-knell of the pamphlet, emblem of 1968, and, with it, that of a certain political idea of the militant culture. A huge gulf separated the strategic dramatization which marked the crisis of May 1968 and the tactics of de-dramatization, which, on the contrary, characterized the 1986 event.

This difference in the activists' relations with the media, is only meaningful if looked at in terms of the question of power. In 1986, the acquisition of power was no longer the movement's structuring principle. This was evident even in the way the movement operated: refusal of hierarchy, rotation of leaders, space occupied by the disorganized as opposed to adherents of political and union groups. The lack of organization was nevertheless not incompatible with self-discipline.

Refusal of hierarchy was best expressed by the rejection of the media star. In May 1968, all the spokespeople were men. Not a single female figure appeared in the public foreground while, driven by the structuralist critique of consumer society, the movement lambasted the sexist mythology and advertising ideology of modern media. In 1986, women are everywhere, speaking in amphitheatres, in the street, but also on radio and television. On the other hand, advertising on French television has never been so overtly sexist, at least according to the criteria of the accusatory discourse of the 1960s. In France media have never been less subjected to the organized critique of a feminist movement in crisis.

The end of the obsession with power coincides with that of the desire for violence. As Roland Barthes wrote following May 1968: 'The university revolt is like "The Capture of Speech" (much as we say "The Capture of the Bastille") . . . violence here concretely and verbally symbolized by the "street", the site of unfettered speech, free contact, counter-institutional space' (Barthes, 1968: 108, 111). In 1986, pacifism is a fact. Both a sign of this non-violence and of the reconciliation of generations is the commitment of parents in organizing the peace keeping during demonstrations, and the appearance of the 'white helmets', the symbol of safety at the head of the march, composed of eminent personalities who have distinguished themselves in the defence of human rights.

The May conflagration, by afflicting the state and the authorities – as Edgar Morin (1968: 11) remarked at the time – was 'an anti-gerontocratic and anti-paternalistic revolt which would influence by generalizing for itself the essence of paternal-patronal power'. In 1986, the power figure is no longer that of the providential man, de Gaulle, but rather the consensual president, Mitterrand, of a society under the placid reign of the social democracy which succeeded the authoritarian right of the 1970s. The President can offer himself the luxury of managing a 'cohabitation' by being in disagreement with his own prime minister's policies.

The movement of 1986 had no stars. But several months afterwards, some of its prominent figures had joined the ranks of candidates in the legislative elections on the presidential party slate. 'Elections, a trap for twerps', cried May 1968, caricaturing the National Assembly columns as prison bars and marching in front of that august temple while booing at it. If the police violence of 1986 cannot be compared to the repressive ideology of the Republican Security Squads of 1968, law and order is present in the efficient armada of clean-up services which leap into action as soon as the demonstrations are over, erasing all traces of dissent from the urban landscape.

Family, school, the media. These three institutional spaces, reproducers of dominant values ('ideological state apparatuses' according to the concept born in the wake of May 1968 (Althusser, 1971)), transformed themselves into sites of negotiation, mediation and reconciliation in the intervening decades.

The last difference which we will pin down is connected to the representation of social alliances which animate the protagonists of the two crises. In 1968, the myth of the liberation of the working class and proletarian ideologies intimately marked the student explosion. The reconciliation of manual and intellectual labour was the utopia which guided the worker–student alliance. Debates resonated with references to the Chinese cultural revolution.

In 1986 the motive for the crisis is, let us remember, a proposal to reform the process of university entrance selection. 'Education is a right; not a privilege'. The students who marched, principally recruited from the lower years of higher education and the upper years of secondary school, are not prompted by a desire to burn their school books and their teachers along with them. Pragmatically, they want to save their education and protect themselves from unemployment in a work market where competition is harsh. Proletarian dreams gave way to the fear of becoming proletarian.

May 1968 nourished itself on the liberation struggles of the Third World. The effigy of Che Guevara, killed in Bolivia in October 1967, dazzled at the time as a symbol of revolutionary commitment and sacrifice for the cause of freedom. At the Tricontinental Congress of Culture held in Havana in January 1968, where numerous intellectuals from all continents met to denounce the cultural imperialism of the United States then at war against Vietnam, the Argentinian writer, Julio Cortazar, launched a watchword: 'All intellectuals belong to the Third World'.

In 1986, the Third World was present in the numbers of young second generation immigrants from north African Arab countries. The status of ethnic communities, the citizenship rights of foreigners, played a decisive role both in the institutional structuring of political debate and in the psychological space of the representation of the other. At the beginning of the 1980s, the rise of racism, intimately linked to the effects of the economic crisis, provoked a response from movements such as SOS Racisme, which revealed itself to be particularly in touch with the sensitivities of young people and their way of conceiving militancy. This movement successfully integrated both the festive and media cultures. While satisfying the emotional needs of intercultural relations, it valorized a democratic dimension of everyday life. Against the notion of pure identity and the chilly withdrawal into national idiosyncrasy, it opened up the utopia of muti-racial conviviality, beginning with the stage settings of its demonstrations and concerts.

1968 had brandished a heroic idea of the Third World. 1986 represented it under the sign of the lived experience of ethnic minorities in the host country. A bristling daily life, always vulnerable to exploding into crisis, in culture shock, always at the mercy of rising new fanaticisms, of religious and political fundamentalism.

## From Revolutionary Crisis to Humanitarian Marketing

If the student movements of 1968 and 1986 confronted two different visions of perceiving society and living with the media, the last two decades were equally animated by a host of new interrogations which may be understood in terms of the rupture and rapprochement between two worlds: the North and the South.

In June 1990, the new President of Brazil, the conservative Collor, took the decision to liberalize the domestic market for computers. Following more than 30 years of protectionist policy, sometimes justified in the name of national independence, sometimes in the name of national security, Brasilia decided to open its borders to foreign manufacturers. National sovereignty henceforth would have to find a common interest with multinational corporations.

The 1970s were entirely dominated by debates on the unequal exchange between the North and South in matters of information and its technology. New world information and communication order, more equitable sharing of the radio frequency spectrum, codes of conduct with a view to regulating the marketing strategies of the food and drug companies, regulation of trans-border computerized data flows, and so on. All this debate put the spotlight on the role of public authorities in the defence of national sovereignty, in an environment where the interests of the multinationals were felt to be violently opposed to those of national identity. Most of the time, however, these debates only led to extremely incomplete measures.

At the height of these debates towards the end of the 1970s, the American delegation to UNESCO and, in its wake, that of Britain – before slamming the door on the international organization – foresaw an irrepressible confrontation between an increasingly authoritarian state imposing more and more limits on information, and a private sector defending its idea of the 'freedom of commercial expression' and the free flow of cultural merchandise.

In the event, this confrontation did not take place, as the public authorities dropped out, preferring to leave the field to market mechanisms. Deregulation and privatization policies succeeded those of welfare state voluntarism. In relations between nations as in relations between groups within each nation, the idea of income redistribution and social justice beat a retreat when faced with the necessity of liberating market forces in order to join the world economy.

The optimism of the 1960s, carried by the conviction that economic democracy would be plentiful, planned to make the benefits of modernity accessible to the largest majority through education, training programmes and, particularly in rural areas, massive literacy campaigns. At the time, the possible use of the new communication technologies, such as satellites, concerned education above all. Illiteracy was seen as an obstacle to economic growth as well as to the development of democracy. Today, increasing priority is placed on *entertainment* as the main use of the new communication apparatus.

More than ever, television plays a regulatory role in day-to-day life. Operating according to the aesthetics of the spectacle, it offers to those who remain on the fringes of market modernity and who benefit the least from its consumer models, the gratification of participating at least vicariously in its desirable symbolic universe – without forgetting that in the crisis of political representation that is becoming more and more generalized, the legitimacy that television confers is enough to make the career of providential politicians.

To be sure, many Third World countries have endowed themselves with their own cultural industries, even becoming competitive on the international programme market. This does not detract from the raw reality of the growing gap between the offer of goods and lifestyles in the televisual shop-window and the cruel drop in the buying power of not only the working classes but also of the middle class, beneficiaries of the modernization policies of the 1960s. Nor does it detract from the growing gap between this extreme pauperization and the extreme sophistication of the security technologies with which residential neighbourhoods have equipped themselves in order to fend off the threat from those left out in the cold.

We certainly know now that television viewers have their own savoir-faire, their own ways of circumventing, of diverting the propositions of the small screen, even of escaping from them altogether. But who can deny that the very mode of technological communication structures choices, fixing the range of priorities and creating a hierarchy in the way society uses its collective resources as well as those of each individual, who is a consumer and a citizen at one and the same time.

The media accompany. Greatly reinforced by the lotteries and fairy-tales which are nourished on half-baked realities, what else can they do? When crisis becomes a chaotic state of normalcy, when money – the founding social link of the market economy – dissolves in the spiral of individual and collective indebtedness, when inflation ensures that between the moment of receiving a salary and depositing it in the bank, money has already lost a large part of its value, when ordinary speculation responds only to the obsession of stable currency, what choice remains?

This new state of everyday disorder best illustrates the slippage in our definition of crisis. A situation saturated with crisis loses its exceptional character in the ordinariness of the exception. As one Peruvian theatre critic wrote at the beginning of the 1990s:

> The crisis ends up establishing itself in the most intimate spheres of our everyday lives. The pauperism and the semi-proletarianism of the middle class, as well as

the fall in the level of consumption of the working classes, have produced a spontaneous series of responses to the crisis, creating a new urban, social and cultural ecology in which we are beginning to reflect and recognize ourselves . . . We are beginning to speak of the creation of a "culture of violence" which touches the sphere of family life, institutions, school and inter-ethnic relations (Salazar del Alcazar, 1990: 38).

This permanent state of crisis is, in effect, the outcome of traits which characterized the accession to modernity of third world societies: the absence or precariousness of the rule of law, the absence or precariousness of structure for regulating the logic of the marketplace, and the subjective internalizing of the instability produced by the arbitrary. This finding is confirmed by the editor of the magazine *Analisis*, published in Bogota, who wrote in June 1990: 'The conflicts produced by narcotics traffic, guerilla fighters, right-wing paramilitary groups, mercenary associations and hired assassins, insert themselves into a series of tensions and problems which have accumulated in our society over the course of centuries. To be sure, the present crisis renders them more evident and multiplies them to the extreme, but we cannot say that it produces them' (*Analisis*, 1990: 3). This representation of crisis, as something rooted in a historic reality, is precisely that which is intensely ignored by the hyper-mediated image of Colombia as the emblem of chaos produced by drug traffic.

Throughout these reflections is deployed a broad-brush portrait of the changes which have affected the South. But we can choose other vantage points: those staked out by the new protagonists, fully fledged actors in the media and crisis scenarios.

The 1970s were marked by the somewhat superstructural and institutional demand for a new world information order. The following decade, to the contrary, saw in a number of Third World countries, and particularly in Latin America (a much better equipped continent, where mass communication systems are as old as those of the advanced industrialized countries), the appropriation of the most diverse communication technologies by social movements inaugurating new forms of social intervention. A significant chronological lag between North and South must be emphasized here. The 1970s in Europe, and even more so in regions such as Québec, abounded with 'alternative media', free radio, community radio and television, and hand-held video (see eg Duquet, 1980; Raboy, 1984). The ensuing decade saw these practices dwindle with the wave of privatization and the rise of market logic, as well as with the crisis of political representation and the idea of public service. The rupture signified by these so-called decentralized or horizontal communication initiatives was to be found in the discovery of new sites of intervention which had been largely disregarded by traditional organizations: the putting down of roots, the day-to-day, the sense of community. The local dimension as opposed to centralism, the ordinary as opposed to the sensational, and experience as opposed to ideas.

Of course, with the withdrawal of international organizations or of the welfare state from these spheres of activity, the logics of efficiency and profitability projected these initiatives on to another plane than that of the 'alternative' everywhere in the world. Instead, they found they had to take account of market forces. They themselves tended to become players in the market. This does not take away from the essential difference separating the North from the South: in the South, the legitimacy of the new communication networks, whether they are radiophonic, televisual, computerized or simply of the press, originate from the intimate link they weave with the networks of popular organization whose end is solidarity in the face of the harshness of everyday life. And this even if the individualism encouraged by the commercial logic of savage capitalism is more rampant in these countries than in those of the North.

The simple confrontation of two historical experiences where the media played a decisive role is, in this regard, enlightening. Both occurred in Latin America: in Chile of the early 1970s, and Nicaragua of the 1980s (see A. Mattelart, 1980; A. Mattelart, 1986; M. Mattelart, 1986).

As much as the dominant references in the Chilean process were rooted in the traditions of class struggle and political parties, based on long-standing, powerful workers' organizations, so was Sandinistan Nicaragua torn between the logic of war or permanent crisis and the pluralistic logic of democracy, between the reproduction of top-down plans for agitation and propaganda and the inventiveness of new social movements (women's, ethnic and Christian) which replaced narrow avant-gardist notions with the demand for a plurality of democratic subjects. As much as radio, video, popular press experiences abounded in the Nicaragua of the 1980s, so had the Chilean left, to varying degrees, difficulty in understanding changes brought to Chilean society by the new technological environment in which mass culture had become an everyday reference. In effect, it was not until the period of resistance to the dictatorship of General Pinochet that the organizations of civil society took upon themselves – with the help of communication supports such as video cassette recorders, radio and television channels – the reconstruction of the fabric of 'public community sociability' to use the term of a Chilean political scientist (Brunner, 1982). As much as the Chilean left had a hard time detaching itself from a notion of mobilization limited to politics as an answer to the violent offensive from the right (which, on the contrary, anchored its resistance in the needs and interests intimately linked to daily life), so were Nicaraguan popular communication experiences immersed in the experiences of people.

Nicaragua was far less covered on television in Europe (notably in France) than in the United States; after all, was not the US one of the belligerents? If the media are fond of crisis, if they consume it so much and more, they are also selective. Thus, they were very prompt to slot this unprecedented revolution into the thorny dossier of Bolshevism. During the entire Cold War period, was not anti-communism the grid of analysis and presentation of the international situation, eluding the North/South opposition in favour of an East/West rift, metamorphosed into a mythic drama of the confrontation of Good and Evil?

Media love a crisis in which they can set the stage. Thus, in the 1980s, we witnessed in France the flowering of a great humanitarian 'charity business' in North/South relations, which, thanks to massive mailings, sponsors, publicity billboards and advertising spots, played solidarity in the marketplace. 'Buy Product X, and you will participate in the struggle against hunger in the Sahel, you will help a child in Mali, etc.'

With the launching of these new marketable forms of private philanthropy, an appeal to consumers' guilt feelings takes over the appeal to the conscience, and the responsibility of citizens. A sense of urgency and instant action gallop far ahead of the long-term view of permanent crisis. It is the end of political representation of the world.

The culminating point of the North-South conception inscribed in spectacle is the sensational violence and marketing of the Paris–Dakar motor race, denounced by more than 200 French, African and international associations. While medical means in Africa are cruelly lacking (one doctor per 160,000 inhabitants), there are 30 doctors on the race circuit. In a film produced by German television and broadcast in France by *Terre des Hommes*, a wounded competitor is seen being cared for in a local hospital with an operating unit helicptered in. A child who lies in the next bed is ignored by the camera (Bernard, 1990).

At the opposite extreme of these organized eruptions which take the Third World as a setting for great exploits, new decentralized cooperative methods are developing, the carriers of a new rapport between cultures and another conception of aid and urgency. On the fringes of heavy state-to-state procedures, short-circuit forms of mutual help are multiplying, direct exchanges from civil society to civil society, from local community to local community, from non-governmental organization to non-governmental organization.

## The Disarray of the Democrats

### Security as the Way out of the Crisis?

In the 1970s, the notion of crisis became the major reference point for analysing the development of the liberal democracies: for example, the oil crisis, and the rupture of economic and social equilibria. The great industrialized countries trembled.

The opening passage of the Trilateral Commission's 1975 report on the governability of democracies gave a good outline of the extent of the disarray. It was signed by Zbigniew Brzezinski, specialist on eastern bloc problems and future adviser to President Carter on matters of national security:

'Is democracy in crisis? This question is being posed with increasing urgency by some of the leading statesmen of the West, by columnists and scholars, and – if public opinion polls are to be trusted – even by the publics. In some respects, the mood of today is reminiscent of that of the early twenties, when the views of Oswald Spengler regarding "The Decline of the West" were highly popular. This pessimism is echoed, with obvious *Schadenfreude*, by various communist observers, who speak with growing confidence of "the general crisis of capitalism" and who see in it the confirmation of their own theories' (Crozier et al., 1975).

Never has history brought forth in so short a time such a scathing denial of words claiming to outline a futurology. But it is not on this aspect that we wish to dwell at present.

The diagnosis made by the report's three authors confirmed the feeling of going off the rails: democracy is in crisis. It was not a case of a simple 'conjunctural' crisis, but of a fully fledged structural crisis; that is to say, a crisis touching the very form of industrialized societies. The causes of this crisis were clearly identified: 'The more democratic a system is, indeed, the more likely it is to be endangered by intrinsic threats. In recent years, the operations of the democratic process do indeed appear to have generated a breakdown of traditional means of social control, a delegitimation of political and other forms of authority, and an overload of demands on government, exceeding its capacity to respond' (Crozier et al., 1975: 8). Among the agitators were oppositional intellectuals and the media. The intellectuals were reproached for asserting 'their disgust with the corruption, materialism, and inefficiency of democracy' and for denouncing the subservience of governments to monopoly capitalism. The challenge they represented was likened to the one that had been formed in another era by 'the aristocratic cliques, fascist movements, and communist parties' (Crozier et al., 1975: 7).

The charge against the media emphasized first of all the autonomy they had acquired with respect to political and financial power. Their impact on social life was judged harmful in that they appeal to emotion by privileging lived experience, thus preventing genuine analysis of the complex game in which political leaders make their moves. The media's conception of public relations was seen to complicate the making of decisions and, above all, their being put into practice. This led the French sociologist, Michel Crozier, in the chapter on the state of democracy in Western Europe, to conclude: 'Journalists' autonomy does not lead necessarily to transparency and truth but may distort the perception of reality' (Crozier et al., 1975: 36). Let us stress in passing that this way of looking at the media/crisis relationship brings us back to the instrumental conception so prevalent in the 1970s and the preceding years, namely a mechanical idea of the impact of the media, as exercising an effect on public and social life and inducing behaviour.

The report's proposed strategy for suppressing the ill-effects of the excesses of democracy ('so as to prevent its suicide') was to compensate for the failure of traditional forms of social control: 'We have come to recognize that there are potentially desirable limits to economic growth. There are also potentially desirable limits to the indefinite extension of political democracy. Democracy will have a longer life if it has a more balanced existence' (Crozier et al., 1975: 115).

At the same time, many industrial democracies formalized similar concepts of a 'New Internal Order' that attested to the revival of normalization and to the remodelling of state surveillance mechanisms. Astutely seizing the pretext of terrorism, these democracies surreptitiously imposed a concept of the 'enemy within' by overhauling 'internal protection procedures to be applied in time of crisis'. And so, on the old continent, one saw the project of a judicial and policing Europe, the increase in anti-terrorism legislation, the shifts in penal notions of complicity and infraction, the redefinition of the 'suspect', the infringement of the right to a defence, the strengthened controls on identification, the cross-border exchange of police files, the encouragement of denunciation, the home searches, the requisitions, the limits to the right to strike, all forms of control over the movement of people – all endeavours to protect the existing order against the risks 'of a destabilized society, capable of reacting in a disorderly or anarchist fashion', to quote the words of the project for reorganization of territorial security promoted at the time by the French state (University of Vincennes, 1980).

With the revival of growth and the economic and political collapse of the East at the end of the 1980s, certitude replaced disarray: the certitude of holding in exclusivity the keys to democracy, of having replenished it. Democracy has now been accomplished in the West. The other realities, of the East and of the South, offer only signs of its absence and are only suitable for dreaming of an exodus towards the rich industrialized nations, those welcoming lands of human rights and liberty. Faced with the bankruptcy of actually existing socialism, the idea that the triumph of the market resolves the question of democracy rushed in, highly legitimized. Capitalism appears as the best of regimes for lack of a better one, the only one capable not only of managing crises but of managing itself through crisis.

In a 1978 interview on the theme of power, Michel Foucault concisely summarized the image of French intellectuals projected from the past: 'Intellectual and intellectual of the left', he said, 'it is nearly the same thing' (Foucault, 1984). As in many of the European countries, but perhaps more than anywhere else, the history of the intellectuals' position with respect to power was confounded in France with that of critical consciousness, of negative thought. This is, in fact, what Michel Crozier meant when, in his diagnosis of the vulnerability of Western European democracies, he dubbed the intellectuals agitators. He also noted, however, the presence and coming rise in prominence of another less risky type of intellectual, more directly linked to the decision-making process. By conferring raw material status upon knowledge and culture, post-industrial society would undermine the intellectual's relationship with society.

The 1980s would effectively see the rise of 'the professionals of practical knowledge', to paraphrase the words of Sartre. The 1980s would especially see the erosion of critical consciousness and the apparent reconciliation of the traditional intellectual class with the existence of the media. Disengagement? or critical revision of previous positions? The answer is a complex one: it refers us back to the complexity of the crisis of political as well as scientific paradigms which set up the notion of ambiguity as the only certitude of our times (see Mattelart and Mattelart, 1992).

*Humanitarianism as the Way out of the Crisis?*

If we took inventory of the expressions or words most frequently used to depict the organizational crisis of liberal democracies vis-a-vis the temptation of security, we would find 'order', 'authority', 'command', and 'social control', at the top of the list. The preoccupation with order was manifest to such a point that the European communist parties appeared at the time, in these diagnoses set out in the first half of the 1970s, as the only organizations which had evaded – thanks to their concept of authority – the disintegration which had overtaken all other institutions. For the same reason, these communist parties were regarded as being the most likely to profit from this breach in the traditional order and, because of this, they were seen as especially dangerous.

That shows how much the notion of central authority held sway over symbolic references; the actors susceptible of providing a way out of the crisis were states and governments. Little mention of the role of civil society.

On the other hand, at roughly the same period of time, the report written at the request of the French President by Simon Nora and Alain Minc on the computerization of society as a policy for getting out of the crisis placed the accent on the role of civil society: 'Any thought that is given to the computer and society', wrote Nora in the preface, 'reinforces the conviction that the stability of modern civilizations depends on a mixture difficult to achieve, ie blending the increasingly powerful assertion of the prerogatives of the state (even if they are more strictly confined) with the growing impatience with restraint that characterizes modern society. For better or for worse, information processing will be one of the major ingredients of this mixture' (Nora and Minc, 1981: xix).

We got the message: this report on the crisis of French society, published in 1978, but commissioned two years previously, interpreted the theme of communication in a broad sense. The growing overlap of computers and telecommunications, baptised telematics, opened according to the authors 'a radically new horizon, by conveying information, that is to say, power'. From this perspective, communication appeared to be one of the guarantors of a 'new overall mode of social regulation'. Information no longer meant simply what was broadcast by the media, it was understood, in a cybernetic sense, to mean the rules, the proscriptions, the knowledge and the know-how that condition and nurture all human activity.

Claiming that communication technologies play a structuring role, this report proposed an industrial strategy for the development of these basic technologies in a context of reinforced competition on the international market, simultaneously with an approach to policy that might check the loss of social consensus and bring citizens back to adhering to the rules of the social game.

In the face of centuries of 'publicly criticized and secretly sought-after centralization', the network society was heralded in, forecasting more subtle modes of consensus management. The so-called telematics revolution questioned 'an elitist breakdown of power in the long term, that is to say, after all, of knowledge and memory'. It would go on to cause an upheaval in 'the nervous system of organizations and of society as a whole'. For, 'processed communication, and its codes, must recreate an "informational agora" expanded to the size of the modern nation' (Nora and Minc, 1981: 140). But the authors took care to warn: 'An irresponsible promotion of social and cultural aspirations, incompatible with the constraints, would reduce the collective plan to its proper size or would cause a strong reaction on the part of the advocates of sovereign power. . . . In order to make the information society possible, it is necessary to have knowledge but also to have time' (Nora and Minc, 1981: 141). This doubly difficult regulation was supposed to unite state intervention and citizen self-management.

What would become of this report, in the wake of the various policies for dealing with crisis that have succeeded one another since that time? Let us allow Eric Le Boucher, specialist at the newspaper *Le Monde* and co-author of one of the first works to treat the computerization of French society, to reply: 'The Nora–Minc report was written at a time when left-wing values occupied the ideological forefront. It tried out a broad and political vision of development. This is no longer the case today. . . . To say that "the computer is but a tool", as is hammered away by the flatterers of "modernity", is to deliberately brush aside all thought about the tool itself, to not understand that the medium is the message, as McLuhan explained, and to forget that technology fashions civilizations. In short, it is to approve without nuance the spread of the cold media of modernity with no plan' (Le Boucher, 1986; see also Le Boucher and Lorenzi, 1979).

## The Permanent Management of Crisis

### Three Crises, Three Measures

'Television lied to me', protested Guy Sitbon, journalist at *Le Nouvel Observateur*, ascertaining upon his arrival in Bucharest at the end of December 1989 how, through its comments and images broadcast live during the crucial days of the Romanian revolution, French television had given a false version of the respective roles of the army and secret police. His most serious charge concerned the misleading of politicians who, trusting the news images of this first live revolution, prepared to intervene in order to reinforce an army under-equipped in relation to the Securitate. 'It has long been admitted that politics is done on television; must we now resign ourselves as well to the fact that diplomacy and war are decided by optical illusion?', concluded this journalist (Sitbon, 1990).

On the occasion of the Romanian event, television was caught red-handed in imposture, simultaneously placing in a crude light the exorbitant mobilizing capacity of media spectacle and the fragility of professional codes which claim to be impartial. The crisis is not only for others. The rise in the legitimacy of media professionals let it be believed that this group, unlike the intellectuals and the politicians, was beyond reproach. We must accept the obvious fact that this is not so.

The Romanian events took place at precisely the same time as the American marines' military intervention in Panama. But if the media made the public vibrate to the spectacle of a crisis unfolding itself before their eyes, in Bucharest and in Timisoara, the treatment of Panama was not accorded the same status. Certainly, the coinciding of the two events did not favour the second, nor did the high drama of the overthrow of the Ceausescu regime and the popular combat against the tyrant. The fact remains that the false dead of Timisoara eclipsed the many thousand real victims of the bombardment of the civilian neighbourhoods of Panama City.

The passion which nurtured the public's rapport with the media in the Romanian case flowed from the enthusiasm for the epic poem of liberty of which the fall of the Berlin Wall was the first stanza. The East well and truly collapsed, and the event was experienced live. As a result, the memory of Uncle Sam's brutal interventions to re-establish order in his backyard under the pretext of restoring democracy, which could still have been a factor in the past, was well deactivated.

The backyard is now a garden of drugs and the image projected by the media of General Noriega, Panamanian head of state, is that of a master dealer, lynch-pin of the 'Colombian Connection'. The intervention set in motion, under the well-served pretext of protecting United States nationals, legitimized itself once again as a drug-traffic chase. The war on drugs disarms all counts of indictment articulated under principles of international law: national sovereignty, diplomatic immunity, non-interference. The European media and public opinion manifested the consensual value of the combat by accepting naturally, as it were, the legitimacy of this intervention. This same consensual value caused the heads of state of the Group of Seven industrial powers unanimously to declare the priority of the war on drugs, at the Paris Summit in July 1989, in the midst of the bicentennial celebrations of the French Revolution.

But above all, on another level, that of the everyday acceptance of the media, the war on drugs undeniably gathers the force of conviction, simultaneously universal and singular on the theme of drugs, which calls on and establishes communication with audiences' concerns linked to the survival of the human species, physical and mental health, integrity of the person, responsibility of the parent, protection of youth, and to the battle against delinquency and insecurity.

Meanwhile, Latin American public opinion did not read the Panamanian crisis in the same way. It restored to this act its political significance. On the one hand, it interpreted it against the violent historical background of imperial intervention and, on the other, it emphasized the striking contrast with the strategies of negotiation and the acceptance of law coming into their own in the East. Spokesperson for this public opinion, the Mexican writer Carlos Fuentes, cited the anachronism of this operation and judged it with respect to the European aggiornamento: 'European perestroika does not have its counterpart in an American perestroika . . . Gorbachev has renounced the policy of spheres of influence. He has renounced interventionism. Bush has done exactly the opposite' (Fuentes, 1989). The desire to preserve the United States' rights to the Canal, which must be returned to Panama in 1999, was badly hidden under the cover of the moral crusade against drugs.

An anachronism, it is true. Instrumentalization for the short-sighted political ends of an imperial power, also true. But when European opinion vibrates at the collapse of authoritarianism in the East, and condemns outright a general sullied by drugs, it shows that the international consensus is in the process of undergoing profound change.

The rise of great and universal mobilizing themes such as the war on drugs goes hand in hand with the crisis of political representation on the international scene. The post-Yalta context, by moving aside the East/West rift which has defined our geopolitical representations, is setting up what geopoliticians already call 'the new global fronts of order and disorder', fronts which have until now been concealed by the polarization of the Cold War: religious fundamentalism, the rush of migration of refugees and immigrants to the countries of the North, the environment, and the new calamities, such as AIDS and drugs (*World Media*, 1990).

These new fronts are developing on a new world map. The Cold War era was marked by a diet of communication and information nourished by a kind of dialectic between the anti-communist ideology of the 'free world' and the holding back of information, the politics of secrecy behind the iron curtain. Here, saturation: there, scarcity.

Towards the year 2000, new signs of power are making themselves felt, transforming the nature of international confrontations. These are now played out in the mastery of exchange. Financial exchange, cultural exchange, the exchange of knowledge and know-how.

But history held in store for us a crisis of a kind that nobody had foreseen. The obsession with a new oil crisis was revived in August 1990. Obsessed with looking for a way out of the economic crisis, the great industrial countries placed all their stakes on the high technologies of information and communication during the 1980s. The way out of the crisis would be technological or not at all, or so it was said. The advent of the 'information society' would consecrate the decline of traditional forms of energy. The new raw material would be 'information', and it would preside over a new division of the planet between 'data-poor' and 'data-rich'. Everything could be measured according to the yardstick of information, to such an extent that these same industrial powers gave up their political representation of the world, relying on, as we have also seen, the metaphysics of East versus West. On the international horizon loomed a 'commercial war' between the three players in the new world economy: Europe, the United States and Japan.

Then, all of a sudden, a major political crisis launched by a middle-sized regional power, Iraq, undermined the infatuation: oil still plays a determining role in the balance of hegemonies. The battle over oil is still a central stake of the world economy. In passing, the rise of resentment with respect to the West recalls that not all inhabitants of the planet recognize themselves in this globalization of the modernity of the rich by means of the market: this modernity with no design, carrier of new sources of exclusion.

Paradoxically, the Gulf events thrust information into the front row of crisis logistics. From the beginning of the conflict, the American cable television network CNN (Cable News Network), became the principal line of communication between the antagonists. Live broadcasting caused national authorities to lose control of the flow of information and delegitimized old-fashioned secret diplomacy and its intelligence networks.

But have the real stakes of conflict become any less opaque? Nothing is less sure, unless one confuses transparency with the fluidity of exchange. One thing is nonetheless certain: the emotional pressure of images is modifying the political decision-making process. Massive audience intervention by way of the television screen has become a strategic item of war in the postmodern age.

The pioneer of the sensationalist press, William Randolph Hearst, saw it clearly. In his crusade for American intervention in the island of Cuba, then a Spanish possession, he despatched a reporter to Havana in 1897. The reporter sent him the following telegram: 'Everything is quiet. There is no trouble here. There will be no war. Wish to return.' To which the great press baron replied: 'Please remain. You furnish the pictures and I'll furnish the war' (cited in Julien, 1968: 65).

## The Professionalization of Anti-crisis

Adam Smith evoked the invisible hand of the market. The visible hand of the state was its counterpart for a long time. In the 1980s, it became possible to speak of the *visible* hand of the market, as market logic eclipsed the logic of public intervention. In the process, business values began to occupy a central place in the social and economic redeployment of our societies. Enterprise ideology took over the social body as a whole. The references that constituted the welfare state – public service, the constraining pressure of social forces, the corresponding modes of intervention – entered into crisis.

The new hegemonic role of business constitutes a new given everywhere in the world. It is inconceivable without high visibility. What has changed is, first of all, the relationship of business and the media, and the resulting mediatization of business' image and of its acts. Following this is the way in which it has integrated a complex apparatus of communication in to its system of management. Communication has come to the rescue of the crisis of Taylorist business, marked by a top-down organization and productivist structure in which information circulated poorly. The new enterprise is that of the flow of communication, communication as a tool of management. Therein lies the key to the new relationship of media, crisis and business. In the range of communication services now on offer, a new type of expertise has achieved social and professional legitimacy: crisis communication, or communication in a hostile environment. Four successive waves of events, or 'hostilities', have helped in its construction during the last 20 years.

The first alarm which would make business react and oblige it to readjust its communication strategies in the event of hard blows was that of the 'terrorist threat'. It started at the beginning of the 1970s. In plain language, it was a matter of responding to kidnappings by urban guerillas of senior executives of American multinational firms. IBM went so far as to distribute among its managers a course drafted along with the International Association of Chiefs of Police, with the eloquent title: 'Security: A New Style of Management' (*Berkeley Barb*, 1974; see also Mattelart and Mattelart, 1979).

Still in the 1970s, a particularly fertile time of strife, other more 'civil' events led the multinationals to re-evaluate their public relations policies: most notably, the accusations against the marketing policies of the food and drug companies levelled by non-governmental organizations and various agencies of the United Nations. These accusations led to the elaboration of codes of conduct by these large corporations. It was here that the old concept of 'public relations' turned into 'public affairs', and that the communication practice known as 'lobbying' made a qualitative leap into professionalism.

The third jolt came from financial deregulation which ushered in an era of mergers and acquisitions. These occurred to such a point that by the end of the 1970s, the PPO or 'public purchase offer' – and particularly the hostile or wildcat PPO, or raid – became in the United States the symbol of the crisis: the PPO as financial and psychological warfare. Companies elaborated communication scenarios both to prey on victims as well as to defend themselves from the predators. Media campaigns accompanied strategies to destabilize the adversary and any publicity stunt was permissible regardless of the manipulation involved.

The fourth event: the emergence of 'major technological risk': pollution, explosion, shipwreck (Lagadec, 1988). The 1970s were marked by such warnings as the chemical accident at Seveso in Italy (1976), the nuclear catastrophe of Three Mile Island in the United States (1979), and the derailing of the train containing chemical products at Mississaugua in Canada (1979). In the 1980s, the concept of 'major technological risk' continued to take shape. The Mexico City catastrophe (explosion of a gas stockpile site and generalized fire in a densely populated area in 1984); the toxic cloud of Bhopal (India) which, early in 1985, caused more than 2300 deaths and more than 6000 wounded, and cost the third largest American chemical group, Union Carbide, more than a third of its business (Shrivastava, 1987); the in-flight explosion of the Challenger space-shuttle in 1986; Chernobyl; the discharge of toxic products into the Rhine following a fire at the Sandoz warehouse in Basle (Switzerland), and all the shipwrecks which followed that of the Amoco-Cadiz (1978) off the shores of Brittany.

All of these events, most of which were highly mediatized, precipitated reflection on the means of crisis management; not just superficially, but also profoundly, that is to say by turning it into an essential element of business management itself. Through these crises, something obvious gradually took shape: the structural incapacity of organizations to cope with the unforeseen. The proposed solution: not only to endow oneself with mechanisms of communication for times of crisis, but also to think in terms of crisis and destabilization in time of peace. As noted the man in charge of creating a new external relations department for the Sandoz firm after the Basle accident: 'We must develop a cybernetic perception of public relations. To do so, businesses have the duty to reflect on their culture, their communication ethic or the choice of their communicators in time of peace' (Lagadec, 1988: 133).

Seen in this systemic light, business is dealt with as an extremely complex interactive system evolving in an increasingly shifting environment, which is what makes one expert on management strategies conclude: 'Management is becoming an art and a practice which consists of managing the irrational on the inside and the unforeseeable on the outside' (Vincent, 1990).

In keeping with the new domination of exchange, business cannot cease communication. Its image is its capital, communication is its identity.

Here we are far from the crisis of the 1970s when the notion of crisis awakened, at the same time, the guilt feelings of those who had to resolve it and the reflex of self-protection by information blackout.

Here we are, in effect, far from the time when crisis was seen as touching the very foundations of the system, affecting the legitimacy of its political forms and its economic regime. With the rise of the cybernetic vision, the idea of crisis becomes increasingly linked to the functioning of the system, while going through occasional mutation and in perpetual readjustment.

The strategies set up to resolve it increasingly proclaim their transparency. It is by virtue of this that they hook up with the engineering of communication. In return, what becomes increasingly opaque, with the new legitimacy conferred on market values, is the model of development and growth on which these crises thrive – a model which is quite banally accepted as the best by default, as no one will take the risk of thinking of another one.

## Note

This chapter has been adapted from the inaugural lecture at the 'Media and Crisis' conference, Laval University, Québec, 4 October 1990 – ed.)

# References

*Actuel* (1986) (Paris) Interview with Daniel Cohn-Bendit, December.

Adams, W.C. (1986) 'Whose Lives Count? TV Coverage of Natural Disasters', *Journal of Communication*, Spring: 105–12.

Adamus, A. (1985) *Zanim byl Sierpien*. Wroclaw: KAW.

Althusser, L. (1971) 'Ideology and Ideological State Apparatuses', in *Lenin and Philosophy and Other Essays*. New York: Monthly Review Press, pp. 127–86.

*Analisis* (1990) Centro de investigacion y educacion popular (CINEP) (Bogota). Special issue, No. 60.

Audley, P. (1983) *Canada's Cultural Industries*. Toronto: James Lorimer.

Bagdikian, B. (1990) *The Media Monopoly* (3rd edn.). Boston: Beacon Press.

Bagnall, J. (1989) 'Killings Reveal Violence against Women Deeply Ingrained', *Montreal Gazette*, 16 December.

Baker, R.K. and Ball, S.J. (1969) *Mass Media and Violence*. Report of the Task Force on Mass Media and Violence to the National Commission on the Causes and Prevention of Violence. Washington: US Government Printing Office.

Barthes, R. (1968) 'L'écriture de l'évènement', *Communications*, 12.

Barthes, R. (1972) *Mythologies*. New York: Hill and Wang.

Bassiouni, M.C. (1981) 'Terrorism, Law Enforcement, and the Mass Media: Perspectives, Problems, Proposals', *Journal of Criminal Law and Criminology*, 72(1).

Bassiouni, M.C. (1982) 'Media Coverage of Terrorism: The Law and the Public', *Journal of Communication*, 33(2): 128–43.

Bauch, H. (1989) 'Wounded', *Montreal Gazette*, 9 December.

Baudrillard, J. (1991) *La guerre du Golfe n'a pas eu lieu*. Paris: Galilée.

Beauchamp, C. (1987) *Le silence des médias: les femmes, les hommes et l'information*. Montreal: Remue-ménage.

Beniger, J. (1986) *The Control Revolution*. Cambridge, MA: Harvard University Press.

Bérard, S. (1991) 'Words and Deeds', in L. Malette and M. Chalouh (eds), *The Montreal Massacre*. Charlottetown: Gynergy Books, pp. 75–81.

*Berkeley Barb* (1974) 'The IBM Papers', 22–8 November.

Bernard, M. (1990) *Paris–Dakar: pas d'accord*. Lyon: Edition Silence.

Beuve-Méry, H. (1980) *Freedom and Responsibility of Journalists*. CIC document no. 90ter. Paris: UNESCO.

Bialecki, I. (1987) 'What the Poles Thought in 1981', in J. Koralewicz, I. Bialecki and M. Watson (eds), *Crisis and Transition: Polish Society in the 1980s*. New York: Berg.

Black, G. (1990) 'A Myth that Lets Butchers off the Hook', *Los Angeles Times*, 10 June.

Bloor, D. (1977) *Knowledge and Social Inquiry*. London: Routledge & Kegan Paul.

Blumler, J.G. (1985) 'The Social Character of Media Gratifications', in K.E. Rosengren, L.A. Wenner and P. Palmgreen (eds), *Media Gratifications Research: Current Perspectives*. Beverly Hills, London and New Delhi: Sage.

Bordewich, F.M. (1977) 'Supermarketing the Newspaper', *Columbia Journalism Review*, 16(3): 24–30.

Bowles, S., and Gintis, H. (1986) *Democracy and Capitalism*. New York: Basic Books.

Brooks, J. (1986) 'Popular and Public Values in the Soviet Press 1921–28'. Paper presented at the Conference on Popular Culture – East and West: Approaches and Theoretical Perspectives, Bloomington.

Bruck, P.A. (1989a) 'Strategies for Peace, Strategies for News Research', *Journal of Communication*, 39(1): 108–29.

Bruck, P.A. (1989b) 'Lesern gehen die Augen auf: Die Gesundheitsanstalt – ausgepackt und enthuellt', *Medien Journal*, 13(4): 140–48.

Bruck, P.A. (forthcoming) 'Tabloid Formats and Reader Address', in P. Dahlgren and C. Sparks (eds), *Journalism and Popular Culture*. London: Sage.

Bruck, P.A. and Raboy, M. (1989) 'The Challenge of Democratic Communication', in M. Raboy and P.A. Bruck (eds), *Communication for and against Democracy*. Montreal: Black Rose Books, pp. 3–16.

Brunner, J.J. (1982) 'La vie quotidienne en régime autoritaire', *Amérique latine* (Paris), October–December.

Brzezinski, Z. (1989) *The Grand Failure: The Birth and Death of Communism in the Twentieth Century*. New York: Scribner.

Bunce, R. (1977) *Television in the Corporate Interest*. New York: Praeger.

Bunyan, J. and Fisher, H.H. (eds) (1934) *The Bolshevik Revolution, 1917–1918. Documents and Materials*. Stanford: Stanford University Press.

Burke, K. (1962) *A Grammar of Motives and a Rhetoric of Motives*. Cleveland: Meridian.

Burnham, J. (1941) *The Managerial Revolution* (reprint). Bloomington: Indiana University Press (1960).

Camus, A. (1955) *The Myth of Sisyphus*. New York: Random House.

Carey, J.W. (1986) 'The Dark Continent of American Journalism', in R.K. Manoff and M. Schudson (eds), *Reading the News*. New York: Pantheon, pp. 146–96.

Carey, J.W. (1989a) 'A Cultural Approach to Communication', in J.W. Carey, *Communication as Culture: Essays on Media and Society*. Boston: Unwin Hyman, pp. 13–36.

Carey, J.W. (1989b) 'Reconceiving "Mass" and "Media"', in J.W. Carey, *Communication as Culture: Essays on Media and Society*. Boston: Unwin Hyman, pp. 69–88.

Chafee, Z., Jr (1942) *Free Speech in the United States*. Cambridge, MA: Harvard University Press.

Chomsky, N. (1989) *Necessary Illusions*. Boston: South End Press.

Cleaver, H. (1991) *The Political Economy of the Persian Gulf Crisis*. Austin: Pamphlet Press.

Cohen, C. (1987) 'Sex and Death in the Rational World of Defense Intellectuals', *Signs*, 12(4): 687–718.

Cohen, J. and Rogers, J. (1983). *On Democracy*. London and Baltimore: Penguin Books.

Comstock, G.A., Rubinstein, E.A. and Murray, J.P. (eds) (1972) *Television and Social Behavior*. Report to the Scientific Advisory Committee. Washington: US Government Printing Office.

Côté, R. (1990) *Manifeste d'un salaud*. Montreal: Editions du Portique.

Crozier, M., Huntington, S.P. and Watanuki, J. (1975) *The Crisis of Democracy. Report on the Governability of Democracies to the Trilateral Commission*. New York: New York University Press.

Curry, J.L. (1988) 'Glasnost: Words Spoken and Words Heard'. Paper presented at the Kennan Institute's Conference on the Gorbachev Reform Program, 20–22 March.

Dagenais, B. (1989) 'Octobre 1970: Le discours social et les médias', *Communication/Information*, 10(2–3): 147–73.

Dagenais, B. (1990) *La crise d'octobre 1970 et les médias: un miroir à dix faces*. Montreal: VLB Éditeur.

Dahlgren, P. (1987) 'Ideology and Information in the Public Sphere', in J.D. Slack et al. (eds), *The Ideology of the Information Age*. Norwood: Ablex Publishing Co.

Dahrendorf, R. (1988) 'Citizenship and the Modern Social Conflict', in R. Holme and M. Elliott (eds), *1688–1988. Time for a New Constitution*. Basingstoke: Macmillan.

DeBoer, C. (1979) 'The Polls: Terrorism and Hijacking', *Public Opinion Quarterly*, 43 (Fall): 410–18.

Debord, G. (1983) *Society of the Spectacle*. Detroit: Black & Red.

Debord, G. (1990) *Comments on 'The Society of the Spectacle'*. Trans. by Malcolm Imrie. London: Verso.

# References

de Grotius, H. (1925) *De jure belli ac pacis libri tres. Prolegomena.* (Originally publishe 1625.) Oxford: Clarendon Press.

de Maistre, J.M. (1830) *Du Pape.* Lyon: Rusand.

de Rudder, C. (1991) 'La grande manipulation', *Le Nouvel Observateur*, 6–12 June: 4–9.

Dicey, A.V. (1885) *Introduction to the Study of the Law of the Constitution.* London: Macmillan.

Dionne, E., Jr (1990) '"Defense Intellectuals" in a New World Order: Rand Analysts Rethink the Study of Conflict', *The Washington Post*, 29 May.

Donahue, J. (1989) 'Shortchanging the Viewer', Washington: Essential Information.

Doyal, L. (1979) *The Political Economy of Health.* London: Pluto Press.

Duquet, A.M. (1980) *Vidéo au poing.* Paris: Hachette.

Edwardson, M. (1986) 'FCC Changes Cut Public's Access to News,' *The Miami News*, 2 September.

Émond, A. (1990) 'Poly: là où le bât blesse', *Le Devoir*, 12 December.

Entman, R. (1989) *Democracy without Citizens.* New York: Oxford University Press.

Ericson, R.V., Baranek, P.M. and Chan, J.B.L. (1987) *Visualizing Deviance: A Study of News Organizations.* Toronto: University of Toronto Press.

Ericson, R.V., Baranek, P.M. and Chan, J.B.L. (1989) *Negotiating Control: A Study of News Sources.* Toronto: University of Toronto Press.

Erikson, K. (1977) *Everything in its Path.* New York: Touchstone Books.

FAIR (1989) *Expose of 'Nightline'.* New York.

FAIR (1990) *Critique of MacNeil–Lehrer News Hour.* New York.

FAIR (1991) Press Release on Gulf War Coverage. New York.

Fiske, J. and Hartley, J. (1978) *Reading Television.* New York: Methuen.

Foucault, M. (1984) 'Du pouvoir' (Interview) *L'Express* (Paris), 6–12 July.

Fournier, L. (1982) *FLQ: histoire d'un movement clandestin.* Montreal: Québec-Amérique.

France (1978) Loi no 78–17 du 6 janvier 1978 relative à l'informatique, aux fichiers et aux libertés.

Fuentes, C. (1989) 'Las lecciones de Panama', *El Pais* (Madrid), 24 December.

Fukuyama, F. (1989) 'The End of History?', *The National Interest* (Summer), pp 3–18.

Garfinkel, H. (1967) *Studies in Ethnomethodology.* Englewood Cliffs: Prentice-Hall.

Garnham, N. (1989) 'The Media and the Public Sphere. Part 2'. Paper presented to the Conference on Habermas and the Public Sphere, University of North Carolina at Chapel Hill, 8–10 September.

Gartner, R. (1990) 'The Victims of Homicide: A Temporal and Cross-Cultural Comparison', *American Sociological Review*, 55: 92–106.

Gerbner, G. (1988) 'Violence and Terror in the Mass Media', in *Reports and Papers in Mass Communication*, 102. Paris. Unesco.

Gerbner, G. (1991) 'The Politics of Media Violence: Some Reflections', in C. Hamelink and O. Linne (eds), *Mass Communication Research: On Problems and Policies.* Norwood: Ablex

Gerbner, G., Gross, L., Morgan, M. and Signorielli, N. (1982) 'Charting the Mainstream: Television's Contributions to Political Orientations'. *Journal of Communication*, 32(2): 100–126.

Gerbner, G., Gross, L., Morgan, M. and Signorielli, N. (1986a) *Television's Mean World: Violence Profile, No. 14–15.* Annenberg School of Communications, University of Pennsylvania.

Gerbner, G., Gross, L., Morgan, M. and Signorielli, N. (1986b) 'Living with Television: The Dynamics of the Cultivation Process', in J. Bryant and D. Zillman (eds), *Perspectives on Media Effects.* Hillsdale: Lawrence Erlbaum Associates Inc

Gerth, H.H. and Mills, C.W. (1953) *Character and Social Structure: The Problem of Institutions.* New York: Harcourt and Brace.

Gitlin, T. (1980) *The Whole World is Watching: Mass Media in the Making and Unmaking of the New Left*, Berkeley: University of California Press.

Gitlin, T. (1983) *Inside Prime Time.* New York: Pantheon.

Gitlin, T. (1990) 'Who Communicates What to Whom, in What Voice and Why, About the Study of Communications?', *Critical Studies in Mass Communication*, 7: 185–96.

Glasgow University Media Group (1976) *Bad News*. London: Routledge & Kegan Paul.

Glasgow University Media Group (1980) *Really Bad News*. London: Routledge & Kegan Paul.

Glasgow University Media Group (1982) *More Bad News*. London: Writers and Readers.

Glasgow University Media Group (1985) *War and Peace News*. London: Open University.

Goffman, E. (1974) *Frame Analysis*. New York: Harper and Row.

Goldblatt, M. (1988) 'Canadian Tabloids Mushroom', *Content*, September–October: 28–9.

Gould, S.J. (1981) *The Mismeasure of Man*. New York: W.W. Norton.

Gramsci, A. (1930) 'State and Civil Society', in Q. Hoare and G.N. Smith (eds), *Selections from the Prison Notebooks*. New York: International Publishers (1971), pp. 210–76.

Gross, L.Z. (1959) *Symposium on Sociological Theory*. New York: Harper and Row.

Habermas, J. (1975) *Legitimation Crisis*. Boston: Beacon Press.

Habermas, J. (1985) 'Modernity – An Incomplete Project', in H. Foster (ed.), *Postmodern Culture*. London and Sydney: Pluto Press, pp. 3–15.

Hall, S. (1977) 'Culture, the Media, and the "Ideological Effect"', in J. Curran, M. Gurevitch and J. Woollacott (eds), *Mass Communication and Society*. London: Edward Arnold, pp. 315–48.

Hall, S. (1980) 'Encoding and Decoding in the Television Discourse', in S. Hall, D. Hobson, A. Lowe and P. Willis (eds), *Culture, Media, Language*. London: Hutchinson, pp. 128–38.

Hallin, D.C. and Mancini, P. (1991) 'Summits and the Constitution of an International Public Sphere: The Reagan–Gorbachev Meetings as Televised Media Events', *Communication*, 12(4): 249–66.

Halloran, J.D. (1977) 'Violence and its Causes', Leicester: Centre for Mass Communication Research.

Hankiss, E. (1990) 'In Search of a Paradigm', *Daedalus*, 119(1): 183–214.

Harden, I. and Lewis, N. (1986) *The Noble Lie. The British Constitution and the Rule of Law*. London: Hutchinson.

Harris, C. (1991) '"CNN Owned Baghdad": News Network Scoops Rivals in US, Canada', *Globe and Mail*, 18 January.

Harvey, D. (1989) *The Condition of Postmodernity*. London: Blackwell.

Held, D. (1987) *Models of Democracy*. London: Polity Press.

Heritage, J. (1985) 'Analysing News Interviews: Aspects of the Production of Talk for an Overhearing Audience', in T.A. van Dijk (ed.), *Handbook of Discourse Analysis*. London: Academic Press.

Herman, E. and Chomsky, N. (1988) *Manufacturing Consent*. New York: Pantheon.

Hertsgaard, M. (1988) *On Bended Knee*. New York: Farrar, Straus, and Giroux.

Hesse, M. (1966) *Models and Analogies in Science*. South Bend: Notre Dame Press.

Hofstadter, R. (1944) *Social Darwinism in American Thought*. Boston: Beacon.

Horkheimer, M. and Adorno, T.W. (1972) *Dialectic of Enlightenment*. New York: Seabury Press.

Horowitz, R. (1989). *The Irony of Regulatory Reform*. New York: Oxford University Press.

Jakubowicz, K. (1985) 'Mass (?) Communication (?). As Contemporary Broadcasting Evolves, Both Terms are Acquiring Quite New Meanings', *Gazette*, 36(1): 39–53.

Jakubowicz, K. (1987) 'Democratizing Communication in Eastern Europe', *InterMedia*, 15 (3): 34–9.

Jakubowicz, K. (1989) 'Political and Economic Dimensions of Television Programme Exchange between Poland and Western Europe', in J. Becker and T. Szecsko (eds), *Europe Speaks to Europe*. London: Pergamon Press.

Jakubowicz, K. (1990a) 'Media and Culture in the Information Society', *Gazette*, 45(2): 71–88.

Jakubowicz, K. (1990b) 'Musical Chairs?: The Three Public Spheres of Poland', *Media, Culture and Society*, 12(2): 195–212.

# References

Jakubowicz, K. (1990c) '"Solidarity" and Media Reform in Poland', *European Journal Communication*, 5(2–3): 333–53.

Jansen, S.C. (1988) 'The Ghost in the Machine: Artificial Intelligence and Gendered Thought Patterns', *Resources for Feminist Research*, 17(4).

Jansen, S.C. (1990) *Censorship: The Knot that Binds Power and Knowledge*. New York: Oxford University Press.

Jerdan, W. (1866) *Men I Have Known*. London.

Johnson, O. (1988) 'The Historical Perspective in the American Study of Soviet Mass Communications'. Paper presented at the 16th Congress of the International Association for Mass Communication Research, Barcelona, July.

Julien, C. (1968) *L'Empire américain*. Paris: Grasset.

Keane, J. (1988) *Democracy and Civil Society*. London: Verso.

Keane, J. (1990) 'Decade of the Citizen' (Interview), *The Guardian*, 1 August.

Keane, J. (1991) *The Media and Democracy*. London: Polity Press and Basil Blackwell Inc.

Kellner, D. (1981) 'Network Television and American Capitalism,' *Theory and Society*, 10(1): 31–62.

Kellner, D. (1989) *Critical Theory, Marxism and Modernity*. Baltimore: Johns Hopkins University Press.

Kellner, D. (1990) *Television and the Crisis of Democracy*. Boulder: Westview Press.

Kellner, D. (forthcoming) *Chronicles of a Television War. Technowar in the Persian Gulf*.

Knight, G. (1989) 'The Reality Effects of Tabloid Television News', in M. Raboy and P.A. Bruck (eds), *Communication for and against Democracy*. Montreal: Black Rose Books, pp. 111–29.

Knight, G. and Dean, T. (1982) 'Myth and the Structure of News', *Journal of Communication*, 32(2): 144–61.

Kolakowski, L. (1989) 'On Total Control and its Contradictions: The Power of Information', *Encounter*, July–August.

'Komunikowanie masowe w Polsce. Proba bilansu lat siedemdziesiatych' (1981) *Zeszyty Prasoznawcze*, 1.

Koralewicz, J. (1987) 'Changes in Polish Social Consciousness during the 1970s and 1980s: Idealism and Identity', in J. Koralewicz, I. Bialecki and M. Watson (eds), *Crisis and Transition: Polish Society in the 1980s*. New York: Berg.

Labedz, K. (1988) 'Prasa NSZZ "Solidarnosc" w latach 1980–1981', *Zeszyty Prasoznawcze*, 4.

Lagadec, P. (1988) *Etats d'urgence. Défaillances technologiques et déstabilisation sociale*. Paris: Seuil.

Lakoff, G. and Johnson, M. (1980) *Metaphors We Live by*. Chicago: University of Chicago Press.

Lapham, L. (1991) 'Trained Seals and Sitting Ducks', *Harper's*, May: 10–15.

*La Presse* (Tunis) (1989) 'Rocard: L'absence de démocratie est un frein au développement', 5 November.

Lash, S. and Urry, J. (1987) *The End of Organized Capitalism*. Cambridge: Polity Press.

Le Boucher, E. (1986) 'Le média froid de la modernité', *Le Monde*, 7 January.

Le Boucher, E. and Lorenzi, H. (1979) *Mémoires volées*. Paris: Ramsay.

*Le Devoir* (1990) 'Des journalistes jugent la couverture des médias lors de la tuerie à Polytechnique', 29 January.

Legault, M. (1990) 'Recherche et réflexion sur le discours de la presse quotidienne face à la violence faite aux femmes à partir de la tragédie de l'École Polytechnique', Laval University, Quebec.

*Le Monde* (1989) '"Pas de démocratie sans développement"', 16 December.

*Le Monde* (1990) 'M. Rocard critique l'information télévisée', 23 August.

*Le Monde Diplomatique* (1991) 'Médias, sociétés et démocratie', Dossier, May: 11–18.

Le Net, M. (1981) *L'État annonceur: techniques, doctrine et morale de la communication sociale*. Paris: Les Editions de l'organisation.

Le Net, M. (1985) *La communication gouvernementale*. Paris: Les Editions de l'Institut de la communication sociale.

kning: Copenhagen, June.

*Oxford English Dictionary* (1971) Compact Edition. Oxford: Oxford University Press.

Paletz, D.L. and Dunn, R. (1969) 'Press Coverage of Civil Disorders: A Case Study of Winston-Salem,' *Public Opinion Quarterly*, 33(3): 328–45.

Paletz, D.L., Fozzard, P.A. and Ayanian, J.Z. (1982) 'The IRA, the Red Brigades and the FALN in *The New York Times*,' *Journal of Communication*, 32(2): 162–71.

Palmgreen, P., Wenner, L.A. and Rosengren, K.E. (1985) 'Uses and Gratifications Charlottetown: Gynergy Books.

Martindale, D. (1960) *The Nature and Types of Sociological Theory*. Boston: Houghton Mifflin.

Mattelart, A. (1979) *Multinational Corporations and the Control of Culture*. Hassocks (Sussex): Harvester Press.

Mattelart, A. (1980) *Mass Media, Ideologies and the Revolutionary Movement*. Hassocks (Sussex): Harvester Press.

Mattelart, A. (ed.) (1986) *Communicating in Popular Nicaragua*. New York: International General.

Mattelart, A. and Mattelart, M. (1979) *De l'usage des médias en temps de crise*. Paris: Alain Moreau.

Mattelart, A. and Mattelart, M. (1990) 'Des nouveaux usages des médias en temps de crise.' Inaugural lecture to the Media and Crisis Conference, Laval University, Quebec, 4–6 October.

Mattelart, A. and Mattelart, M. (1992) *Re-Thinking the Media*. Trans. by J. Cohen and M. Urquidi. Minneapolis: University of Minnesota Press.

Mattelart, M. (1986) *Women, Media and Crisis*. London: Comedia/Routledge.

*Media, Culture and Society* (1991) 'Postmodernism'. Theme issue, 13(1).

Meinecke, F. (1957) *Machiavellism: The Doctrine of Raison d'État and its Place in Modern History*. New Haven: Yale University Press.

Meyrowitz, J. (1985) *Non Sense of Place: The Impact of Electronic Media on Social Behavior*. New York and Oxford: Oxford University Press.

Michnik, A. (1990) 'The Two Faces of Europe', *The New York Review of Books*, December.

Mickolus, E.F. (1980) *Transnational Terrorism: A Chronology of Events, 1968–1979*. Westport: Greenwood Press.

Miège, B. et al. (1986) *Le JT: Mise en scène de l'actualité à la télévision*. Paris: La Documentation française.

Milburn, M.A., Bowley, C., Fay-Dumaine, J. and Kennedy, D.A. (1987) 'An Attributional Analysis of the Media Coverage of Terrorism'. Paper presented at the 10th Annual Meeting of the International Society of Political Psychology, San Francisco, July 6.

Morin, E. (1968) 'Pour une sociologie de la crise', *Communications*, 12: 2–16.

Morin, E. (1976) 'Pour une crisologie', *Communications*, 25: 149–63.

Morrow, F. (1985) 'The US Power Structure and the Mass Media'. Unpublished PhD dissertation, University of Texas.

Mrozowski, M. (1987) 'Ideological Clash in Polish Television', *Media Development*, 2.

Munro, R. (1990) 'Who Died in Beijing and Why,' *The Nation*, 11 June.

Negt, O. and Kluge, A. (1972) *Oeffentlichkeit und Erfahrung*. Frankfurt: Suhrkamp.

Nora, S. and Minc, A. (1981) *The Computerization of Society*. Cambridge, MA: MIT Press.

*Nowe Drogi* (Warsaw) (1983) Special issue.

Offe, C. (1984) '"Crisis of Crisis Management": Elements of a Political Crisis Theory', in *Contradictions of the Welfare State*, Cambridge, MA: MIT Press, pp. 35–64.

Oledzki, J. (1984) 'Towards the Democratization of Mass Communication'. Paper presented at the 14th Congress of the International Association for Mass Communication Research, Prague.

Onyegin, N. (1986) 'Construction of the "Facts" of Political Violence: A Content Analysis of Press Coverage.' Unpublished MA thesis, University of Pennsylvania.

Ossowski, S. (1967) 'O osobliwosciach nauk spolecznych', *Dziela*, PWN, Warsaw.

Ougaard, M. (1990) 'The Internationalisation of Civil Society'. Center for Udviklingsfors-

*Le Temps* (Tunis) (1989) 'La Tunisie est résolue à gagner le pari de la démocratie', 5 November.

*L'Évènement du jeudi* (1991) 'Le procès des journalistes'. (Paris) 2–8 May, p. 50–52.

Levy, L. (1985) *Emergence of a Free Press*. New York and Oxford: Oxford University Press.

Lewis, A. (1991) 'To see ourselves . . .', *The New York Times*, 6 May.

Lippmann, W. (1922) *Public Opinion* (reprint). New York: Macmillan (1957).

Malette, L. and Chalouh, M. (1991) *The Montreal Massacre*. Trans. by Marlene Wildeman. Research: The Past Ten Years', in K.E. Rosengren et al. (eds), *Media Gratifications Research: Current Perspectives*. Beverly Hills, London and New Delhi: Sage.

Parenti, M. (1986) *Inventing Reality: The Politics of the Mass Media*. New York: St Martin's Press.

Parsons, T. (1966) *Societies: Evolutionary and Comparative Perspectives*. Englewood Cliffs: Prentice-Hall.

Passent, D. (1990) 'Do ostatniego slowa', *Polityka* 1.

Pearl, D., Bouthilet, L. and Lazar, J. (eds) (1982) *Television and Behavior: Ten Years of Scientific Progress and Implications for the Eighties*. Rockville: National Institute of Mental Health.

Pêcheux, M. (1988) 'Discourse: Structure or Event?', in C. Nelson and L. Grossberg (eds), *Marxism and the Interpretation of Culture*. Urbana: University of Illinois Press, pp. 633–50.

Perigoe, R. (1990) 'The Media and Minorities', *Content* (September–October): 10–13.

Phillips, D.P. and Hensley, J.E. (1984) 'When Violence Is Rewarded or Punished: The Impact of Mass Media Stories on Homicide', *Journal of Communication*, 34(3): 101–16.

Philpot, R. (1991) *Oka: dernier alibi du Canada anglais*. Montreal: VLB Editeur.

Pisarek, W. (1978) *Prasa – chleb nasz powszedni*. Wroclaw: Ossolineum.

Pisarek, W. (1988) 'Communication for Development: Four Strategies in the People's Poland'. Mimeo.

Pozzo di Borgo, O. (ed.) (1964) *Ecrits et discours politiques*. Paris.

Raboy, M. (1984) *Movements and Messages: Media and Radical Politics in Quebec*. Toronto: Between The Lines.

Raboy, M. (1990a) *Missed Opportunities: The Story of Canada's Broadcasting Policy*. Montreal and Kingston: McGill-Queen's University Press.

Raboy, M. (1990b) 'Pourquoi avoir publié de tels propos?', *Le Devoir*, 10 April.

Raboy, M. (1990c) 'Crise des médias, crises de société: les femmes, les hommes et l'École Polytechnique de Montréal'. Paper presented to the Media and Crisis Conference, Laval University, Quebec, 4–6 October.

Raboy, M., and Bruck, P.A. (eds.) (1989) *Communication for and against Democracy*. Montreal: Black Rose Books.

Raina, P. (1981) *Independent Social Movements in Poland*. London: London School of Economics and Political Science.

Ramonet, I. (1991) 'La télévision loin des fronts', *Le Monde diplomatique*, February.

Raphals, P. (1990) 'Mohawks Rouse the Captive Nations', *The Nation*, 15 October: 413–16.

*Raport o stanie komunikacji spolecznej (sierpien 1980 – 13 grudnia 1981)* (1982). Krakow: Osrodek Badan Prasoznawczych.

Reuillard, V. (1990) 'L'usage des médias en période de crise'. Laval University, Quebec.

Rorty, R. (1986) 'The Contingency of Language', *London Review of Books*, 17 (17 April): 3–6.

Rowan, F. (1984) *Broadcast Fairness*. New York: Longman.

Roy, M. (1970) 'Les médias d'information et le terrorisme', *L'Actualité*, November.

Ryan, C. (1971) *'Le Devoir' et la crise d'octobre 1970*. Montreal: Leméac.

Said, E.W. (1979) *Orientalism*. New York: Vintage Books.

Said, E.W. (1981) *Covering Islam: How the Media and the Experts Determine How We See the Rest of the World*. New York: Pantheon Books.

Saint-Jean, A. (1991) 'Burying Women's Words: An Analysis of Media Attitudes', in L. Malette and M. Chalouh (eds), *The Montreal Massacre*. Charlottetown: Gynergy Books, pp. 61–5.

Salazar del Alcazar, H. (1990) 'El teatro peruano de los 80: las marcas de la historia y de la violencia de estos dias', *Conjunto/Casa de las Americas* (Havana), January–March.

Salutin, R. (1991) 'Thoughts of a Gulf War Watcher', *This Magazine*, May: 35–7.

Scanlon, J. (1990) 'What Can I Say When Words Can Kill? The Ultimate Public Relations Assignment – Spokesperson During a Hostage Incident'. Paper presented to the Media and Crisis Conference, Laval Univeristy, Quebec, 4–6 October.

Schiller, H.I. (1989) *Culture, Inc*. New York: Oxford University Press.

Schlesinger, P. and Lumley, B. (1985) 'Two Debates on Political Violence and the Mass Media: The Organisation of Intellectual Fields in Britain and Italy', in T.A. van Dijk (ed), *Discourse and Communication*. Berlin: Walter de Gruyter, pp. 324–49.

Schmid, A.P. and de Graaf, J. (1982) *Violence as Communication: Insurgent Terrorism and the Western News Media*. London and Beverly Hills: Sage.

Schneider, F. (1966) *Pressefreiheit und politische Offentlichkeit*. Neuwied.

Schuetz, A. (1967) *The Phenomenology of the Social World*. Evanston: Northwestern University Press.

Selucky, R. (1972) *Economic Reforms in Eastern Europe: Political Background and Economic Significance*. New York: Praeger.

Shrivastava, P. (1987) *Bhopal, Anatomy of a Crisis*. Cambridge, MA: Ballinger.

Signorielli, N. (1986) 'Selective Viewing: Limited Possibilities', *Journal of Communication*, 36(3): 64–76.

Signorielli, N. (1990) 'Television's Mean and Dangerous World: Continuing the Cultural Indicators Perspective', in N. Signorielli and M. Morgan (eds), *Cultivation Analysis*. Newbury Park: Sage.

Signorielli, N. and Morgan, M. (eds) (1990) *Cultivation Analysis*. Newbury Park: Sage.

Sitbon, G. (1990) 'La télé m'a menti', *Le Nouvel Observateur*, 11–18 January.

Smith, D. (1978) 'K is mentally ill', *Sociology*: 22–53.

Sorokin, P.A. (1928) *Contemporary Sociological Theories: Through the First Quarter of The Twentieth Century*. New York: Harper and Row.

Sproule, M.J. (1980) *Argument, Language and its Influence*. New York: McGraw-Hill.

Stephens, M. (1985) 'Sensationalizing and Moralizing in 16th and 17th Century Newsbooks and News Ballads', *Journalism History*, 12 (3–4): 92–5.

Sun, Lin (1989) 'Limits of Selective Viewing: An Analysis of "Diversity" in Dramatic Progamming'. Unpublished MA thesis, University of Pennsylvania.

Szarzynski, P. (1989) 'Oficyny bez adresu', *Polityka*, 9.

Szpocinski, A. (1987) 'Changes in Systems of Values in Polish Radio Programmes on Historical Subjects', *European Journal of Communication*, 2(1): 33–52.

Thompson, E.P. (1990) 'END and the Beginning: History Turns on a New Hinge', *The Nation*, 29 January: 117–18 and 120–22.

Thompson, R.J. (1990) *Adventures on Prime Time: The Television Programs of Stephen J. Cannell*. New York: Praeger.

Timasheff, N. (1955) *Sociological Theory: Its Nature and Growth*. New York: Random House.

Trait, J.C. (1970) *FLQ 70: Offensive d'automne*. Montreal: Editions de l'Homme.

Trudeau, P. (1970) 'Les terroristes veulent nous diviser, ne tombons pas dans leur piège', *Le Devoir*, 19 October.

Tuchman, G. (1978) *Making News: A Study in the Construction of Reality*. New York: The Free Press.

Turki, D. (1990) 'Crise du Golfe: Le Président Saddam Hussein et la presse américaine', *Réalités* (Tunis), 264 (14–20 September) 22–3, 36.

Tusa, J. (1989) 'Marketing Politics on TV', *The Independent*, 17 May.

UNESCO (1980) *Many Voices, One World*. Report of the International Commission for the Study of Communication Problems (MacBride Commission). London: Kogan Page.

United Nations (1988) *Human Rights: Compilation of International Instruments* (5th edn.) Geneva: United Nations Publications.

United States Congress (1982) *Hearing Before the Subcommittee on Telecommunications, Consumer Protection, and Finance of the Committee on Energy and Commerce, House of Representatives, Ninety-Seventh Congress, First Session, October 1981.* Washington: US Government Printing Office.

University of Vincennes (1980) *Le Nouvel Ordre Intérieur.* Paris: Alain Moreau.

Vincent, C.P. (1990) *Des systèmes et des hommes.* Paris: Les Editions de l'organisation.

Voyenne, B. (1982), *L'information aujourd'hui.* Paris: Editions Armand Colin.

Walicki, A. (1990) 'Czy PRL byla panstwem totalitarnym', *Polityka*, 20.

Warren, P. (1991) 'La politique hollywoodienne a encore de beaux jours devant elle', *Le Devoir*, 9 April.

Weiss, P. (1989) 'Bad Raps for TV Tabs', *Columbia Journalism Review*, 28 (1) (May–June): 38–42.

Welborn, D. (1984) *Implementation and Effects of the Government in the Sunshine Act.* Draft Report for the Administrative Conference of the United States. Washington.

White, M. (1976) *Social Thought in America.* New York: Oxford University Press.

Williams, G.A. (1989) 'Enticing Viewers: Sex and Violence in *TV Guide* Program Advertisements', *Journalism Quarterly*, 66(4): 970–73.

Williams, R. (1977) *Marxism and Literature.* Oxford: Oxford University Press.

Williamson, J. (1978) *Decoding Advertisements: Ideology and Meaning in Advertising.* New York: Marion Boyars.

Wolfe, A. (1973) *The Seamy Side of Democracy.* New York: McKay.

Wolfe, A. (1977) *The Limits of Legitimacy.* New York: Free Press.

*World Media* (1990). Special issue, 15 December.

Wurth-Hough, S. (1983) 'Network News Coverage of Terrorism: The Early Years', *Terrorism*, 6(3): 403–521.

Yang, N. and Linz, D. (1990) 'Movie Ratings and the Content of Adult Videos: The Sex–Violence Ratio', *Journal of Communication*, 40(2): 28–41.

# Index